英汉双语版

社会学导论

杨淑琴　主编

Introduction to Sociology

上海交通大学出版社
SHANGHAI JIAO TONG UNIVERSITY PRESS

内容提要

本书共分八章,分别是导论、社会学理论的起源与发展、社会组织、文化、社会化、社区、社会工作和社会问题。全书的主体部分为中文,书中出现的主要概念另配英文解释。每章开始部分设置课前阅读,章后设置延伸阅读,均为英文,旨在拓宽学生的知识面,激发读者的思考能力。本教材适合社会学专业学生选用。

图书在版编目(CIP)数据

社会学导论：英汉双语版 / 杨淑琴主编. — 上海：
上海交通大学出版社，2023.11
ISBN 978－7－313－27924－8

Ⅰ. ①社… Ⅱ. ①杨… Ⅲ. ①社会学－高等学校－教材－英、汉 Ⅳ. ①C91

中国版本图书馆 CIP 数据核字(2022)第 237058 号

社会学导论（英汉双语版）
SHEHUIXUE DAOLUN（YING-HAN SHUANGYU BAN）

主　　编：杨淑琴

出版发行：上海交通大学出版社		地　　址：上海市番禺路 951 号	
邮政编码：200030		电　　话：021－64071208	
印　　刷：上海新华印刷有限公司		经　　销：全国新华书店	
开　　本：787mm×1092mm　1/16		印　　张：14.75	
字　　数：280 千字			
版　　次：2023 年 11 月第 1 版		印　　次：2023 年 11 月第 1 次印刷	
书　　号：ISBN 978－7－313－27924－8		音像书号：ISBN 978－7－88941－572－9	
定　　价：58.00 元			

前　言

编写本教材是为了满足中外合作办学相关专业社会学课程的教学需要。

本教材的特色有如下四点:第一,为了帮助非英语专业的学生掌握社会学专业英语词汇,本教材在各章节重复出现重要的英语词汇。第二,对关键词的英文注释,非汉语直译,而是对汉语内容的有益补充。第三,为了帮助学生感受社会学相关英文著作的原汁原味,每章前后增加了课前阅读与延伸阅读。第四,由社会学专业教师提供阅读资料的英文音频。感谢上海工程技术大学教学建设项目资助本教材的出版;感谢上海交通大学出版社的支持。

本教材由上海工程技术大学教师杨淑琴编写,由昆山杜克大学教师河鋐定(Hyun Jeong Ha)录制英文阅读资料的音频;全书由杨淑琴统稿,如有错误疏漏,敬请教材使用者批评指正。

编者

2022 年 9 月

扫一扫,可听本书

课前阅读和延伸阅读朗读

目　录

1 导论
Introduction

Introduction to Sociology

Sociology is the study of human social relationships and institutions. Sociology's subject matter is diverse，ranging from crime to religion，from the family to the state，from the divisions of race and social class to the shared beliefs of a common culture，and from social stability to radical change in whole societies. Unifying the study of these diverse subjects of study is sociology's purpose of understanding how human action and consciousness both shape and are shaped by surrounding cultural and social structures.

Sociology is an exciting and illuminating field of study that analyzes and explains important matters in our personal lives，our communities，and the world. At the personal level，sociology investigates the social causes and consequences of such things as romantic love，racial and gender identity，family conflict，deviant behavior，aging，and religious faith. At the societal level，sociology examines and explains matters like crime and law，poverty and wealth，prejudice and discrimination，schools and education，business firms，urban community，and social movements. At the global level，sociology studies such phenomena as population growth and migration，war and peace，and economic development.

Sociologists emphasize the careful gathering and analysis of evidence about social life to develop and enrich our understanding of key social processes. The research methods sociologists use are varied. Sociologists observe the everyday life of groups，conduct large-scale surveys，interpret historical documents，analyze census data，study video-taped interactions，interview participants of groups，and conduct laboratory experiments. The research methods and theories of sociology yield powerful insights into the social processes shaping human lives and social problems and prospects in the contemporary world. By better understanding those social processes，we also come to understand more clearly the forces shaping the personal experiences and outcomes of our own lives. The ability to see and understand this connection between broad social forces and personal experiences — what C. Wright Mills called "the sociological imagination" — is extremely valuable academic preparation for living effective and rewarding personal and professional lives in a changing and complex society.

Students who have been well trained in sociology know how to think critically about human social life，and how to ask important research questions. They know how to design good social research projects，carefully collect and analyze empirical data，and formulate and present their research findings. Students trained in sociology also know how to help others understand the way the social world works and how it might be changed for the better. Most generally，they have learned how to think，evaluate，and communicate clearly，creatively，and effectively. These are all abilities of tremendous value in a wide variety of vocational callings and professions.

Sociology offers a distinctive and enlightening way of seeing and understanding the social world in which we live and which shapes our lives. Sociology looks beyond normal，taken-for-granted views of reality，to provide deeper，more illuminating and challenging understandings of social life. Through its particular analytical perspective，social theories，and research methods，sociology is a discipline that expands our awareness and analysis of the human social relationships，cultures，and institutions that profoundly shape both our lives and human history.

（Reference：sociology.unc.edu/undergraduate-program/sociology-major/what-is-sociology/）

1.1　什么是社会学 What Is Sociology

"什么是社会学?"一直是社会学家(sociologist)力图回答而又难以回答的问题。由于各国国情(national conditions)不同、个人面临的处境(plight)各异，因此对于这个问题的答案也各不相同。不仅不同历史时期的社会学家有意见分歧，即使同一时期不同的社会学家也众说纷纭，甚至同一个社会学家在不同时期也有不同看法。进入 21 世纪后，我们面对一个更加充满变革的社会:经济下滑、失业、精神疾病等社会问题(social problem)时有发生，一个充满不确定性的(probabilistic)世界展现在我们面前。如何应对这些问题成为社会学家们共同面临的挑战(challenge)。

Sociology is a subject that never stands still and, from the outside at least, its constantly changing theories may appear quite unfathomable. But the task of sociology is to understand and explain the ever changing social world, and to do so sociologists can not afford to cling to comfortable yet increasingly outdated ideas.

1.1.1 社会学的研究对象 Objectives of Sociology

社会学是对人类生活（human life）、群体（population）和社会（society）的研究。其研究对象极其广泛，从陌生人的短暂接触到全球化（globalization）都可成为社会学关注的领域。社会学在约两百年的发展历史中积累了为数众多的定义（definition），从这些定义中可以归纳出社会学的主要研究对象有社会现象（social phenomenon）、社会形式（social form）、社会组织（social organization）、社会进步（social progress）、社会关系（social relations）、社会行为（social behavior）、人类文化（human culture）等。

While some sociologists conduct research that may be applied directly to social policy and welfare, others focus primarily on refining the theoretical understanding of social processes. Subject matter can range from micro-level analyses of society to macro-level analyses.

以上内容概括起来，主要分属于两大类型：

第一类认为社会学是研究社会整体的科学。持这类观点的主要代表是奥古斯特·孔德（August Comte）、赫伯特·斯宾塞（Herbert Spencer）、埃米尔·迪尔凯姆（Emile Durkheim）等人。其中孔德、斯宾塞在研究整体社会时，强调的是一般的社会现象（general social phenomenon），而迪尔凯姆则强调特殊的社会现象（specific social phenomenon），即"社会事实"（social fact）。正是在这些观点的基础上，形成了社会学中的实证主义（positivism）路线。

第二类认为社会学是研究个人及其社会行动（social action）的科学。持这类观点的主要代表是马克斯·韦伯（Max Weber）等人，在这种观点的基础上，形成了社会学中的反实证主义（anti-positivism）路线。

这两类观点对后世影响至深，后世的许多看法多为这两类观点的变形或混成。按照上述分类，中国社会学界对社会学的定义，大体有以下几种看法。

（1）侧重以作为有机整体（organic integrity）的社会本身为研究对象。持这类看法的代表人物与观点有以下几种：

严复于1897年翻译了赫伯特·斯宾塞1873年出版的 *The Study of Sociology*，并将中文译本取名为《群学肄言》。他认为社会学是用科学方法研究社会的治和乱、盛和衰的原因，揭示社会"治"的方法和规律的学问。严复这样给社会学下定义，既与孔德、斯宾塞关于社会学的见解一致，又具有中国特色。严复翻译出版《群学肄言》是社会学进入中国的标志性事件之一。

> *The Study of Sociology*, by English philosopher, biologist, anthropologist, and sociologist, Herbert Spencer, was originally published in 1873. Spencer was known for his contributions to evolutionary theory and for applying it outside of biology, to the fields of philosophy, psychology, and within sociology. In particular, this work is a survey of the foundations of sociology, by one of its founders, within which he applies the idea of natural selection to the group survival and institutional structures.

1949 年以前，中国的马克思主义社会学家（Marxism sociologist）李大钊、瞿秋白、李达、许德珩等人认为社会学是研究社会发展（development of society）普遍规律（universal law）的科学。他们对社会学所下的定义大体相仿：李大钊（1920）认为社会学是一种科学，研究社会上各种现象及其原则与一切社会制度的学问，且用科学的方法，考察社会是何物，发明一种法则，以支配人间的行动。李达（1980：237）认为"社会学者，社会科学之一，其研究之目的在探求社会进化（social evolution）之原理；其研究之方法，在追溯过去以说明现在，更由现在以逆测将来"。许德珩（1936）认为社会学是研究人类社会之构造（social construction），社会构造之存在、发展、变革及其相互联系，分析构成人类社会生活的诸要素及诸要素的性质、诸要素之间相互作用的关系，探求社会变革的因果关系和法则，以推知社会进行的方法，预测将来的一种学问。

费孝通等人认为社会学是研究社会整体及其规律的科学。在他主持和指导的中国社会学重建后出版的第一本《社会学概论（试讲本）》中，他从社会整体的角度来下定义，认为社会学是从变动着的社会系统的整体出发，通过人们的社会关系和社会行为来研究社会的结构、功能、发生、发展规律（law of development）的一门综合性的（synthetic）社会科学（Social Science）。

（2）侧重以作为社会主体的个人及其社会行为为研究对象。持这种观点的在中华人民共和国建立前主要以孙本文为代表。他深受芝加哥学派（Chicago School）的符号互动理论（symbolic interactionism）的影响，认为社会学的各种定义虽没有什么错误，但或失之抽象，或失之广泛，或失之含糊，或失之狭隘，似均非适当的定义。比较目前可认为适当的定义，即是以社会学研究社会行为的科学（孙本文，1935）。

上述关于社会学研究对象的种种不同观点，都是由于研究者对社会的观察角度不同造成的。社会学对象问题上的众说纷纭，是这门学科从不成熟走向成熟过程中的必然现象。

那么，到底什么是社会学呢？综上所述，我们可以给社会学下这样一个定义：社会学是关于社会的科学，它的研究对象极其丰富，包括人类行为（human behavior）、社会整体、个人及其社会行为、群体及其群体生活、文化、社会组织与社会制度、社会关系等。

> Sociology can be defined as the general science of society. It refers to social behavior, society, culture, patterns of social relationships, social groups, and social interactions.

1.1.2 社会学与其他学科的关系 Sociology and Other Disciplines

Social research has influence throughout various industries and sectors of life，such as among politicians，policy makers，and legislators，educators，planners，administrators，developers，business magnates and managers，social workers，non-governmental organizations，and non-profit organizations，as well as individuals interested in resolving social issues in general. As such，there is often a great deal of crossover between social research，market research，and other statistical fields.

社会科学(social sciences)的发展趋势(trend of development)表明:社会科学的各门学科都是相互开放的体系,跨学科的学术交流(interdisciplinary academic communication)与研究项目越来越引起社会科学家们的注意,社会科学家们已经明确意识到了各学科之间的相互交流与渗透。社会学在对特定领域的社会现象(social phenomenon)进行研究时,也要依靠其他学科已经取得的研究成果;在研究方法的选择上也要受到其他学科的影响与制约。

1. 社会学与哲学 Sociology and Philosophy

从社会学产生和发展的历史来看,它是从哲学(philosophy)的母体中分化出来的。社会学约两百年的发展史,正是它逐渐摆脱思辨的(speculative)历史哲学(philosophy of history)和社会哲学(philosophy of society)母体之影响、不断用现代科学方法武装自己、日益增加经验研究(empirical research)和应用研究(application research)的比重,从而成为一门独立学科(independent discipline)的发展过程。

2. 社会学与经济学 Sociology and Economics

经济学(economics)是研究商品和服务的生产(production)、交换(exchange)、分配(distribution)和消费(consumption)规律的科学。当社会学家们探究经济生活(economic life)时就会发现,经济学毕竟是社会的一部分;经济生活的这种社会性,导致了社会学一门分支学科"经济社会学"(economic sociology)的产生。

Economic sociology is the application of sociological concepts，methods，techniques，and ideologies to analyze the trade，distribution，and consumption of services and goods in an economy. It details the relationship between the economic activities，the society and the changes in the firms involved in the production.

3. 社会学与政治学 Sociology and Politics

政治学(politics)是研究政治哲学(political philosophy)和政府体制(government system)及其两者之间关系的学科。目前,政治学家(politician)越来越关注社会学的研究领域,而社会学的研究也越来越多地应用于政治决策(political decision-making)。政治学家和社会学家的兴趣正在逐步汇聚、交叉和渗透。也正是在这一过程中,政治学和社会学的交叉学科"政治社会学"（political sociology）应运而生。

> Political sociology is the study of power and the relationship between societies, states, and political conflict. It is a broad subfield that straddles political science and sociology, with "macro" and "micro" components.

4. 社会学与心理学 Sociology and Psychology

心理学（psychology）是研究人类的心理现象（mental phenomena）与心理规律的科学。社会学与心理学的共同研究领域是"社会心理学"（social psychology），它是研究社会环境如何影响个人行为的学科。社会心理学与社会学都非常重视从社会环境（social environment）与个体相互作用的关系上来分析问题；社会学借助社会心理学的理论和研究成果，进入"人—社会"系统的分析；社会心理学则借助社会学（sociology）成功地把个体心理活动置于社会分析（social analysis）的基础之上。

> Social psychology is the study of how individual or group behavior is influenced by the presence and behavior of others. The major question social psychologists ponder is this: How and why are people's perceptions and actions influenced by environmental factors, such as social interaction?

5. 社会学与人类学 Sociology and Anthropology

作为一门文化科学，人类学（anthropology）与社会学的关系最为密切。两者的区别主要在于两点：一是就研究内容而言，人类学主要研究完整的、小规模的社会，而社会学则侧重于研究当代大工业社会；二是就研究方法来讲，人类学家（anthropologist）主要使用直接观察法（direct observation）和案例分析法（case study）进行研究，而社会学家则经常依靠统计量表（statistic scale）和调查问卷（questionnaire）来收集资料。

1.1.3　社会学的研究方法 Methods of Sociology

1. 观察法 Observation

> Observation is the active acquisition of information from a primary source. In science, observation can also involve the perception and recording of data via the use of scientific instruments. Observations can be qualitative, that is, only the absence or presence of a property is noted, or quantitative if a numerical value is attached to the observed phenomenon by counting or measuring.
>
> However, because human senses are limited and subject to errors in perception, such as optical illusions, scientific instruments were developed to aid human abilities of observation, such as clocks, telescopes, microscopes, thermometers, cameras, and tape recorders.

Human observations are also biased toward confirming the observer's conscious and unconscious expectations and view of the world; we human being always "see what we expect to see". In psychology, this is called confirmation bias.

(1) 观察法是指研究者根据一定的研究目的、研究提纲或观察表,用自己的感官和辅助工具去直接观察被研究对象,从而获得资料的一种方法。科学的观察具有目的性(purposeful)、计划性(planned)、系统性(systematic)和可重复性(repeatable)。观察一般利用眼睛、耳朵等感觉器官去感知观察对象(object of observation)。由于人的感觉器官(sense organ)具有一定的局限性(limitation),观察者往往要借助各种现代化的仪器(instrument),如照相机、录音机、显微录像机等来辅助观察。

(2) 观察法的分类(classification of observation)有如下几种:①按照观察者是否参与被观察对象的活动,可分为参与观察(participant observation)与非参与观察(non-participant observation)。②按照对观察对象控制性强弱或观察提纲的详细程度,可分为结构性观察(structured observation)与非结构性观察(unstructured observation)。③按照是否具有连贯性,可分为连续性观察(continuous observation)和非连续观察(discontinuous observation)。④按照观察地点和组织条件,可分为自然观察(naturalistic observation)和实验观察(experimental observation)等。

(3) 观察法的作用(functions of observation)主要有如下三点:①扩大人们的感性认识(perceptual awareness)。②启发人们的思维。③带来新的发现。

(4) 观察法的优缺点(pros and cons of observation)。

观察法的优点:①它能通过观察直接获得资料,无需其他中间环节。因此,由观察获取的资料比较真实。②在自然状态下的观察,能获得生动的资料,有助于激发研究者的研究想象力。③观察具有及时性(timeliness)优点,能捕捉到正在发生的现象。④观察能搜集到一些无法言表的材料,可以引发更深入的研究和探寻。

观察法的局限性:①受时间的限制,某些事件的发生是有一定时间限制的,过了这段时间就不会再发生。②受观察对象限制。如研究青少年犯罪问题,有些研究对象如秘密团伙一般是不会让别人观察的。③受观察者本身限制。一方面人的感官都有生理限制,超出这个限度就很难直接观察。另一方面,观察结果也会受到主观偏见(bias)的影响。④观察者只能观察外表现象和某些物质结构,不能直接观察到事物的本质和人们的思想意识。⑤观察法不适用于大面积调查。

2. 调查法 Survey Methods

A survey method is a process, tool, that can be used to gather information in research by asking questions to a predefined group of people. Survey methods can be qualitative or quantitative depending on the type of research and the type of data you want to gather in the end.

（1）调查法是科学研究中最常用的方法之一。它是有目的、有计划、有系统地搜集有关研究对象现实状况或历史状况材料的方法。调查方法也是社会科学研究中常用的基本研究方法，它综合运用历史法（historical method）、观察法（observation）等方法以及访谈（interview）、问卷（questionnaire）、个案研究（case study）、测验（test）等科学方式，对社会现象进行有计划的、周密的和系统的了解，并对调查搜集到的大量资料进行分析（analysis）、综合（synthesis）、比较（comparison）、归纳（induction），从而为人们提供规律性的知识。

（2）调查法的特点（characteristics of survey methods）：①间接灵活；②途径多样；③系统严密；④实施方便。

（3）中国社会调查研究的发展（social surveys and research in China）从一个侧面显示了中国社会学成长发展的历程，因此有必要认真分析一下。

中国早期的社会调查研究。中国社会学早期代表人物，曾任中国科学院副院长的陶孟和曾在 20 世纪 30 年代时说，在中国，采用科学方法研究社会状况，只不过是近 10 年的事。从教育和科学研究系统看，中国的社会调查研究活动大多起始于 20 世纪初的一些教会学校或一些学校中的外籍教授。他们为指导学生学习，从事一些小规模的调查研究。例如：1917 年清华学堂美籍教授狄德莫（C. G. Dittmer）指导学生在北京西郊调查 195 户居民的生活费用。1918—1919 年，美籍教师甘溥（S. D. Gamble）与燕京大学（Yenching University）教授步济时（I. S. Burgess）等曾仿照美国春田社会调查（The Springfield Survey）的成例，调查北京社会状况，于 1921 年在美国出版《北京，一种社会调查》（*Peking, A Social Survey*）。这是高等学校城市社会调查研究的开端。

> The Springfield Survey was a massive study of local schools, prisons, and other institutions undertaken in 1914 by the Russell Sage Foundation with the help of hundreds of local volunteers in Springfield, USA. The survey was initiated by a group of Springfield citizens who were dissatisfied by social conditions in the city. More than 120 volunteers collected data. It was a process that lasted from March through early July 1914. Another 600 people helped present the survey results in an exhibition held in November and December at the Illinois State Arsenal.

沪江大学（现上海理工大学）的社会学教授葛学溥（D. H. Kulp）指导学生在广东潮州调查了有 650 名村民的凤凰村，1925 年在美国出版了书名为《华南农村生活：家庭主义的社会学》（*Country Life in South China：The Sociology of Familism*）的调查报告。这是高等学校乡村生活社会调查开始的标志。

从此之后，社会调查研究的活动逐渐盛行，出版的作品也逐渐增多，到 1935 年前后发展到了高峰。

中国社会调查研究的第二个发展阶段。20 世纪 30 年代中期至 1952 年，是中国社会调查研究的第二个发展阶段，其特点是开创了"社会调查"的新境界。社会调查又称社区研究

(community study),或称社区分析。它是首先由燕京大学社会学系以吴文藻为首的一批师生们发起的。

费孝通对中国社会调查研究的贡献。中国社会学研究自 1979 年恢复以来至今,可以认为在调查方法与方法论上走入了第三个阶段。

结合中国社会发展的不同时期,最为系统、最有创新意义、在方法和方法论上做出重要发展的,要数费孝通领导的社会调查(social survey)或称作社区研究。

费孝通研究的起点是对农村做微观的解剖。这项工作始于 20 世纪 30 年代,费孝通对江村(开弦弓村)这个位于太湖边的约 360 户住户的小村子进行了调查。调查的目的是认识中国农民的生活及其变化,了解中国农村社会的特点,探索中国农村社会现代化的道路。经过调查,费孝通提出了"人多地少,工农相辅""发展农村工业是提高农民生活水平的必由之路"等看法。

1936 年,费孝通在开弦弓村作了第一次调查,写出了《江村经济》(*Peasant Life in China*)一书。之后,费孝通于 1957 年重访江村,之后竟然九访江村,并于 1986 年作了《江村五十年》一文,系统、全面地把开弦弓村 50 年来的变化,作了概括的叙述。费孝通这种追踪调查的精神,是社会学者深入社会,进行社会实践,科学地认识社会,艰苦而认真地探索社会发展规律(law of social development)精神的可贵表现。这种研究精神和探索社会规律的活动,也是研究工作坚持理论、实践紧密相结合的典范。

1.2　理论视角 Theoretical Perspectives

社会学是一门完善的学科,但它并不是一门用统一的方式看待世界的学科。虽然社会学家们在某些基本原则上持相同立场(standpoint),但是,在现代社会中,社会学家们并未形成一种单一、占统治地位的理论观点。认识社会,不能仅仅凭借我们的经历和经验,必须借助理论。每一种社会学的理论视角(theoretical perspectives)都帮助我们更深刻地认识社会。

> Most of us see the world in terms of the familiar features of our own lives, our families, friendship and working lives, for example. But sociology insists that we take a broader view in order to understand why we act in the ways we do. It teaches us that much of what we regard as natural, inevitable, good and true may not be so, and that things we take for granted are actually shaped by historical events and social processes. Understanding the subtal yet complex and profound ways in which our individual lives reflect the contexts of our social experience is basic to the sociologist's outlook.

在试图理解社会如何运转的问题上,不同的社会学家对于人类社会生活之基本特征,有着不同的假设(hypothesis)。有些人认为秩序与稳定比冲突与变迁更重要，而另一些人则持相反观点。一些人主要考察社会的宏观制度结构(macro-institutional structure)，另一些人则更关心小群体的人际互动(interpersonal interaction)。这些选择决定了社会学家的理论视角。下面来看社会学的三个主要理论视角。

1.2.1　功能主义的理论视角 Perspective of Functionalism

功能主义的基本原则是在生物学占据统治地位的 19 世纪发展起来的。那时有关人体、微生物以及遍布全球的动植物的知识不断增长。查尔斯·达尔文吸收了这些知识并以"自然选择"来解释物种进化。受这些知识启发的早期的社会思想家自然地将生物学(biology)的一些概念运用到了社会中。后来的一些学者吸收了"社会与生物有机体相似"这一功能主义的基本思想，并且对其进行了提炼和补充。迪尔凯姆常被视为当代功能主义的奠基人。他把社会看作一个由道德价值观上的共识来规范的一种特殊的有机体。功能主义还是英国文化人类学(cultural anthropology)的创建者们所持的主要理论视角。

Functionalism holds that society is a complex system whose various parts work together to produce stability and that society should investigate their relationships. For example, we can analyse the religious beliefs and customs of a society by showing how they relate to other institutions because the different parts of a society always develop in close relation to one another. They argue that the parts of society work together, just as the various parts of human body do, for the benefit of society as a whole. For example, to study a bodily organ such as the heart, we need to show how it relates to other parts of the body.

罗伯特·默顿(Robert Merton)将塔尔科特·帕森斯(Talcott Parsons)的功能主义理论进行了改进，使其更有利于经验研究。他的理论是从分析社会结构中的一个特定单位入手的。默顿指出社会系统中并非所有组成部分都发挥着正功能，当社会结构中的某一部分阻止了整个社会或其组成部分的需求满足时，它则是反功能的(dysfunctional)。

当宗教把社会成员团结在一起的时候，它就在发挥着正功能；当军队在保护一个社会免受伤害时，它也是正功能的；当一部政治机器通过提供关于政府和社会服务的信息而将外来移民整合入社会之中的时候，它同样发挥着正功能。然而，当宗教在北爱尔兰等地区激起政治纷争时，当军队耗尽了医疗和教育机构等更紧迫的社会需求所需的资源时，当一部政治机器靠贪污和腐败为生时，他们发挥的却又是反功能。

同样需要着重指出的是，社会结构单位发挥的功能并不局限于正式的或预期的功能，除了已意识到的或显功能(manifest function)之外，一个社会结构单位还具有尚未意识到的，或者是未预料到的潜功能(latent function)。

例如，大学的一个显功能是使年轻人接受教育，为将来承担专业化的工作打下基础。而大学的一个潜功能则是把一部分人口排除在劳动力市场之外，从而减缓经济生活中的压力。

功能主义在许多问题上受到了批评,主要是因为它所反映的社会观从本质上是保守的(conservative)。由于它强调共享价值观并且将社会看成是由为整体利益共同发挥作用的各部分所组成的,功能主义似乎给不赞同这些社会价值观并企图改变它们的人们只留了极少的空间。批评家指责功能主义在很大程度上忽视了人们对社会的不满和社会冲突(social conflict)。由于功能主义是如此依赖秩序、稳定和共识,它甚至可能曲解了社会的真正本质。批评家们指出,与生物体不同,社会的各个部分并不总是为了整体利益而通力合作的。社会中的某些组成部分处于冲突之中,某些部分的获利则是以其他部分的利益受损为代价的。

> Since the 1980s the popularity of functionalism has waned as its limitations have become apparent. Many functionalist thinkers focused on stability and social order, minimizing social decisions and inequalities based on factors such as class, race and gender. Functionalism also placed too little emphasis on the role of creative social action within society.

对功能主义最严厉的批评来自被称为冲突论者(conflict theorists)的社会学家。他们认为功能主义视角在研究稳定的社会时也许是十分有用的。但放眼今天之世界,社会在飞速变迁,冲突不是例外而是规律;因此,从冲突的视角(perspective of conflict)看社会才更合理。

1.2.2 冲突论的理论视角 Perspective of Conflict Theory

冲突论是社会学史上与功能论并驾齐驱的另一种宏观的社会学理论。现代冲突论在很大程度上是建立在对结构功能论(structural functionalism)的批判的基础上的。当结构功能论如日中天的时候,很多冲突论者对功能论者有关社会整合(social integration)和社会协调(social cooperation)的社会均衡论(theory of equilibrium)观点进行了指责和批判。

> Like functionalists, sociologists using conflict theories emphasize the importance of social structures. They highlight the importance of divisions in society and, in doing so, concentrate on issues of power, inequality and competitive struggles. They tend to see society as composed of distinct groups, each pursuing its own interests, which means the potential for conflict is always present. Conflict theorists examine the tensions between dominant and disadvantaged groups, looking to understand how relationships of control are established and maintained.
>
> Both Marx and later Marxist approaches have been highly influential in conflict theory, though it is important to note that by no means all conflict theories are Marxist.

社会冲突理论(theory of social conflicts)以刘易斯·科塞(Lewis Coser)、拉尔夫·达伦多夫(Ralf G. Dahrendorf)为代表,重点研究社会冲突的起因、形式、制约因素及影响,是作为对结构功能主义理论的反思和对立物提出的。他们强调,人们因有限的资源、权力和声望而发生的斗争是永恒的社会现象,也是社会变迁(social change)动力的主要源泉。

如果说结构功能主义强调的是社会的稳定(stability)和整合(integration),代表社会学的保守派(the conservatives),那么冲突理论则是强调社会冲突对于社会巩固和发展的积极作用,代表社会学的激进派(the radicals)。该理论在 20 世纪 60 年代后期流行于美国和一些西欧国家。

美国社会学家科塞是第一位试图将功能论与冲突论整合起来的社会学家。1956 年,他出版了《社会冲突的功能》(*The Functions of Social Conflict*)一书,对社会冲突进行了较为系统的分析。什么是冲突? 科塞解释说,冲突是价值观、信仰以及对于稀缺的地位、权利和资源在分配上的争斗。冲突产生于社会报酬的分配不均以及人们对这种分配不均表现出的失望,只要不直接涉及基本价值观或共同观念,那么,它的性质就不是破坏性的,而只会对社会有好处。这就是科塞强调的冲突的五项正功能:①冲突对社会与群体具有内部整合的功能;②冲突对于社会与群体具有稳定的功能;③冲突对新社会与群体的形成具有促进功能;④冲突对新规范和制度的建立具有激发功能;⑤冲突是一个社会中重要的平衡机制(equilibrium mechanism)。

Lewis Coser was the first sociologist to try to bring together structural functionalism and conflict theory; his work was focused on finding the functions of social conflict. Coser said that conflict might serve to solidify a loosely structured group. In a society that seems to be disintegrating, conflict with another society, inter-group conflict, may restore the integrative core. Conflict with one group may also serve to produce cohesion by leading to a series of alliances with other groups. Conflicts within a society, intra-group conflict, can bring some ordinarily isolated individuals into an active role.

Conflicts also serve a communication function. Prior to conflict, groups may be unsure of their adversary's position, but as a result of conflict, positions and boundaries between groups often become clarified, leaving individuals better able to decide on a proper course of action in relation to their adversary.

科塞认为,弹性比较大、比较灵活的社会结构容易出现冲突,但对社会没有根本性的破坏作用,因为这种冲突可以导致群体与群体间接触面的扩大,也可以导致决策过程中集中与民主的结合及社会控制的增强,它对社会的整合和稳定起着积极的作用。相反,僵硬的社会结构采取压制手段,不允许或压抑冲突,冲突一旦积累、爆发,其程度势必会更加严重,将对社会结构产生破坏。为此,科塞提出,要建立完善的社会安全阀制度(safety valve mechanism)。这种制度一方面可以发泄积累的敌对情绪,另一方面,可以使统治者得到社会信息,体察民情,避免灾难性冲突的爆发,破坏社会整体结构。显然,科塞把冲突看作促进社会整合与适应性的过程,所强调的社会变迁是改良性的局部社会调整,而非社会革命,其安全阀机制的探讨也不过是为资产阶级统治者献计献策而已。因此,可以说,科塞与帕森斯最终是殊途同归,都是要维护资本主义社会(capitalist society)的运行和发展。

1.2.3 符号互动论的理论视角 Perspective of Symbolic Interaction

互动论是社会学中另一种颇为引人注目的理论视角,它更关注于社会的微观方面,因此,倾向于该视角的社会学家通常被称为微观社会学家。一般认为,乔治·米德(George H. Mead)是该理论的奠基人。他提出的符号互动论是互动论理论视角的基础。所谓符号互动(symbolic interaction),就是指一种主张从人们互动的日常自然环境去研究人类群体生活的社会学和社会心理学理论派别。这种理论又称象征相互作用论或符号互动主义(symbolic interactionism)。

Symbolic interactionism springs from a concern with language and meaning. American social philosopher George Herbert Mead argues that language allows us to become self-conscious beings — aware of our own individuality and able to see ourselves "as others see us". The key element in this process is the symbol. A symbol is something that stands for something else. Non-verbal gestures and forms of communication are also symbols. Waving at someone or making a rude gesture have symbolic value. Symbolic interactionism directs our attention to the details of interpersonal interaction and how that detail is used to make sense of what others say and do. Sociologists influenced by symbolic interactionism often focus on face-to-face interactions in the context of everyday life.

该理论源于美国实用主义(pragmatism)哲学家威廉·詹姆斯(William James)和米德的著作。从哲学上看,符号互动论与美国的实用主义、德国和法国的现象学(phenomenology)联系最为密切,与逻辑实证主义(logical positivism)、结构功能主义、文化决定论(cultural determinism)、生物决定论(biological determinism)、刺激—反应行为主义(stimulate-response behaviorism)、社会交换理论(social exchange theory)以及均衡理论(general equilibrium theory)的各种形式相对立,而与心理分析理论(theory of psychological analysis)、现象学社会学(phenomenological sociology)、民俗学(folklore studies)、方法论(methodology)、角色理论(role theory)、戏剧理论(dramaturgical theory),以及人本主义(humanism)和存在主义(existentialism)的心理学、哲学,具有某些相容性。戈夫曼(Goffman)是符号互动论在当代的主要代表人物之一。

符号互动论的基本假定(basic assumption)主要有:①人对事物所采取的行动是以这些事物对人的意义(significance)为基础的;②这些事物的意义来源于个体与其同伴的互动,而不存于这些事物本身之中;③当个体在应付他所遇到的事物时,他通过自己的解释去运用和修改这些意义。

1934年,米德出版了《心灵,自我与社会》(*Mind, Self, and Society*)一书,阐述了符号互动论的主要观点:

(1)心灵、自我和社会不是分离的结构,而是人际符号互动的过程。

(2)语言是心灵和自我形成的主要机制。

(3)心灵是社会过程的内化,事实上内化的过程就是人的"自我互动"过程,人通过人际互动学到了有意义的符号,然后用这种符号来进行内向互动并发展自我。社会的内化(internalization)过程,伴随着个体的外化(externalization)过程。

(4)行为是个体在行动过程中自己设计的,并不是对外界刺激的机械反应。

(5)个体的行为受他自身对情境定义的影响。

(6)在个体面对面的互动中有待于协商的中心对象是身份和身份的意义,个人和他人并不存在于人自身之中,而是存在于互动本身之中。

According to the University of Chicago Press, George Herbert Mead is widely recognized as one of the most brilliantly original American pragmatists. Although he had a profound influence on the development of social philosophy, he published no books in his lifetime. This makes the lectures collected in *Mind*, *Self*, *and Society* all the more remarkable, as they offer a rare synthesis of his ideas. This collection gets to the heart of Mead's meditations on social psychology and social philosophy. Its penetrating, conversational tone transports the reader directly into Mead's classroom as he teases out the genesis of the self and the nature of the mind.

符号互动论倾向于自然主义、描述性和解释性的方法论,偏爱参与观察、生活史研究、人种史、不透明的互动片段或行为标本等方法,强调研究过程(study process)而不是研究固定、静止、结构的属性,必须研究真实的社会情境,而不是通过运用实验设计或调查研究来构成人造情境。符号互动论不运用正式的数据搜集法和数据分析法,而代之以概括性和一般方法论的指令。

应用符号互动论有助于对许多问题的理解,如对社会越轨(social deviance)、精神疾病(mental disorders)、集体行动(collective action)、儿童社会化(socialization of children)、疾病与痛苦(illness and painfulness)的理解等。

1.2.4 对三种理论视角的简要评价 Comments on Three Theoretical Perspectives

社会学的三种理论视角使我们清楚地认识到,社会学并不是一门有着严格定义和统一世界观的学科,当然,更不是一门追求狭隘性和封闭性的学科。

社会学的三种理论视角所显示的差异性并不是起源于矛盾或对抗,每种视角都考察了同一社会现实的相关方面,而给对方以补充。因此,绝不能说哪种视角是对的,哪种视角是错的。每一位社会学家都从自己的个人兴趣出发考察社会现实和社会关系,这不可避免地会将他们的个人偏见带入社会学理论。但是,当我们考察社会现象时,这三种理论视角依然会给我们有益的启示。

Social theorists, they speculate, they develop theories, and their theories deal with social realities and social relationships. Of course, there are important differences between everyday theorizing and that of social theorists. The best sociological theories often stem from deep personal interests of theorists. Various social theorists find different aspects of the social world important and interesting, and it is in those areas that they are likely to devote their attention. Thus, bias became an ever present danger that both theorists and those who read theory must keep in the forefront of their thinking.

1.3 为什么要学习社会学 Why We Study Sociology

1.3.1 社会学的地位 Position of Sociology

社会学在社会科学中的地位,是随着社会学学科的发展而历史地变化着的。在创立时期,社会学刚刚从哲学的怀抱里解脱出来,社会学实际上是社会科学的代名词,同时它又在一定程度上有社会哲学(social philosophy)或历史哲学(philosophy of history)的色彩,带有某种包罗万象、凌驾于各门社会科学之上的印记。例如,孔德认为社会学的目标是一切现有知识的综合。斯宾塞也认为社会是各种社会科学的综合或总和,他的《社会学原理》(Principles of Sociology)包含了对政治、经济、宗教等多种学科的研究。

孔德特别是斯宾塞还认为,社会学是一种研究社会第一原理(first principle)的科学,是各种社会科学的根本科学(fundamental science)。例如,他们两人都主张社会有机体论(social organism),并把社会各组成部分相互之间以及部分与整体之间保持和谐作为社会根本原理(hypostasis)。不过他们各自的着眼点有所不同,孔德强调整体,斯宾塞则强调个体。

社会学的原理具有普遍性(universality),适用于一切社会生活;各门社会科学的原理则只有特殊性,仅适用于特殊的社会现象。这种观点,事实上把社会学与其他各门社会科学的关系看作一般与特殊的关系。

随着社会学进入形成时期,它逐渐摆脱了哲学的怀抱,越来越明确地确定了自己的范围和方法,成为与其他社会科学并列的独立科学。迪尔凯姆、韦伯等人虽然对社会学的说法各异,但都认为社会学与其他社会科学一样,都研究社会生活现象的一个方面,它与其他社会科学处于平等地位。

目前,大多数社会学家都认同这样一种表述,即社会学所研究的原理,就是一种普通的根本的原理。社会学的主要目标是推进我们对生活世界(living world)的理解。这是一个崇高的目标,而这个目标也表明了社会学作为一个学科门类在诸学科之中的地位。

Sociology has several practical implications for our lives. First, sociology gives us an awareness of cultural differences that allows us to see the social world from many perspectives. If we properly understand how others live, we also acquire a better understanding of what their problems are. Second, sociological research provides practical help in assessing the results of policy initiatives. Third, many sociologists concern themselves directly with practical matters as professionals. Fourth, and most importantly, sociology can provide us with self-enlightenment or increased self-understanding. The more we know about the overall workings of our society, the more likely we are to be able to influence our own futures.

1.3.2　社会学的功能 Functions of Sociology

社会学研究的前提是从既成的社会事实出发，描述（describe）它的状况，解释（interpret）它的原因，预测（predict）未来的变化。它以自己的研究成果对科学地管理社会和制订正确的社会政策提供有根据的、经过论证的实际建议。可见，社会学是人类认识社会和改造社会的强有力工具，它的主要功能表现为以下三个方面：

（1）描述（description）。这是指社会学使用科学的方法，客观而忠实地搜集、整理和记录关于社会现象及其过程的信息，为深入地认识和有效地管理社会提供可靠的感性经验（perceptual experience）资料。具体地说，社会学在描述社会现象（social phenomenon）方面既定性（qualitative）又定量（quantitate），它可以及时向人们提供相对真实可靠和有效的社会信息。

（2）解释（interpretation）。这是指社会学研究过程借助概念（concept）、范畴（category）进行理论抽象（theoretical abstraction），将描述功能得出的感性经验（perceptual experience）上升到理性认识（rational cognition），从而对社会现象的形成、发展及其过程做出科学的解释。它包括对社会现象进行客观的因果性考察和人的社会行为动机的意义理解。如果说描述功能只是告诉人们"是什么""怎么样"；那么解释功能就是进一步告诉人们"为什么"。社会学的解释功能表现出了社会学理论的综合能力。

（3）预测（prediction）。社会预测（social prediction）是社会学的又一项重要功能，这是对前两种功能的进一步运用。当社会学用经验研究法（empirical research）把社会事实描述出来，再加以理论解释（theoretical explanation）以后，实际上就已经掌握了各变项之间的相关关系及相关程度。

1.3.3　社会学的想象力 Sociological Imagination

Sociological imagination is an outlook on life that involves an individual developing a deep understanding of how their biography is a result of historical process and occurs within a larger social context.

The term was coined by American sociologist C. Wright Mills in his 1959 book *The Sociological Imagination* to describe the type of insight offered by the discipline of sociology. In the book，Mills attempted to reconcile two different and abstract concepts of social reality—the "individual" and "society". Mills defined sociological imagination as "the awareness of the relationship between personal experience and the wider society". Anthony Giddens in his book *Sociology* says：

The application of imaginative thought to the asking and answering of sociological questions. Someone using the sociological imagination "thinks himself away" from the familiar routines of daily life.

学习社会学式的思考,意味着要培养我们的想象力。一名社会学家必须能够摆脱他们个人情境的即时性,而将事件置身于一个广阔的社会背景之中。当今世界正经历百年未有之大变局,在此背景下,社会学想象力(sociological imagination)如何帮助我们理解时代与自我。美国社会学家查尔斯·赖特·米尔斯(Charles Wright Mills)提出,社会学想象力是"对体验与更广泛社会的清晰意识"。在1959年出版的《社会学的想象力》(*The Sociological Imagination*)中,米尔斯试图调和"个人"与"社会"这两个不同的抽象概念。米尔斯认为,社会学想象力不仅有助于人们分析自身所处的社会生活现状,也有助于人们看见未来的可能性。加强社会学想象力,个体需要从当前的境遇中抽离出来,转换思考的视角,社会学的想象力对于个体发展具有重要作用。

延伸阅读 Further Reading

思考 Thinking it through：
中国社会学得以在燕京大学发展的因素有哪些?

Yenching University and the Development of Sociology in China

1. Yenching University

Yenching University was a university in Beijing，China，that was formed out of the merger of four colleges between the years 1915 and 1920.

The term "Yenching" comes from an alternative name for old Beijing, derived from its status as capital of the state of Yan，one of the seven Warring States that existed until the 3rd century BC.

John Leighton Stuart was appointed as the principal of the university in January 1919. As the university was initially short on funds，he turned to fundraising worldwide. The university bought the royal gardens of a Qing Dynasty prince to build a scenic campus and employed gardeners from the Imperial gardens. In 1926，the campus was completed. Stuart determined to create a university that served the Chinese nation. He attracted major Chinese and Western scholars to teach.

Here are two sociologists. One was a professor and the other was a student at Yenching University.

(1)Wu Wenzao 吴文藻(1901—1985).

Wu Wenzao was a Chinese sociologist，anthropologist，ethnologist. He was born in Jiangyin，Jiangsu. He was admitted into Tsinghua University at 1917.

In 1925，he was admitted into Columbia University，and in 1928 he got his PhD in the Department of Sociology. In 1928，the Harvard-Yenching Institute was jointly founded by Yenching University and Harvard University for the teaching of the humanities and social sciences in East Asia.

In 1929，he married Bing Xin，when they were studying in the United States. In 1933，he became the dean of sociology department in Yenching University.

(2)Fei Xiaotong 费孝通(1910—2005).

Fei Xiaotong or Fei Hsiao-tung，was a Chinese anthropologist and sociologist. He was a pioneering researcher and professor of sociology and anthropology. As one of China's finest sociologists and anthropologists，his works on these subjects were instrumental in laying a solid foundation for the development of sociological and anthropological studies in China，as well as in introducing social and cultural phenomena of China to the international community. His last post before his death in 2005 was as Professor of Sociology at Peking University.

At Yenching University，which had China's best sociology program，he was stimulated by the semester visit of Robert E. Park，the University of Chicago sociologist. For an M. A. in anthropology，Fei went to nearby Tsinghua University where he studied with Pan Guangdan. Fei's first fieldwork experience，in the rugged mountains of Guangxi in the far south，ended tragically after Fei's leg was crushed by a tiger trap，and his young bride Wang Tonghui（王同惠）died seeking help.

Sociology became a subject of academic interest in China in 1920s，and in 1948 sociologist Fei Xiaotong published a book，*From the Soil*，that sought to establish a framework for detailing Chinese society and its moral and ethics.

By 1930, the school was among the top universities in China, its teaching distinguished itself by a considerable academic freedom. During the Second World -War, the area was occupied by Japan and the university was moved to Chengdu, Sichuan. After the People's Republic of China was established in 1949, Yenching University remained open. In 1952, Yenching University was closed up, and its arts and science faculties were merged into Peking University and other state-operated institutions, its politics and law faculties were merged into China University of Political Science and Law, its economics faculties were merged into Central University of Finance and Economics, its sociology faculties were merged into Minzu University of China, and other faculties merged into other institutions. At the same time, its engineering section was merged with Tsinghua University, and Peking University moved from central downtown Beijing to take over the former Yenching University campus in the city's Haidian District.

2. Sociology in China

In 1979, Deng Xiaoping noted the need for more studies of the Chinese society and supported the reestablishment of the discipline. That year, in March, Chinese Sociological Association (CSA) was reestablished. Since then, sociology has been widely accepted as a useful tool for the state, and sociology graduates have often been employed in government institutions. Reestablishment of the field was also aided by the growing cooperation between Chinese and American sociologists.

In the People's Republic of China, the study of sociology has been developing steadily since its reestablishment in 1979. Chinese sociology has a strong focus on applied sociology, and has become an important source of information for Chinese policymakers. Chinese sociology, concentrates on policy-oriented, empirical research, to justify its support by the state. A notable example of the use of sociology by state planners was the impact of works by Fei Xiaotong on the policies of industrialization and urbanization of the rural countryside.

In 2003, a large Chinese General Social Survey program has begun. This is a big thing in the history of sociology in China.

2 社会学理论:起源与发展
Sociological Theory:Origin & Development

Sociological Theory:Origin & Development

Like the subjects it studies, sociology is itself a social product. Sociology first emerged in western Europe during the eighteenth and nineteenth centuries. In this period, the political and economic systems of Europe were rapidly changing. Monarchy, the rule of society by kings and queens, was disappearing, and new ways of thinking were emerging. Religion as the system of authority and law was giving way to scientific authority. At the same time, capitalism grew. Contact between different societies increased, and worldwide economic markets developed. The traditional ways of the past were giving way to a new social order. The time was ripe for a new understanding.

The Influence of the Enlightenment

The Enlightenment in eighteenth and nineteenth century Europe had an enormous influence on the development of modern sociology. Also known as the Age of Reason, the Enlightenment was characterized by faith in the ability of human reason to solve society's problems. Intellectuals believed that there were natural laws and processes in society to be discovered and used for the general good. Modern science was gradually supplanting traditional and religious explanations for natural phenomena with theories confirmed by experiments.

The earliest sociologists promoted a vision of sociology grounded in careful observation. Auguste Comte (1798—1857), a French philosopher who coined the term sociology, believed that just as science had discovered the laws of nature, sociology could discover the laws of human social behavior and thus help solve society's problems. This approach is called positivism, a system of thought still prominent today, in which scientific observation and description is considered the highest form of knowledge, as opposed to, say, religious dogma or poetic inspiration. The modern scientific method, which guides sociological research, grew out of positivism.

Alexis de Tocqueville（1805—1859），a French citizen，traveled to the United States as an observer beginning in 1831. Tocqueville thought that democratic values and the belief in human equality positively influenced American social institutions and transformed personal relationships. Less admiringly，he felt that in the United States the tyranny of kings had been replaced by the tyranny of the majority. He was referring to the ability of a majority to impose its will on everyone else in a democracy. Tocqueville also felt that，despite the emphasis on individualism in American culture，Americans had little independence of mind，making them self-centered and anxious about their social class position.

Another early sociologist is Harriet Martineau（1802—1876）. Like Tocqueville，Martineau，a British citizen，embarked on a long tour of the United States in 1834. She was fascinated by the newly emerging culture in the United States. Her book *Society in America*（1837）is an analysis of the social customs that she observed. This important work was overlooked for many years，probably because the author was a woman. It is now recognized as a classic. Martineau also wrote the first sociological methods book，*How to Observe Morals and Manners*（1838），in which she discussed how to observe behavior when one is a participant in the situation being studied.

Classical Sociological Theory

Of all the contributors to the development of sociology，the giants of the European tradition were Emile Durkheim，Karl Marx，and Max Weber. They are classical thinkers because the ideas they offered more than 150 years ago continue to influence our understanding of society，not just in sociology but in other fields as well（such as political science and history）.

Emile Durkheim

During the early academic career of the Frenchman Emile Durkheim（1858—1917），France was in the throes of great political upheaval. Durkheim was fascinated by how the public degradation of Jews by non-Jews seemed to calm and unify a large segment of the divided French public. Durkheim later wrote that public rituals have a special purpose in society. Rituals create social solidarity，referring to the bonds that link the members of a group. Some of Durkheim's most significant works explore what forces hold society together and make it stable.

According to Durkheim，people in society are glued together by belief systems. The rituals of religion and other institutions symbolize and reinforce the sense of belonging. Public ceremonies create a bond between people in a social unit. Durkheim thought that by publicly punishing people，such rituals sustain moral cohesion in society.

Durkheim also viewed society as an entity larger than the sum of its parts. He described this as society sui generis (which translates as "thing in itself"), meaning that society is a subject to be studied separately from the sum of the individuals who compose it. Society is external to individuals, yet its existence is internalized in people's minds—that is, people come to believe what society expects them to believe. Durkheim conceived of society as an integrated whole—each part contributing to the overall stability of the system. His work is the basis for functionalism, an important theoretical perspective.

One contribution from Durkheim was his conceptualization of the social facts. Durkheim created the term social facts to indicate those social patterns that are external to individuals. Things such as customs and social values exist outside individuals, whereas psychological drives and motivation exist inside people. Social facts, therefore, are the proper subject of sociology; they are its reason for being.

A striking illustration of this principle was Durkheim's study of suicide. He analyzed rates of suicide in a society, as opposed to looking at individual (psychological) causes of suicide. He showed that suicide rates varied according to how clear the norms and customs of the society were, whether the norms and customs were consistent with each other and not contradictory. Anomie (the breakdown of social norms) exists where norms were either grossly unclear or contradictory; the suicide rates were higher in such societies or such parts of a society. It is important to note that this condition is in society—external to individuals, but felt by them. In this sense, such a condition is truly societal.

Durkheim held that social facts, though they exist outside individuals, nonetheless pose constraints on individual behavior. Durkheim's major contribution was the discovery of the social basis of human behavior. He proposed that society could be known through the discovery and analysis of social facts. This is the central task of sociology.

Karl Marx

It is hard to imagine another scholar who has had as much influence on intellectual history as Karl Marx (1818—1883). Along with his collaborator, Friedrich Engels, Marx not only changed intellectual history but also world history.

Marx's work was devoted to explaining how capitalism shaped society. He argued that capitalism is an economic system based on the pursuit of profit and the sanctity of private property. Marx used a class analysis to explain capitalism, describing capitalism as a system of relationships among different classes, including capitalists (also known as the bourgeois class), the proletariat (or working class), the petty bourgeoisie (small business owners and managers), and the lumpenproletariat (those "discarded" by the capitalist system, such as the homeless). In Marx's view, profit, the goal of capitalist endeavors, is produced through the exploitation of the working class. Workers sell their labor in exchange for wages, and capitalists make certain that wages are worth less than the goods the workers produce. The difference in value is the profit of the capitalist. In the Marxist view, the capitalist class system is inherently unfair because the entire system rests on workers getting less than they give.

Marx thought that the economic organization of society was the most important influence on what humans think and how they behave. He found that the beliefs of the common people tended to support the interests of the capitalist system, not the interests of the workers themselves. Why? The answer is that the capitalist class controls the production of goods and the production of ideas. It owns the publishing companies, endows the universities where knowledge is produced, and controls information industries—thus shaping what people think.

Marx considered all of society to be shaped by economic forces. Laws, family structures, schools, and other institutions all develop, according to Marx, to suit economic needs under capitalism. Like other early sociologists, Marx took social structure as his subject rather than the actions of individuals. It was the system of capitalism that dictated people's behavior. Marx saw social change as arising from tensions inherent in a capitalist system—the conflict between the capitalist and working classes. Marx's ideas left us an important body of sociological thought springing from his insight that society is systematic and structural and that class is a fundamental dimension of society that shapes social behavior.

Max Weber

Max Weber (1864—1920) was greatly influenced by and built upon Marx's work. Whereas Marx saw economics as the basic organizing element of society, Weber theorized that society had three basic dimensions: political, economic, and cultural. According to Weber, a complete sociological analysis must recognize the interplay between economic, political, and cultural institutions (Parsons 1947).

Weber also theorized extensively about the relationship of sociology to social and political values. He did not believe there could be value-free sociology because values would always influence what sociologists considered worthy of study. Weber thought sociologists should acknowledge the influence of values so that ingrained beliefs would not interfere with objectivity. Weber professed that the task of sociologists is to teach students the uncomfortable truth about the world. Faculty should not use their positions to promote their political opinions, he felt; rather, they have a responsibility to examine all opinions, including unpopular ones, and use the tools of rigorous sociological inquiry to understand why people believe and behave as they do.

An important concept in Weber's sociology is verstehen (meaning "understanding"). Verstehen, a German word, refers to understanding social behavior from the point of view of those engaged in it. Weber believed that to understand social behavior, one had to understand the meaning that a behavior had for people. He did not believe sociologists had to be born into a group to understand it (in other words, he didn't believe "it takes one to know one"), but he did think sociologists had to develop some subjective understanding of how other people experience their world. One major contribution from Weber was the definition of social action as a behavior to which people give meaning.

(Reference: triumphias.com/blog/sociological-theory-origin-development/)

2.1　社会学理论的产生 Origin of Sociological Theories

在这一章,我们将按照起源、古典和当代三个阶段的划分来介绍社会学理论的发展。

2.1.1　第一位社会学家奥古斯都·孔德

The First Sociologist August Comte

"Sociology" was defined independently by French philosopher of science Auguste Comte in 1838 as a new way of looking at society. Comte had earlier used the term "social physics," but it had been subsequently appropriated by others. To distinguish his own approach from the others, he coined the term "sociology". Comte endeavored to unify history, psychology, and economics through the scientific understanding of social life.

一个研究领域的建立,不可能是出于一个人的努力。但是,由于孔德首先创造了"社会学"这个术语,所以他通常被称为社会学的创始人(founder of sociology)。他这样做,是想把自己的思想与他人的观点区分开来。

1. 生平

孔德于 1798 年出生于法国南部城市蒙彼利埃。他于 1814 年进入巴黎综合工业学校学习。由于一场师生间的冲突,孔德在巴黎综合工业学校的学业没有完成,就离开了学校。1817 年,孔德开始了与圣西门(Saint Simon)的合作,成为圣西门的秘书。圣西门对孔德的影响是多方面的,因为孔德主要思想的形成和成熟就在这一时期。

不过,在思想领域常常会发生类似的情况,在合作的状况下,要清楚地区分各自的思想贡献是非常困难的,这也经常导致合作者的分裂。孔德的情况也不例外。他不能忍受圣西门的控制欲和对他思想的占用。两人合作期间,通常孔德负责撰文,而圣西门就直接在文章上署上自己的名字予以发表。此外,圣西门越来越倾向于先知式的思想家风格也让孔德无法忍受。1824 年孔德和圣西门彻底决裂。1825 年孔德开始撰写他的主要著作《实证哲学教程》(*The Course in Positive Philosophy*)。这套 6 卷本巨著耗费了孔德 18 年的时间,直到 1842 年才全部完成。在这段时间里,孔德的学术生涯始终处于低迷状态。虽然《实证哲学教程》第一卷的出版得到了学术界的赞许,但是到第六卷完成时,连找到一家出版社都非常困难。这主要是因为和圣西门的决裂,使孔德失去了和学术界联系的渠道;其次也和他傲慢、独断的个性有关。

完成《实证哲学教程》之后的孔德,仍然得不到学术界承认,转而向工人阶层和其他团体讲授他的思想。这一时期,孔德越来越偏离了自己的主要思想,越来越夸大自己先知般的领袖特质,并自封为"人道教的教主"。1857 年孔德去世。

2. 思想

就像自然科学能够解释物质世界一样,孔德也探索建立了一门能够解释社会世界规律的科学。孔德认为,与物质世界要服从一些不变的法则一样,社会也遵循着一套自己的法则。就具体的研究方法而言,孔德提出了四种研究方法,即观察(observation)、实验(experiment)、比较(comparison)和历史分析(historical analysis)。

关于观察,孔德认为,观察本身不能作为科学研究的独立程序,观察必须受到理论的指导。事实上,在科学活动中,有效的观察从来都受到预设(preset)理论的约束。唯有如此,观察才能具有明确的目标和主题。不过,孔德似乎更多是满足于从理论上说明观察对于实证科学的意义,随后他就转向了理论阐述活动。因此在他的社会理论当中,并没有多少出于观察本身的认识。

关于实验,孔德提出,社会学很难做到像自然科学那样设计出人为的实验。但是他认为,存在着使自然的正常过程得以扭曲的"自然实验",也就是通常说的病理现象。作为反证,这些病理现象恰恰可以展示正常过程的内在机制,从而需要引起社会学家的重视。

对于比较法,孔德的理解要比我们现在的认识宽泛得多。在他看来,比较不仅仅涉及到"可比性"事物之间的比较,更具有类比的色彩。

至于历史分析的方法,则更多的是和他的社会动力学研究联系在一起。因为在那里,他所提出的"三个社会发展阶段的法则"恰恰是通过对社会历史的分析发展出来的。

(1)社会静力学(social statics)。如果我们需要对孔德的社会学思想加以概括的话,最核心的一点是,他明确地将社会体系理解为有机体(organism)。所谓有机体就意味着总体大于部分之和。比较起部分的简单叠加,由不同部分构建起来的有机体,具有了新的结构和功能。在其中每个部分也因此相互联系并承担起特定的功能。显而易见,孔德的这个思想启发了后来的结构功能主义。在他的思想体系中,对社会体系的结构性描述就属于社会静力学部分,至于社会结构的运动发展则要留到社会动力学(social dynamics)部分去处理。

Social statics is a branch of social physics that deals with the fundamental laws of the social order and the equilibrium of forces in a stable society. It is an approach to sociology focusing on the distinctive nature of human societies and social systems in abstract rather than empirical terms. The studies of social statics and dynamics are the two fundamentals of Comte's study of the organic phase or social stability. The studies of social statics and dynamics are not two distinct classes of facts but are two components of a theory. These studies are not separate but are complementary to each other as static is the study when society is in equilibrium and dynamics is the study of evolution which is a slow and steady process. This slow and steady process can only occur during the phase in which the society is in equilibrium and not disequilibrium or critical phase. Despite the fact that it seemed desirable for methodological and heuristic purposes to separate the study of statics and dynamics, in empirical reality they were correlative. Comte believed that social structures could not be reduced to the properties of individuals. Rather, social structures are composed of other structures and can be understood only as the properties of, and relations among, these other structures.

社会静力学讨论的第一个问题是:什么是社会体系最基本的单位?孔德明确指出,作为个体的人不能作为社会体系的基本单位。这就意味着,我们所发现的诸种社会法则不能最终归结为人性的法则。换句话说,我们不可能从关于个体的心理、生物法则推导出关于社会的法则。他认为,构成最基本社会单位的只能是家庭。社会的所有其他单位最终都是从家庭演化而成。

由此,社会静力学讨论的第二个问题就是,当社会体系经历着从最基本的单元家庭向复杂社会形式演变时,社会体系进变过程中最基本的问题是什么?回答这个问题,就需要和孔德的社会有机体(social organism)思想联系在一起。按照社会有机体的思想,有机体的进化过程必然受到两个反方向运动的影响。在一个方向上,有机体的演化表现为基本单元的不断分化、组合,从而产生新的更高层次的单元,而这也就意味着有机体内部结构的重新调整和原有有机体结构的瓦解。在社会体系的演化过程中,最基本的问题就是,在社会单元不断分化的状态中,如何实现社会结构的重新整合?可以预见,一旦这种整合没有得到有效的维持,就会出现社会体系的病理现象。

孔德认为,这种对社会体系加以重新整合的力量,只能是政府日趋集中的权力和社会层面上普遍共享的道德准则。在他看来,社会体系内部不断分化的部分,必然助长一种威胁有机体存在的个人主义和私人利益,从而抑制了全体的精神。为此,必须通过政府权威的日趋集中来抑制此种分裂倾向。同时仅仅依靠政府的物质力量还远远不够,还需要培养一种有利于社会整合的普遍道德准则(universal moral code)。

(2)社会动力学。在社会动力学部分,孔德提出了著名的"三个阶段的法则"(the law of

three stages）。

Social dynamics refers to the pattern of the revolutionary progress in which the sequence of the development is necessary and inevitable. The term "Progress" refers to the orderly development of the society, which is according to the natural law. Hence, the order and progress or statics and dynamics are co-related to each other. According to Comte, social dynamics describe the successive and necessary stages in the development in the human mind and the society. Moreover, it is natural that the social systems, such as institutions are interrelated and interdependent, so they can make a harmonious whole. Comte placed greater emphasis on the study of social dynamics, or social change.

他认为，从宏观的历史视野来看，人类社会体系的发展经历了三个不同的阶段。在每个阶段，主导的思想体系（ideological system）、精神领袖（spiritual leader）、社会的基本单元（basic unit）和社会结构（social structure）都是迥然有别的。

The law of three stages is an idea developed by Auguste Comte in his work *The Course in Positive Philosophy*. It states that society as a whole, and each particular science, develops through three mentally conceived stages: the theological stage, the metaphysical stage, and the positive stage.

三个阶段依次为神学阶段（the theological stage）、形而上学阶段（the metaphysical stage）和实证阶段（the positive stage）。

在神学阶段，主导的思想体系关注于超自然的事物和精神力量。社会最基本的控制性单元是血缘关系形成的组织，社会结构的整合主要依靠小的血缘性群体和宗教的精神力量。这个阶段大致是在文艺复兴前期进入形而上学阶段，开始从自然的而非超自然的角度来解释社会。

The first and earliest stage is called the theological stage. Starting at the very beginning of human beings and social groups, Comte believed that in this stage, people viewed the world and events as a direct expression of the will of various gods. In other words, ancient people believed that everything around them was a sign of active gods influencing their lives.

在形而上学阶段，主导的思想体系排斥对超自然事物的关注，转而通过思想的理性推导去阐述被认为隐藏在现象背后的本质。主导的精神权威是哲学家。社会最基本的控制性单元是国家，社会结构的整合主要通过国家的军队和法律来实现。

The second stage is called the metaphysical stage. Comte said that this stage started around the Middle Ages in Europe, or somewhere around the 1300s. In this stage, people viewed the world and events as natural reflections of human tendencies. They still believed in divine powers or gods, and that these beings are more abstract and less directly involved in what happens on a daily basis. Instead, problems in the world are due to defects in humanity.

在实证阶段，主导的思想体系是受到实证哲学指导的实证科学，它拒绝对现象背后的所谓本质加以抽象地理性思辨，而要求把认识限定在经验观察所涉及到现象层面。

孔德相信思想是决定社会发展的根本力量。正是思想的演进决定着社会基本结构的演进。实证主义认为：科学只能关注可以观察的实体即可以直接通过经验了解的实体。以细致的感官观察为基础，人们可以推断出能够解释现象的规律。只有到了第三个阶段即实证阶段，才可能实现对社会的科学认识，从而利用科学的力量实现社会的完善与进步。

作为先驱式的人物，孔德对社会学理论发展所具有的意义可以归结为两点：①他首先提出了"社会学"这个名称，从而为社会学作为独立学科（independent discipline）存在奠定了基础；②借助于和生物有机体（biological organism）的类比，他发展出关于社会结构和社会演进动力的一套理论模型，对日后的结构功能主义具有启示意义。但是孔德的社会学思想缺乏明确的经验基础，具有比较强的思辨性，这是他对社会学思想的发展缺乏实质性贡献的原因所在。孔德的思想是他所处时代的反映。

Comte's thinks reflected the turbulent events of his age. Comte looked to create a science of sociology that could discover the laws of the social world, just as natural science had discovered laws of the natural world. Although he recognized that each scientific discipline has its own subject matter, he thought that similar logic and scientific method could be applied to them all. Finding laws that govern human societies could help us to shape our desnity and improve the welfare of all humanity.

2.1.2　赫伯特·斯宾塞 Herbert Spencer

1. 生平

1820 年斯宾塞出生于英格兰的德比市。13 岁之前，他一直由父亲在家中教育（homeschooling），经历了短短几个月的正式教育后，他又转入叔叔家接受私人教育。终其一生，他接受的教育主要来自于家庭和成年以后的学术交往。尽管如此，在数学和自然科学方面，斯宾塞都获得了广泛的知识。1837 年，斯宾塞谋求到了一个铁路工程师的职务，这也证明了他所受教育的成功。1841 年工程完工，斯宾塞回到家乡德比，开始为当时的激进主义报刊撰写文章。1848 年他成为《经济学人》(*The Economist*)的副主编。1851 年,他出版了第一部著作《社会静力学》(*Social Statics*)。

1853 年斯宾塞的叔叔去世,留给他一大笔遗产。自此以后,斯宾塞得以辞去编辑职务,专心从事学术作品撰述和学术交流活动,并留下了数千页的文稿。1854 年斯宾塞出版《心理学原理》(*Principles of Psychology*),1874 年出版《社会学原理》(*The Study of Sociology*)。和孔德不同,斯宾塞在他的有生之年就获得了巨大的学术成功。实际上,《心理学原理》就曾经被哈佛大学和剑桥大学选作教材。

2. 思想

(1)社会有机体论。斯宾塞明确承认在这个问题上受到孔德的影响,即他同样是按照生物有机体的视角来理解宏观的社会系统。由此,他认为生物学和社会学是平行的两门科学,而且生物学是社会学的基础。从社会有机体出发,斯宾塞也认为,有机体的发展必然出现功能不断分化的现象,在提高有机体复杂程度的同时,也带来了内部整合的压力。

斯宾塞还详细地考察了生物有机体和社会有机体二者之间的相同点和不同点。在他看来,二者之间的相同点在于:生物有机体和社会有机体的生长、发展都迥然有别于无机物(inorganic substance)的变化。对于生物有机体和社会有机体来说,简单的规模增长往往就意味着结构的复杂程度加深,而这也就意味着功能上的分化。这是斯宾塞对于结构功能主义理论的共享。

> Though Spencer made some valuable contributions to early sociology, not least in his influence on structural functionalism, his attempt to introduce Darwinian ideas into the realm of sociology was unsuccessful. It was considered by many, furthermore, to be actively dangerous.

当然,斯宾塞也指出了二者之间的一些不同点,最主要的是:在生物有机体那里,部分与部分之间的联结通常非常紧密,而在社会有机体中,个体成员之间的联系却有可能是非常偶然和边缘化的。生物有机体中,部分与部分之间的交流其实主要是一个化学的过程,而在社会有机体里,成员之间的沟通主要是通过符号系统来实现的。

关于社会互动(social interaction),斯宾塞支持自由意志论(indeterminism)的基本原则。他认为:在不侵犯他人权利的情况下,个体可以根据自己的选择而做事。不只保守派(the conservatives)利用斯宾塞的理论来宣扬自己的观点。很多社会学家都套用他的理论来解释阶级战争。

(2)社会类型学(social typology)。在其社会系统发展的理论基础上,斯宾塞对不同社会类型做出了区分。其中最著名的一组区分就是军事社会(military society)和工业社会(industrial society)的区别。在斯宾塞看来,二者之间的主要区别在于,军事社会是以管理过程为主导,表现为高度集中的权力系统;而工业社会则是生产过程占主导,表现为低度集中的权力系统。

Spencer developed a theory of two types of society, the militant and the industrial society. Militant society was simple and undifferentiated, structured around relationships of hierarchy and obedience; Industrial society was complex and differentiated, based on voluntary.

我们可以从几个方面进一步进行这种比较:

在管理方面,军事社会的主要社会目标是进行防御或者战争,政治目标是维持中央集权;而工业社会的主要社会目标则是对内提供生产和服务,政治目标是降低权力集中程度,减少权威对生产环节的干预。

在生产过程方面,军事社会高度控制生产环节,并努力使之与进行防御和战争的目标保持一致;而对于工业社会来说,生产过程中始终保持着程度不一的自由,并努力使生产的功能能够和社会宏观结构的调整、发展保持一致。

在分配方面,军事社会中所有的物质流动都围绕着权力中心来展开,信息的流动则主要表现为从国家到个体的单向流动;至于工业社会,物质的流动可以在组织、其他团体和个人之间相对自由地展开,能够有效避免国家的随意干预;在信息流方面,除了由从国家到个人的流动,也保持从个人到国家的流动。

需要说明的是,斯宾塞并没有把这种社会类型学理解为截然分立的两个不同类型。实际上,他更愿意强调同一个社会在这两种倾向之间的摆动。导致一个社会更多地倾向于军事社会的原因主要在于外部的威胁和内部的整合压力。这两者带来的压力越大,一个社会就越倾向于军事社会;反之,当外部的威胁和内部的整合压力缓解时,社会就更倾向于工业社会。

2.2　古典社会学理论的发展 Development of Classical Theories

斯宾塞的社会学思想并不比同时代的其他社会学家更为逊色,但是区分社会学理论的起源阶段和古典阶段,并把斯宾塞归结为起源阶段的主要理由仍然成立。对于当代的社会学家来说,阅读孔德和斯宾塞并不必然能完整构成学科教育的组成部分。但是没有哪个严肃的社会学家敢否认我们归为古典阶段的几位社会学家对社会学理论发展所具有的重要意义。

2.2.1　卡尔·马克思 Karl Marx

1. 生平

卡尔·马克思于 1818 年 5 月 5 日出生于德国的特里尔市。1835 年他进入波恩大学学习,一年后转入著名的柏林大学。1841 年马克思以博士论文《德谟克利特的自然哲学和伊壁鸠鲁的自然哲学的差别》（The Difference Between the Democritean and Epicurean Philosophy of Nature）获得博士学位。随后他开始为《莱茵报》（Rhenish Newspaper）撰稿，并最终成为它的主编。1843 年，与燕妮·冯·维斯特华伦（Jenny Von Westphalen）结婚后，马克思夫妇移居巴黎。在巴黎，马克思开始对政治经济学产生兴趣。这一时期，马克思最著名的作品是《1844 年哲学经济学手稿》（Economic and Philosophic Manuscripts of 1844），这份直到 20 世纪才由苏联当局发表的手稿，引起国际学术界对青年马克思主义人学思想（Marxist human theory）的讨论。

　　1845 年，马克思从巴黎迁往布鲁塞尔（Brussels）。在这里，马克思、恩格斯合作完成了《德意志意识形态》（German Ideology）一书。这本书继续了前一著作的主题，批判青年黑格尔派（Young Hegelian School）耽于在幻想中改造世界。与之相反，马克思则主张通过现实的实践活动推翻资本主义社会。1848 年马克思完成著名的《共产党宣言》（The Communist Manifesto）。随后他回到巴黎，很快又前往伦敦，过着漂泊他乡的生活，并在伦敦度过了余生。

> The *Communist Manifesto* is an 1848 pamphlet by German philosophers Karl Marx and Friedrich Engels. Commissioned by the Communist League and originally published in London just as the Revolutions of 1848 began to erupt, the Manifesto was later recognized as one of the world's most influential political documents. It presents an analytical approach to the class struggle and the conflicts of capitalism and the capitalist mode of production. In 2013, The *Communist Manifesto* was registered to UNESCO's Memory of the World Program along with Marx's *Capital*, Volume I.

　　实际上，从 1849 年开始，马克思就退出了公共政治生活，转入到非常勤勉的学术研究当中。在将近 15 年的时间里，他大量阅读，并写下许多摘录和评论。1867 年，马克思最主要的著作《资本论》第一卷（Capital，Vol 1）发表。

　　1864 年国际工人协会（International Workingmen's Association）在伦敦成立，马克思迅速成为该协会的领袖。国际工人协会后改名为共产国际（Communist International）。1871 年巴黎公社（the Paris Commune）运动再次激起马克思巨大的政治热情。但是随着巴黎公社最后的失败，这一运动对马克思来说，只留下他的另一部伟大作品《法兰西内战》（The Civil War in France）。1881 年燕妮去世。1883 年 2 月马克思的小女儿也去世了。1883 年 3 月 14 日，马克思逝世。

2. 思想

　　马克思总是把经济问题与社会制度（social system）联系在一起加以思考。因此，他的经济学著作也具有深刻的社会学的洞察力。在马克思看来，人类社会的第一个特征就是，人不同于其他动物那样服从于自身的自然规律，从而和自然本身保持一致；人之所以为人，恰恰在于他必须从环境中制造出所需的生活资料（means of living）。这个制造过程就是人在特定技术水平上，通过构建起特定的社会关系从而实现的。与之相关的第二个特征是，随着人的创造活动的进展，人的需要也是不断发展的。因此，只有随着这个过程的不断深化，人才能超出对生存的简单物质需求，不断发展出其他更高层次的需求。第三个特征指的是人类的生产活动建立在劳动分工（division of labor）的基础上。马克思认为，劳动分工导致生产水平的提高，必然带来产品的剩余，从而产生出私有制（private ownership）。由此，劳动分工开始以土地或者资本的私有制为前提，而这就意味着社会结构等级的分化和与之相关的剥削（exploitation）和异化（alienation）等现象。

马克思认为，只要存在着生产资料（means of production）的私有制，就必然存在剥削和异化。在这样的社会中，被统治阶级只能通过自己的劳动力来交换基本的生活资料，以便使统治阶级获利。这也就意味着只能通过集体所有制（collective ownership），才能在根本上解决这个问题。最后一个特征和意识形态（ideology）联系在一起。人的思想和价值观念最终来自于人们的劳动实践活动。意识形态是关于世界的系统的观点，并且为统治阶级的权力所支撑，从而成为了统治阶级维护自身利益的重要手段。

> Alienation: The breakdown of, the separation from, the natural interconnection between people and their productive activities, the products they produce, the fellow workers with whom they produce those things, and with what they are potentially capable of becoming.

总之，马克思认为：资本主义发展的动力源于资本再生产过程（process of reproduction）中对劳动者的剥削和异化。马克思是作为对资本主义进行最深刻最彻底最科学地批判的批判家而闻名于世的。不过，对资本主义弊端的揭示、矛盾的考察和灭亡的预言，虽是马克思的资本主义批判的主要内容，但并非其全部内容。事实上，他对资本主义的历史贡献的肯定，亦是其资本主义批判的重要内容，也是其历史唯物主义（historical materialism）大厦不可分割的部分。

马克思在批判资本主义的基础上提出了一个基本的社会结构理论。按照这个理论，社会的基础是与生产力（productivity）一定发展阶段相适应的生产关系的总和（relations of production）组成的经济基础（economic base）。二者之间，生产力处于主导地位，因为决定何种生产关系能够最终确立的，恰恰是生产力发展水平。当二者处于相互适应的阶段，则社会基本结构保持稳定。而一旦生产力的发展超出了既存生产关系的范围，它就必然导致代表这一新兴生产力的社会阶级和生产关系中的既得利益阶级之间爆发阶级斗争。马克思相信，无论这个过程有着怎样的曲折，最终代表新兴生产力的阶级必将取得胜利，从而对旧的生产关系加以全面的改造。要使这种改造真正彻底，胜利的阶级还必须控制社会结构的第二个层级，即上层建筑（superstructure）。

Economic Base：To Karl Marx, the economy, which conditions, if not determines, the nature of everything else in society.

Superstructure：To Karl Marx, secondary social phenomena, like the state and culture, that are erected on an economic base that serves to define them. Most extremely, the economy determines the superstructure.

Ideology：A system of ideas and ideals, especially one which forms the basis of economic or political theory and policy.

马克思相信，改变这一社会状态的方法只能是共产党领导下的无产阶级革命（proletarian revolution）。共产党的目标就是废除私有制。为了实现这个目标，无产阶级第一步必须掌握国家的政权。一旦取得了政治地位，接下来就可以废除土地私有制（private ownership of land）和继承权（inheritance）、将信贷、银行、交通和一切工厂收归国家所有；实行普遍的劳动义务制；消除城乡差别等。马克思称这个向共产主义社会过渡的阶段为"无产阶级的革命专政"（revolutionary dictatorship of the proletariat）。至于共产主义，则预示的是一个人彻底解放和自由，国家完全消亡，从而实现社会自我管理的社会。马克思的研究对世界产生了深远影响。

2.2.2 马克斯·韦伯 Max Weber

Max Weber was a German sociologist, historian, jurist, and political economist. His ideas profoundly influenced social theory and research. He is recognized as one of the fathers of sociology along with Auguste Comte, Karl Marx, and Émile Durkheim.

1. 生平

马克斯·韦伯于 1864 年 4 月 21 日出生于德国的埃尔福特市。其父老马克斯·韦伯是当地的一名法官兼律师，后从政于柏林，先后担任了州议会和帝国议会的议员。韦伯年幼时就在家庭举办的各类招待宴会上认识了当时德国一流的知识分子。1882年，韦伯高中毕业，考入海德堡大学（the University of Heidelberg）学习法律专业。1884 年，韦伯转入柏林大学（现柏林洪堡大学）就读，在这一时期，他完成了博士论文。受到德国社会政治协会的资助和委托，韦伯对易北河东部地区农业工人的状况进行了调查，并完成大部头的《易北河东部农业工人状况》一书。

1892 年，韦伯接受了柏林大学的讲师职务，并与玛丽安·施尼特格尔（Marianne）完婚。1894 年，这对年轻的夫妇迁往弗赖堡大学（University of Freiburg），韦伯在那里担任了政治

经济学(Political Economy)教授。1897 年,韦伯与其父之间长期积累的矛盾爆发为一次激烈的争吵。事后不久老韦伯就去世了。此后,韦伯陷入了长期的精神崩溃状态,无法从事学术研究和教学工作。1900 年,韦伯从海德堡大学(University of Heidelberg)退休。

> Spirit of capitalism: In the West, unlike any other area of the world, people were motivated to be economically successful, not by greed, but by an ethical system that emphasized the ceaseless pursuit of economic success. The spirit of capitalism had a number of components including the seeking of profits rationally and systematically, frugality, punctuality, fairness, and the earning of money as a legitimate end in itself.

第一次世界大战爆发后,韦伯成为海德堡地区一家医院的行政官员。随后他对德国的战时政策加以批判,认为德国如不限制自己的目标,无限制的潜艇战必将使美国参战,到那时德国必败无疑。

1918 年韦伯接受维也纳大学(University of Vienna)聘请,重新回到课堂。1919 年他改任慕尼黑大学(Ludwig Maximilian University of Munich)教授。在慕尼黑大学,韦伯发表了两篇著名的演说《作为职业的科学》(Science as a Vocation)和《作为职业的政治》(Politics as a Vocation)。在这一时期,他还完成了《经济与社会》(*Economy and Society*)的一部分,并作了一系列讲座,后收入《经济通史》(*General Economic History*)一书。1920 年夏天,韦伯因患肺炎去世。

2. 思想

> Max Weber defined sociology as the science whose object is to interpret the meaning of social action and thereby give a causal explanation of the way in which the action proceeds and the effects which it produces. Action in this definition is meant the human behavior when and to the extent that the agent or agents see it as subjectively meaningful.

韦伯是一位知识广博的人,他的著作涵盖了经济学、法学、哲学、比较史学以及社会学等诸多领域,所以不能将他仅视为一位社会学家。通过一系列经验研究(empirical study),韦伯提出了现代工业社会的一些基本特征。

与其他早期的社会学思想家不同,韦伯认为社会学应该关注社会行动而非社会结构。他坚信人类的动机(motivation)和信念(faith)是变革背后的动因,思想、价值和信念具有推动社会变革的力量。

社会科学方法论(the methodology of social sciences)。在社会科学方法论上,韦伯明确提出要保持价值中立(value neutrality)。这是个很容易引起激烈争论的主张。韦伯的意思是:研究者个人的价值取向(value orientation)和经济利益(economic benefit)不应该影响社会科学分析的过程。研究过程必须是理性的(rational)、系统的(systematic),即采用明晰的概念对经验材料(empirical materials)加以归类,使用正确的论据规则和进行严格的逻辑推理（logical reasoning）。按照韦伯的观点，社会科学不应该为任何一种道德观念提供证明，事实上它也没有能力提供出这样的证明。因为社会科学不可能科学地证明何种价值规范或行为模式是正确的或最好的，而只能对之进行客观的（objective）、中立的（neutral）描述。也就是说，我们不可能从实然（reality）推导出应然（necessity）。韦伯进一步提出，社会科学研究的目的不是普遍、抽象的一般规律，而是为社会行动提供解释性的理解。在这一点上，韦伯深受德国新康德主义（neo-Kantianism）的影响。

> Value neutrality, as described by Max Weber, is the duty of sociologists to identify and acknowledge their own values and overcome their personal biases when conducting sociological research.
>
> In order to be value-neutral, sociologists must be aware of their own moral judgments and values, and avoid incorporating them into their research, their conclusions, and their teaching.

既然社会科学的最终目的不是普遍的规律，那么应该如何对之加以研究呢？对此，韦伯提出了他著名的理想类型（ideal type）概念。理想类型来自于经验概括，但不同于一般的概念，而是经过社会学家的主观提炼，从而完成对一个纯粹的理性行为过程的构建。实际上，韦伯并没有对理想类型给出清晰的定义。

> Weber himself wrote："An ideal type is formed by the one-sided accentuation of one or more points of view and by the synthesis of a great many diffuse, discrete, more or less present and occasionally absent concrete individual phenomena, which are arranged according to those one emphasized viewpoints into a unified analytical construct…" It is a useful tool for comparative sociology in analyzing social or economic phenomena, having advantages over a very general, abstract idea and a specific historical example.

在韦伯看来，人的行为可以归为四种类型。当然，这样的分类并不表示这些行为类型之间有着绝对的界限，界限只存在于理想类型那里。

第一种行为类型是工具理性行为（instrumental rational action），它以客观的、理想科学的知识为基础，突出了实现特定目标必须使用的手段。

> Instrumental rational action involves the pursuit of ends that the actor has chosen for himself；Thus, his action is not guided by some larger value system. However, it is affected by the actor's view of the environment in which he finds himself, including the behavior of people and objects in it.

第二种行为类型是价值理性行为（value rational action），即个人不再是根据最有效实现目标的手段，而是根据基本的价值规范来确定自己的行为，比如某些信教者因为遵奉教义而避免饮酒。

> Value rational action occurs when an actor's choice of the best means to an end is chosen on the basis of the actor's belief in some larger set of values.

第三种行为类型是传统型行为（traditional action），即由根深蒂固的习俗惯例决定的行为。有相当一部分人类行为属于这个范畴，因为人们通常以历代相传的惯例来应对惯常的情景。在韦伯看来，传统社会中决定人们行为的基本类型就是传统型，并且这一行为类型和工具理性行为、价值理性行为处于排斥的状态。这是因为，在传统社会中，人们按照习俗要求来安排自己的行为，一般都会排除以客观资料为基础的计算和对手段、目的的逻辑判断。另一方面，由于传统行为预先已经决定了人们的行为选择，也就不存在价值理性行为所要求的对价值的明确承担。

> Traditional action refers to action taken on the basis of the ways things have been done habitually or customarily.

第四种行为类型是情感型行为（affectual action），它的典型例子可以在愤怒的球迷、打骂孩子的父母身上看到。

> Affectual action refers to non-rational action that is the result of emotion.

2.2.3 埃米尔·迪尔凯姆 Émile Durkheim

> Émile Durkheim was a French Jewish sociologist. He formally established the academic discipline of sociology and is commonly cited as one of the principal architects of modern social science, along with both Karl Marx and Max Weber.

1. 生平

1858 年，迪尔凯姆出生于法国的埃皮纳尔。1879 年，迪尔凯姆成功考进了巴黎高等师范学院（Ecole Normal Super Paris）。在那里，他感受到哲学和历史学的魅力，并深受当时法国著名历史学家德·库朗热（De Coulanges）的影响。1882—1887 年，迪尔凯姆在巴黎周围的学校任教，其间在德国进修一年。这些经历帮助迪尔凯姆和法国教育部门的官员建立起重要的个人联系，这对于他最终在波尔多大学开讲社会学课程有着重要的影响。迪尔凯姆在波尔多大学教席上出版了他的主要著作《社会分工论》

（*The Division of Labor in Society*）等。正是这些著作最终确立了迪尔凯姆的经典作家地位。同时期由他创办、主编的《社会学年鉴》(*Annual Review of Sociology*)也使他的声望进一步得以提高。

The institutionalization of sociology as an academic discipline, however, was chiefly led by Émile Durkheim, who developed positivism as a foundation for practical social research. While Durkheim rejected much of the detail of Comte's philosophy, he retained and refined its method, maintaining that the social sciences are a logical continuation of the natural ones into the realm of human activity, and insisting that they may retain the same objectivity, rationalism, and approach to causality. Durkheim set up the first European department of sociology at the University of Bordeaux in 1895, publishing his *Rules of the Sociological Method* (1895).For Durkheim, sociology could be described as the "science of institutions, their genesis and their functioning."

1902 年，迪尔凯姆转入巴黎索邦大学(Sorbonne University)。1906 年，他的职位是科学和教育学教授。1913 年，他的职位变成了教育科学和社会学教授。迪尔凯姆因此成为了第一位社会学教授(professor of sociology)。这对于社会学最终在当代学科分类体系中确立其地位有着重要的意义。可以这样说，如果不是因为迪尔凯姆卓越的学术贡献和崇高的学术地位，社会学要成为学科分类体系中一门成熟的学科，还有更长的道路要走。而迪尔凯姆明确的方法论思想，尽管有着种种缺陷，却为社会学克服起源阶段思辨大于经验研究的缺陷，发挥了重要的作用。在这一时期，迪尔凯姆借助于其教学和主办的《社会学年鉴》，成功地吸引了一批有才智的青年投身于社会学研究。

第一次世界大战对迪尔凯姆的事业造成了巨大的打击，尤其是在他的儿子安德烈阵亡时。迪尔凯姆再也没能从打击中恢复过来。1917 年，迪尔凯姆去世。

2. 思想

与孔德一样，迪尔凯姆也认为必须要用科学的方法客观地研究社会。他认为社会学的第一原则就是把社会事实(social facts)当作事务来研究。但是，与孔德的著作相比，迪尔凯姆的著作对于现代社会学产生了更为持久的影响。在迪尔凯姆看来，所谓社会事实，就是那些塑造我们个体行动的社会生活的诸多方面，例如家庭规矩(family norms)，宗教礼仪(religious rituals)、法律条文(law articles)、经济状况(economic situation)等等。社会事实是行动、思考和感觉的方式。它对个体施加强制性力量(coercive power)，但是人们却经常不承认社会事实的约束作用的强制性(coercion)，这是因为人们一般会主动顺从社会事实，盲目地相信自己的行动是出于自我选择。事实上，社会事实能够以多种方式制约(restrict)人类行动，从直接的惩罚(如犯罪)到社会拒绝(行为不被社会接受)再到人际互动时的误解(如语言误用等)。社会事实可以是物质的(material)，如一个国家的国旗；也可以是非物质的(immaterial)，如自由(freedom)、爱(love)。非物质的社会事实(immaterial social facts)看不见、摸不着，不能被直接观察，必须通过间接地分析它们的效果来研究。研究社会事实必须要摒弃主观偏见和意识形态,因此是很难的。

> In sociology, social facts are values, cultural norms, and social structures that transcend the individual and can exercise social control. Durkheim defined the term. For Durkheim, social facts consist of manners of acting, thinking and feeling external to the individual, which are invested with a coercive power by virtue of which they exercise control over him. Durheim viewed it as a concrete idea that affected a person's everyday life.
>
> Durkheim's examples of social facts included social institutions such as kinship and marriage, currency, language, religion, political organization, and all societal institutions we must account for in everyday interactions with other members of our societies. Deviating from the norms of such institutions makes the individual unacceptable or misfit in the group. Durkheim's discovery of social facts was significant because it promised to make it possible to study the behavior of entire societies, rather than just of particular individuals.

《社会分工论》是迪尔凯姆的博士论文,也是他的第一部重要作品。在这部著作中,迪尔凯姆对社会变迁进行了分析,他认为工业时代的到来意味着一种新的团结(solidarity)形式的出现。

> *The Division of Labor in Society* is the doctoral dissertation of the French sociologist Émile Durkheim, published in 1893. It was influential in advancing sociological theories and thought, with ideas which in turn were influenced by Auguste Comte. Durkheim described how social order was maintained in societies based on two very different forms of solidarity — mechanical and organic, and the transition from more primitive societies to advanced industrial societies.

所谓社会团结(social solidarity),指的是构成社会各部分之间的协调问题,也就是使社会结合起来而免于混乱的原因。在他看来,社会团结最基本的纽带就是集体意识(collective conscience)。只有当个体成功融入社会群体,并且接受一套共享的价值观或习俗时,团结才能得以维持。按照《社会分工论》的说法,"同一个社会中普通市民所共有的全部信仰和观点构筑了一个有自身生命的确定系统,可以将它们称作集体或共同意识。"应该说,这不是一个特别清晰的概念,但它对于理解迪尔凯姆的思想来说,却是关键性的。迪尔凯姆坚持认为,对社会现象的认识,绝不能通过将之还原到个体水平的事实来加以解释。从这个意义上说,集体意识指的就是使特定社会系统得以维持的,为社会成员共享的价值体系。它之所以是超出个体的社会现象,是因为它既不能由个体产生,也约束着个体的行为和观念。尽管集体意识可能存在着多种表现形式,在《社会分工论》中,迪尔凯姆主要选择了法律作为它的表现形式。

Durkheim's grand theory involves a concern for the historical transformation from more primitive mechanical societies to more modern organic societies. What differentiates these two types of society is the source of their solidarity, or what holds them together. The key here is the division of labor.

Collective conscience：The ideas shared by the members of a collectivity such as a group, a tribe, or a society.

迪尔凯姆对比了两种团结形式，即机械团结（mechanical solidarity）与有机团结（organic solidarity），并把它们同劳动分工（division of labor）联系起来。迪尔凯姆的无机（机械）社会和有机社会的区分，本质上是对传统和现代两种社会形态的说明。

根据迪尔凯姆的说法，劳动分工程度低的传统文化是以机械团结为特征的。大多数社会成员所从事的职业相似，共同的经验和信念把他们结合在一起，这些共享信念具有压制性的力量。在无机社会中，社会规模相对较小，成员数量有限，基本的结构单位为独立的血缘组织（consanguineous organization）。血缘组织之间的联系松散而稀少，每个单位彼此类似，并且独立地满足各自成员的需要。在这种社会形态中，社会团结表现为强烈的集体意识，即严酷的制裁性法律。在这里，法律之所以是严酷的，是因为任何对集体意识的背离都被看作对社会所有成员和神灵的背叛，从而遭受到严酷的惩罚。由此可见，在无机社会中，个体的自由、选择度很低，人们为集体意识所左右。

In mechanical solidarity, society is held together by the fact that virtually everyone does essentially the same things. In other words, there is little division of labor in primitive society and this fact holds society together. In this society, people care deeply about collective ideas. Furthermore, the ideas are very powerful and people are likely to act in accord with them.

迪尔凯姆将人口密度（population density）与成长（growth）作为由传统社会到现代社会的关键要素。当无机社会变迁到有机社会，一方面社会规模的扩大，成员扩张，另一方面成员之间发展出彼此区别、相互依赖的社会分工体系。工作的专门化（specialization）和社会分化（social differentiation）的深化导致了一种新的等级制的有机团结。以有机团结为特征的社会是靠人们在经济上的独立和承认其他人的贡献的重要性来维系的。由于劳动分工的发展，人们更加相互依赖，经济交换关系和相互依赖取代了共享信念。集体意识也随之变得更为抽象和软弱。从法的角度上说，集体意识的这种变化表现为从严酷的刑法转变为主要对契约关系加以调整的民法。它的惩罚性更少，更强调以非惩罚的方式纠正对规范的侵犯，从而将违反者重新整合进相互依赖的网络中。在有机社会中，个体拥有更大的自由，集体意识也表现出对人格尊严的更多尊重。

> In more modern organic solidarity a substantial division of labor has occurred and people come to perform increasingly specialized tasks. In this society, fewer people are affected by the collective conscience, more people are able to evade it partially or completely. The collective conscience is not as important and most people don't seem to care about it so deeply.
>
> Durkheim dealt with changes in the material world in the way in which we divide up and do our work.

当社会形态从无机向有机转化时,社会分工的扩展以及相应的集体意识的转变,并非总是一帆风顺的。现代世界的变革过程非常迅速而激烈,这导致了许多社会难题的出现。在传统、道德、宗教和日常生活方式瓦解时,却没有明确的新价值观产生出来,这就是迪尔凯姆所说的失范状态(anomie):这是一种由现代生活所引起的失落感或绝望感。现代社会的发展极大动摇了传统道德标准(traditional moral criteria)。这使得现代人感受到他们的日常生活缺乏意义。

在《社会分工论》中,迪尔凯姆对失范现象以及如何克服失范的方法讨论的并不充分,他只是强调了个人对集体生活的重新融入。在 1902 年出版《社会分工论》的第二版时,他在新加的"序言"部分,补充了关于职业群体和发展职业伦理(professional ethics)的论述。在他看来,职业群体(occupational groups)将提供过去由家庭、教会所提供的娱乐、教育和社会化(socialization)的功能。职业群体把从事相关职业从而可能拥有类似生活经验的人们联合起来。在其中,人们能够感到重新融入了社会,减轻了专业化工作带来的心理压力和社会异化。也就是说,通过职业群体,由专业人士组成的社会能够重新和集体意识联系起来。

2.3 社会学理论的当代发展
Contemporary Development of Sociological Theories

社会学古典阶段的社会学家除了我们以上介绍的马克思、韦伯和迪尔凯姆以外,通常还包括齐美尔(Georg Simmel,1858—1918)、帕累托(Vilfredo Pareto,1848—1923)等人。所谓当代阶段(contemporary era),一般以 1937 年帕森斯(Talcott Parsons,1902—1979)发表《社会行动的结构》(*The Structure of Social Action*)为标志。在这个阶段,社会学作为一门成熟的学科在大学教育体系中牢牢地确立了地位,同时也形成了极其丰富的理论流派(theoretical perspectives)。接下来,我们按照功能主义(functionalism)、冲突论(conflict theory)、法兰克福学派(Frankfurt school)、符号互动论(symbolic interactionalism)和现象学社会学(phenomenological sociology)等几个方面,对当代社会学理论做简单的介绍。

2.3.1 功能主义 Functionalism

功能主义认为社会是一个非常复杂的体系。这个体系的各个组成部分协同工作产生了稳定和团结。按照功能主义的观点，社会学应该研究社会各组成部分之间以及与社会整体的相互关系。孔德和迪尔凯姆等功能主义者（functionalist）经常使用有机体（organism）类比的概念，把社会的运行比作一个活的有机体的运转。他们认为：社会的各组成部分也是为了社会整体的利益而协同工作，像人体的各个部分一样。功能主义者强调道德共识（moral consensus）对于维护社会稳定（maintain social stability）的重要性。当社会的大多数成员分享一种共同的价值观时，这种道德共识会帮助社会达成社会平衡（social equilibrium）。

> Functionalism holds that society is a complex system whose various parts work together to produce stability and that sociology should investigate their relationships. —Giddens

1. 塔尔科特·帕森斯 Talcott Parsons

> Talcott Parsons was an American sociologist, best known for his social action theory and structural functionalism. Parsons is considered one of the most influential figures in sociology in the 20th century. He is generally considered a structural functionalist. Parsons' contributions to sociology in the English-speaking world were his translations of Max Weber's work and his analyses of works by Max Weber, Émile Durkheim, and Vilfredo Pareto. Their work heavily influenced Parsons' view and was the foundation for his social action theory.

很大程度上，韦伯之所以在英语世界获得崇高的学术地位要归功于帕森斯。在求学期间，帕森斯曾作为交换生就读于海德堡大学。在那里，他对韦伯的思想进行了详细的研究，并于 1930 年将《新教伦理和资本主义精神》翻译成英文。1937 年，帕森斯发表《社会行动的结构》一书，阐释了他的社会功能主义思想。1998 年，国际社会学学会把这本书列为 20 世纪排名第三的社会学最重要的著作。在这本书中，帕森斯把一般行动系统区分为四个子系统，分别是文化系统（cultural system）、社会系统（social system）、人格系统（personality system）和行为有机体（behavioral organism）。

> *The Structure of Social Action*（SSA）is Parsons' most famous work. Its central figure was Weber, and the other key figures in the discussion were added, little by little, as the central idea took form. Parsons first achieved significant recognition with the publication of *The Structure of Social Action*（1937）, his first grand synthesis, combining the ideas of Durkheim, Weber, Pareto, and others. The International Sociology Association listed it as the third most important sociological book of the 20th Century in 1998.

按照帕森斯的观点,文化系统由符号系统构成,即宗教信仰、语言和价值观念等。这些社会价值必须通过社会化的过程被社会成员内化为自己的价值观,从而成为保持社会团结的强大力量。社会系统的基本分析单位则是角色互动,指的是两个或两个以上行动者形成的相对稳定的互动关系。在这里,行动者既可能是个体,也可能是团体。在人格系统(personality system)层面,帕森斯关注的是个体的需求、动机和态度。帕森斯认为,人们都是以自己的利益最大化作为行动的基本动机的。行为的有机体(behavioral organism)指的是作为动物性存在的个体,既包括人所生存的生物环境也包括自然环境。在行为有机体层面,中枢神经系统和动力系统构成最基本的单位。按照这样一个理论模型,帕森斯就可以对人的社会行为进行描述和说明。行为者的目标由标准化的角度期待界定下来,为了实现这一目标,行为者必须具有一定的条件。

Cultural system: The Parsonsian action system that performs the latency function by providing actors with the norms and values that motivate them for action.

Social system: The Parsonsian action system responsible for coping with the integration function by controlling its component parts; a number of human actors who interact with one another in a situation with a physical or environmental context.

Personality system: The Parsonsian action system responsible for performing the goal-attainment function by defining system goals to attain them.

Behavioral organism: One of Parsons's action system, responsible for handing the adaptation function by adjusting to and transforming the external world.

此后,帕森斯试图通过一组模式变量,来分析不同的角度期待和关系结构,将自己的理论提炼为著名的"AGIL 模型"。按照功能主义的社会模型,社会被理解为一个由执行不同功能的部分联结成的整体,不同部分之间彼此依赖、相互平衡。AGIL 模型将社会系统为实现自身平衡而必须处理的纷繁复杂的问题和要求提炼为四个方面或者说必须具备的四种基本功能:adaption(适应)意味着任何社会结构必须从外界获取足够的资源,并在社会系统内分配这些资源;goal attainment(目标实现)指的是社会系统必须有能力确定系统目标的次序,并调整足够的资源实现这些目标;integration(整合)为了保证社会系统的有效运行,还必须对系统内不同行为者之间行为进行调节、控制,限制冲突的发生,这就是整合功能;latency(保持)意味着社会系统必须向社会成员灌输(indoctrination)社会价值观,以促进成员之间的有效互动。

作为当代社会学理论中的经典作家,帕森斯一方面对社会学理论的发展具有重要的影响,但另一方面,他的理论模型从一开始就遭到了众多批评。主要的批评在于如下几点:①他的 AGIL 模型是一个静态的模型,无法分析社会发展的过程。②他的理论不能解释角色冲突问题。③他没有明确指出社会重新恢复平衡所需的机制。④最关键的一点是,他的理论包含一个重要的价值判断(value judgment),即认为保持社会系统的功能平衡是最理想的社会状态。这一点在那些接受了马克思主义社会冲突理论的学者看来是很成问题的。

2. 罗伯特·金·默顿 Robert King Merton

Robert King Merton was an American sociologist. He is considered a founding father of modern sociology. He spent most of his career teaching at Columbia University. He was awarded the National Medal of Science for his contributions for having founded the sociology of science in 1994.

另一位重要的功能主义者是罗伯特·默顿。他是帕森斯指导的第一批博士生当中的一个。帕森斯本人也提到过，他和默顿常常被视为功能主义学派的领袖。然而和他导师过分的理论偏好有所不同，默顿对经验调查、统计分析一类的经验研究投入了大量精力。正是这种研究经历，使得默顿能够从经验研究的角度，为功能主义提出了"中层理论"（middle-range theory）的设想。他的主要著作都收入了论文集《社会理论与社会结构》（*Social Theory and Social Structure*）。

Although both Merton and Parsons are associated with structural functionalism, there are important differences between them. Merton was more favorable toward Marxian theories than was Parsons. Merton can be seen as having pushed structural functionalism more to the left politically.

按照默顿的观点，对于社会学的发展来说，重要的并不是去发展无所不包的理论体系，而应该首先致力于发展"中层理论"。所谓"中层理论"应该是具有相对有限的研究主题，并根据相应的理论假设发展出经验研究，从而能够对理论假设提供证明。由此，才能够从这些得到经验研究支持的"中层理论"出发，逐步建构更全面的理论体系。由此可见，"中层理论"对于默顿来说，构成了经验研究（empirical research）和宏大理论（grand or all-inclusive theory）之间的桥梁。

Merton fashioned his theory very similarly to that of Max Weber's *Protestant Ethic and the Spirit of Capitalism*（1905）. Merton believed that his middle range theories bypassed the failures of larger theories, which are too distant from observing social behavior in a particular social setting.

此外，默顿还对功能主义加以发展，提出了一系列颇有影响的功能分析概念。

The function can be explained as the result or consequence of people's action. These consequences can be either latent function or manifest function in any social institution. The distinction is explained by Robert K. Merton in his book, Social Theory and Social Structure, in 1949.

(1)"反功能"(dysfunctions)。在帕森斯那里,AGIL 模型所描述的基本功能都是实现社会结构的整合与平衡。而恰恰是这一点遭到了冲突理论的强烈反对。为此,默顿区分了功能与反功能,并发展出"反功能"的概念。社会行为的"反功能"意味着某些事物(组织)可能削弱对社会结构的整合与平衡。举例来说,现代社会的基本组织是科层制(bureaucracy),科层制对于实现某些目标来说缺乏效率;但另一方面,对官僚性规则的过度依赖也会削弱成员的认同。从迪尔凯姆开始,对社会功能的研究往往就是强调它们对社会整合(social integration)发挥的作用。默顿提出的"反功能"使我们认识到,即使某些社会事物对某些群体具有正面的功能,但对另一些群体则可能具有"反功能"。

Dysfunctions are unintended or unrecognized, and have a negative effect on society. They can be manifest or latent.

(2)显性功能(manifest functions)和隐性功能(latent functions)。显性功能指的是活动参与者已经知晓并预想达成的结果,而隐性功能指的是参与者没有意料到或者注意到的后果。

Manifest functions are the consequences that people observe or expect. It is explicitly stated and understood by the participants in the relevant action.

Latent functions are those that are neither recognized nor intended. A latent function of a behavior is not explicitly stated, recognized, or intended by the people involved.

在帕森斯和默顿两位最著名的功能主义拥护者的影响下,在很长一段时间里,功能主义者的思想是社会学最主要的理论传统,特别是在美国。但是,近年来因为功能主义的局限性已经显而易见,所以它的流行逐渐减弱。一个常见的批评是:功能主义过分强调了有助于社会整合的因素,忽视了导致分裂和矛盾的因素。对于稳固和秩序的强调意味着社会中基于阶级、种族和性别等因素的分裂或不平等被最小化了。而且,功能主义对社会内部的创造性不够重视,赋予了社会本身所不具备的品质。

2.3.2　冲突理论 Conflict Theory

如果说功能主义有比较明确的学派意味,那么冲突理论很难说构成了一个真正的学派。被划为冲突理论流派的几位社会学家并不构成为一个派别。只能说,他们在一些基本的理论预设上有着类似的倾向，即都强调社会结构中的冲突的一面，并因此而对功能主义持批评态度。

类似于功能主义者，社会学使用冲突理论来强调社会内部结构的重要性。他们也提出了一个模型来解释社会的运作方式。与功能主义者相比，冲突理论家突出社会中分化的重要性，拒绝接受对共识的强调。冲突论者（conflict theorist）倾向于把社会看作是由追求不同利益的不同群体组成的，这意味着矛盾是永远潜在的，总有一些群体（阶层）会比其他群体（阶层）获得更多的利益。冲突理论考察社会强势与弱势群体（vulnerable groups）之间的紧张状态，并试图去理解统治关系是如何建立以及维持的。

> Like functionalists, sociologists using conflict theories emphasize the importance of social structures. They also advance a comprehensive model to explain how society works. However, conflict theories reject functionalism's emphasis on importance of divisions of society and, in doing so, concentrate on issues of power, inequality and competitive struggle. Conflict theorists examine the tensions between dominant and disadvantaged groups, looking to understand how relationships of control are established and maintain.

很多冲突理论家都认为，他们的观点来自马克思，但也有些人同时也受到韦伯的影响。当代德国社会学家达伦多夫（Ralf Dahrendorf）就是一个很好的例子。

1. 拉尔夫·达伦多夫 Ralf Dahrendorf

> Ralf Dahrendorf is best known in sociology for his conflict theory, heavily influenced by Marxian theory. While his conflict theory was influenced by Marxian ideas, Dahrendorf was never a Marxist. He describes himself as a liberal. He has led a life in which he has developed theory and applied it to practical matters in academia and, more importantly, in the larger society.

按照达伦多夫（1929—2009）的观点，社会中始终存在着一种冲突的倾向。冲突的双方分别是一个社会当中有权力的团体和没有权力的团体。冲突的原因则是不同团体为了寻求各自的利益。在一些社会中，有权力团体的地位相对稳固，但是在另一些社会中，这种相对的稳固的状态终究会被打破，从而发生社会变迁。在这个意义上讲，社会冲突是人类社会演变的关键因素。

显而易见，对于达伦多夫来说，权力对于理解社会结构有着根本的意义。所谓权力，本质上就是一种控制力，掌权者因此得以确定基本的社会秩序（social order），向无权力者索取利益。而这就必然引起无权力者的反抗。因此，达伦多夫认为，这种利益的冲突是不可避免的。如果说，社会规范在功能主义那里构成为社会整合的基本因素，对于达伦多夫来说，它同样具有这样的功能。区别在于，社会规范（social norms）并不像功能主义认为的那样是中立、为社会各阶层普遍共享的，而是受到权力的支撑并为权力服务的。

　　既然围绕着权力和利益的冲突是社会结构中的普遍现象，那么在什么时候、什么条件下潜在的冲突结构才会导致真正的社会冲突呢？达伦多夫在他的代表作《工业社会的阶级和阶级冲突》（*Class and Class Conflict in Industrial Society*）中试图解答这个问题。

　　首先涉及的是阶级动员的概念。人们潜在的权力欲望和利益冲突必须通过形成特定的组织才能得到实现。为了形成组织，除了需要一个或一群创立者和特定的指导纲领外，外在的社会条件也是很关键的。越是享受政治自由的国家，阶级动员的可能性就越大；反之，越是缺乏政治自由的国家，通过政治动员引发社会冲突的可能性就越小。此外，还需要三个方面的因素：①潜在的群体成员是否在地理上彼此接近？②他们是否容易沟通？③是否能够吸引到足够背景类似的人参与进群体？如果能够满足这三个条件，则社会冲突的可能性就非常大了。在这些理论阐述的背后，我们还需要考虑个体对共同利益的认同水平问题。实际上，如果社会结构中的流动性大，个体就越不容易对阶级、群体身份形成稳定的认同，则社会冲突越不容易发生。

　　至于社会冲突的强度问题，达伦多夫认为，一些特定的社会条件决定着它的水平。其中最重要的是，不同社会组织中那些居于高位的人是否在其他社会组织中同样据有高位。或者说，社会地位（social status）究竟是重叠的还是交叉的。重叠的社会地位意味着：在特定组织中获取高位的人可以将自己的这种优势地位向其他社会生活领域延伸，从而形成了高度垄断的权力结构（authority structure）；反之，交叉的社会地位意味着，不同社会组织中的高位由不同群体所占据，权力结构相对分散。显而易见，越是垄断的权力结构，它的社会冲突强度越高；越是分散的权力结构，社会冲突的强度越低。与之相关的另一个因素则是社会中处理冲突的制度化（institutionalization）水平。也就是说，如果该社会能够为社会冲突提供相对中立的"游戏规则"，则冲突的强度也将减低。

　　按照这样的理论分析，达伦多夫对发达工业社会中的社会冲突进行了分析。他认为，随着所有权和管理权的分离以及社会冲突制度化水平的提高，在发达工业社会（developed industrial society）中，社会冲突将趋于减弱。实际的经验研究也表明，发达工业社会中的工人更经常地与工会保持联系，但不太会质疑国家的政策。

　　关于冲突，马克思谈到的主要是就阶级而言的利益差别，而达伦多夫则把它们与权威和权力联系起来。在所有社会中都存在握有权威的人与几乎被权威排斥的人，以及统治者与被统治者的分化。

2. 刘易斯·阿尔弗雷德·科塞 Lewis Alfred Coser

　　Coser was the first sociologist to try to bring together structural functionalism and conflict theory; his work was focused on finding the functions of social conflict. Conflict with one group may also serve to produce cohesion by leading to a series of alliances with other groups. Conflicts within a society can bring some ordinarily isolated individuals into an active role. Conflicts also serve a communication function.

科塞转入社会学研究颇具戏剧色彩。他于1933年进入巴黎大学（University of Paris）研究比较文学。他的计划是根据法国、英国和德国的社会结构来对三个国家的文学进行比较研究。结果，一位教授指出，这已经不是比较文学而是社会学了。自此以后，科塞一直从事于社会学研究并成为美国著名的社会学家。早年的生活经历使科塞确立了知识分子社会批评的责任感。

科塞（1913—2003）是第一位试图将功能主义与冲突论进行整合的社会学家。他的工作聚焦于社会冲突的功能（functions of social conflict），并于1956年发表了《社会冲突的功能》（*The Functions of Social Conflict*）一书。他认为社会冲突不仅可以使原本处于疏离状态的个体变得更有活力，而且可以发挥沟通的功能。科塞还对社会冲突的起源和根源进行了更详尽的研究。科塞赞同齐美尔（Georg Simmel，1858—1918）的观点，认为人具有好斗和敌对的冲动，因此亲密关系中总是爱恨交集的，越是亲近的关系越有机会发展出憎恨。但是，就社会冲突来说，科塞认为它的根源因社会结构的不同而不同。为此，他将冲突分为外部冲突和内部冲突：

（1）外部冲突建立在群体特性的基本因素上，即彼此在若干重要特征上相互区别的群体形成外部的敌对状态。

（2）内部冲突则指的是，当一个社会中的诸多社会角色彼此交叉，特定个体在承担不同社会角色时，这些社会角色本身存在着的冲突。科塞认为，这种状态有助于保持社会的稳定。

由此，我们可以推论：①越是压抑不同观点的社会，冲突越可能和基本的社会价值联系在一起；②社会群体的彼此依赖性越强，则社会冲突的可能就越低。

2.3.3 符号互动和现象学社会学
Symbolic Interactionism and Phenomenological Sociology

符号互动主义起源于对语言和意义的关注。严格地说，符号互动理论和现象学社会学分属于不同的理论派别。这里之所以放在一起介绍，是因为这两个学派都强调了社会建构和社会行动的意义框架。人的行为不同于动物之处在于：人的互动始终发生在由语言符号构成的意义背景当中。没有这样的意义结构，人的行为是难以想象的。因此，在理解社会结构、社会行为方面，意义结构具有重要的作用。这一点为符号互动学派和现象学社会学所共享。

1. 乔治·赫伯特·米德 George Herbert Mead

米德（1863—1931）认为自我发展是社会经验累积而成，强调环境对人类行为的影响，提出社会自我（social self）理论。米德被认为是第一个对社会学的发展做出重要贡献的美国社会学家，而他的主要著作是在他去世后，其学生整理他的笔记所得，即《心灵、自我与社会》（*Mind，Self and Society*）一书。

我们已经看到，在功能主义那里，人的行为是按照动机（motivation）、价值规范（criteria

of value)等变量(variable)来解释的。换句话说,个体的人格只是这些因素的因变量(dependent variable)而已。米德则认为,不能将个体视为对动机、价值规范等因素消极反应的因变量。米德宣称语言使我们成为具有自我意识的人,意识到我们自己的个体性,能够像别人观察我们那样从外部认识自己。个体有能力根据互动关系发展出自我,从而在不同的动机、价值规范之间做出选择。按照这种观点,米德对人的自我观念进行了进一步的区分。出于有机体对外界或他人的自发反应的部分,构成人的"主我"(I),是行为的自发冲动和倾向;"宾我"(me)则指导着人的社会化自我的行动,它是根据"我"所理解的他人对"我"的看法而形成的。用米德的话说,就是他人的态度构成了有组织的"宾我",然后,个体以"主我"对其做出回应。"宾我"强调了人行为的社会层面,而"主我"突出了人行为的自发性和一定的创造性。

The Self: The ability to take oneself as an object.

I: The immediate response of the self to others; the incalculable, unpredictable, and creative aspect of the self.

Me: The individual's adoption and perception of the generalized other; the conformist aspect of the self. Unlike the I, people are very cognizant of the me, they are very conscious of what the community wants them to do. All of us have substantial me, but those who are conformists are dominated by the me. Society controls us through the me which allows people to function comfortably in the social world while the I makes it possible for society to change. Because of the mix of I and Me, both individuals and society function better.

为了说明个体在自身确立起社会身份(social identity)的过程,米德详细分析了自我互动的过程。按照米德的观点,自我互动是人们确立和承担起社会角色的关键过程。在这个过程中,人们通过与自己对话的方式,通过想象、回忆的方式再现或预示社会场景,从而将他人对自我的角色期待带入到对自我的塑造过程中来。比如说,我们可能回忆起曾经发生过的情景,并将其中自我的表现和他人的评价通过想象再现出来。这也就意味着,个体能够对自己的行为加以有意识地控制。米德亦是开创符号互动论的社会学家,并发展出自我发展三阶段的理论。

Mead believes that the self emerges in 3 key stages in childhood. The first is the play stage in which the child plays at being someone else. The child might play at being Spider-Man or Mommy. In doing so, the child learns to become both subject (who the child is) and object (who Spider-Man is) and begins to build a self. In the next stage, the game stage, the child begins to develop a self in the full sense of the term. Instead of taking the role of discrete others, the child takes the role of everyone involved in a game. Mead used the example of baseball, in which the child may play one role, but must know what the other eight players are supposed to do and expect from her. Another famous concept created by Mead is the generalized other. The generalized other is the attitude of the entire community, in the example of the baseball game, the attitude of the entire team. A complete self is possible only when the child moves beyond taking the role of individual significant others and takes the role of the generalized other. It is also important for people to be able to evaluate themselves from the point of view of the group as a whole and not just from that of discrete individuals.

第一个阶段被称为"前嬉戏阶段"(play stage),表现为无意义的模仿行为。这些行为之所以被称为无意义的,是因为在这个阶段,儿童缺乏感受他人态度的能力。

第二个阶段是"嬉戏阶段"(game stage),出现于儿童的晚期。在这个阶段,儿童通过角色扮演游戏开始学习建构社会角色。但是,在这个阶段,儿童一次只能扮演一个特定的角色,缺乏对整个社会场景中涉及的多种角色的考虑。

第三个阶段是"概化他人"(generalized other)阶段,米德以垒球比赛为例加以说明。垒球比赛是团体性的竞赛,因此任何一名球员不仅需要了解并承担起自身的角色,还必须按照整个团队的立场和期待来调整自己的行为。米德认为,只有在概化他人的能力被内化之后,个体才成为合格的个体进入社会当中。

我们还需要说明的是米德的符号理论。米德认为,人类在互动中依赖共享的符号(symbol)和理解。人类生活在一个充满符号的世界中,人类个体之间所有的交往在本质上都是符号的交换。所谓符号,就是用来指称其他事务的某一事务。这一点源于米德对举止的看法。所谓举止(manner),尽管是整个行动的组成部分,但是它也构成行为的一个标识。

A symbol is something that stands for something else.

比如说,当某个男孩向女孩献花,这个行为就构成了他对女孩感情的一个外在标识。这个时候献花就不仅仅是献花这个行为本身,还构成为一个有意义的符号,被献花的女孩就可以据此来调整自己的行为。从这个例子我们可以看到,米德所理解的符号其实就是社会化了(socialized)的反应方式。当构成意义的某个行为发生时,作为符号它将引起可以合理预期的他人的反应(response)。因此,符号理论也贯穿了米德对社会互动(social interaction)的说明。正是通过对符号的吸收,人才能合理地预期他人的反应,从而能够承担起"他人的角色",概化他人,并因此而形成"主我"和"宾我"。

符号互动主义的视角使我们能够洞察在日常生活过程中我们行动的本质,但是因为它忽视社会中的权利和结构以及它们是如何限制个体行动的等重大问题而一直受到批评。

2. 欧文·戈夫曼 Erring Goffman

Goffman made substantial advances in the study of face-to-face interaction, elaborated the "dramaturgical approach" to human interaction and developed numerous concepts that have had a massive influence, particularly in the field of the micro-sociology of everyday life. Much of his work was about the organization of everyday behavior, a concept he termed "interaction order". He contributed to the sociological concept of framing (frame analysis), to game theory (the concept of strategic interaction), and to the study of interactions and linguistics. His influence extended far beyond sociology: for example, his work provided the assumptions of much current research in language and social interaction within the discipline of communication. Overall, his contributions are valued as an attempt to create a theory that bridges the agency-and-structure divide—for popularizing social constructionism, symbolic interaction, conversation analysis, ethnographic studies, and the study and importance of individual interactions.

按照柯林斯的说法，20 世纪美国的社会学家当中，默顿是最著名的人物，帕森斯是最卓越的综合理论家，而戈夫曼（1922—1982）则对理论进步贡献最大。通过对微观层次社会交往过程的卓越分析，戈夫曼发展出了著名的"戏剧理论"。他的代表作包括《日常生活中的自我呈现》(*The Presentation of Self in Everyday Life*)、《互动仪式》(*Interaction Ritual*)、《框架分析》(*Frame Analysis*)、《印象管理》(*Impression Management*)、《精神病院》(*Asylums*)等。

戈夫曼之所以借用戏剧分析(dramaturgical analysis)来说明自己的观察，是因为他的研究重点关注人在日常生活中的角色表演和印象管理(impression management)，也就是说人们是如何在日常生活中相互呈现，同时有意识地试图引导和控制对方形成对自己的看法。与之相关的概念还包括前台(onstage area)和后台(backstage area)。显而易见，人们的社会互动和印象管理的具体过程主要发生在前台，这里还涉及到各种道具，比如说参加某个工作招聘的面试，应试者会努力在着装、携带的物品上体现自己适合该份工作的素质。至于后台，则是练习印象管理技巧的隐蔽场所。戈夫曼认为，后台是社会戏剧的表演者不再扮演角色，因而呈现其真实自我的地方。

Goffman describes the theatrical performances that occur in face-to-face interactions. He holds that when someone comes in contact with another person, he attempts to control or guide the impression the other person will form of him, by altering his own setting, appearance and manner. At the same time, the second person attempts to form an impression of, and obtain information about, the first person. In his dramaturgical analysis, he saw a connection between the kinds of "acts" that people put on in their daily lives and theatrical performances. In a social interaction, as in a theatrical performance, there is an onstage area where actors (people) appear before the audience; this is where positive self-concepts and desired impressions are offered. But there is also a backstage—a hidden, private area where people can be themselves and drop their societal roles and identities.

通过对微观交往层次的分析，戈夫曼希望能够将基本的互动秩序发展为独立的存在和研究领域。也就是说，这个领域有着自身独特的游戏规则。在他的《互动仪式》一书中，戈夫曼试图对各种面对面的互动秩序按照由小到大的顺序加以说明，其中包括个人交际、邂逅、表演和庆典等活动。在他看来，尽管这些互动秩序都发生在微观层次，但是和宏观的社会秩序直接相关。这是因为宏观的社会秩序归根到底是由无数的微观层次的社会交际来构成的。此外，这种微观的互动秩序也构成个体人生际遇的核心内容。

Goffman's *Interaction Ritual*：is a collection of six essays. The first four were originally published in the 1950s, the fifth in 1964, and the last was written for the collection. They include "On Face-work" (1955); "Embarrassment and Social Organization" (1956); "The Nature of Deference and Demeanor" (1956); "Alienation from Interaction" (1957); "Mental Symptoms and Public Order" (1964); and "Where the Action Is" (1967).

需要说明的是，在对符号互动过程的阐述中，戈夫曼（Erring Goffman）最主要描述和分析了引导和控制他人对自身产生印象的过程，而对其中自我的互动和形成缺乏系统地论述，尽管他也申明了扮演他人角色的重要性。他的研究兴趣主要不在于个体对自己说了什么，而是如何成功地控制了情景，从而引导对方形成对自己的看法。

值得注意的是，戈夫曼最后提议符号互动理论的研究应该关注"弱势群体"（vulnerable groups）。由此，他就指明符号互动理论可以对权力问题加以研究。这种研究涉及到处于弱势地位和强势地位的人之间的互动模式，从而使得微观社会学同样有可以对宏观层次的社会冲突理论提供新的洞见。

3. 哈罗德·加芬克尔 Harold Garfinkel

现象学社会学的理论渊源当然要追溯到著名的德国哲学家胡塞尔（Edmund G. A. Husserl，1859—1938）与舒茨（Alfred Schutz，1899—1959）。胡塞尔把现象学描述为科学中的科学（science of all sciences），按照胡塞尔的观点，现象学（phenomenology）是通过对存在假设的悬置，从而展开的对纯粹意识内容（pure consciousness）的分析。比如说，我可以感知到电脑在我面前的存在。现象学则将此种存在判断悬置起来，分析电脑在我感觉中的呈现。而我之所以能够区分一台真实存在于我面前的电脑和一台我虚构的电脑,也恰恰是因为前者在我意识的呈现中表现出来的某种"实质"(essence)。对这种实质的分析也属于现象学的领域。

> Phenomenology is the study of structures of consciousness as experienced from the first-person point of view. The central structure of an experience is its intentionality, its being directed toward something, as it is an experience of or about some object. An experience is directed toward an object by virtue of its content or meaning（which represents the object）together with appropriate enabling conditions. As a philosophical movement it was founded in the early years of the 20th century by Edmund Husserl and was later expanded upon by a circle of his followers at the universities of Göttingen and Munich in Germany. It then spread to France, the United States, and elsewhere, often in contexts far removed from Husserl's early work.

将胡塞尔的现象学和社会学联系起来的,主要是奥地利哲学家舒茨。舒茨1967年出版了《社会世界的现象学》(*The Phenomenology of the Social World*)一书。对于舒茨来说,个体在日常生活中赋予情景的意义是最重要的。事实上,人们的互动之所以可能,普遍的社会秩序之所以可能,都因为人们普遍共享了未被言明的情景意义。他的理论后来发展成为社会意义建构理论。

如果说,在胡塞尔和舒茨那里,现象学的思辨色彩浓于社会学的分析,那么加芬克尔提出的"常人方法学"(ethnomethodology)则是在社会学当中引入现象学思想的主要代表。

1945年,加芬克尔(Harold Garfinkel)完成了一项对陪审团法庭(jury court)讨论录音的分析。使他感到惊奇的是,陪审团成员都拥有大量共享的关于社会运行组织事件的知识,并且正是这些知识使得他们能够形成有效的互动和讨论,从而顺利完成陪审团的工作。正是这一点在日后成为常人方法学关注的重点。

所谓常人方法学(也称民族学方法论,本土方法论),是社会成员理解他们生活的社会世界的意义的方法。由于无数的日常生活都被理解为理所当然,人们在日常互动中实际上是无需关注到此类问题的。倒是在普遍共享的社会知识受到破坏,基本的社会互动秩序不复存在时,人们才会关注到日常交往得以可能的潜在意义结构。

> Ethnomethodology is a sociological approach, originally developed by Harold Garfinkel, studies how the process of social interactions produces social order. In order to analyze how individuals account for their conduct, ethnomethodologists may intentionally unsettle communal norms to evaluate how such individuals respond and strive to restore order to the community.
>
> Ethnomethodology examines resources, practices and procedures via which a society's members interpret their daily lives, and the mutual recognition of which within certain contexts engenders orderliness. The ethnomethodological approach focuses on the capacities of people as

members of a collective rather than their individuating traits as distinct persons. It is primarily not a theory seeking to analyze social life.

常人方法学的问题论域：①作为社会学主要关注内容的社会结构问题逐渐被淡化，反对把社会关系和人际关系物化和神秘化；②当常人方法学以平常人的心态对面对日常生活时，发现日常生活呈现的不是结构、模式等抽象形式，而是可以直接感知并且发生最普遍的"交谈行为"，并认为只有研究人们在日常生活中的交谈行为，才能真正地进入生活世界，真正地接触到人们的日常经验过程。

2.4 社会整合理论
Social Integration Theory

2.4.1 于尔根·哈贝马斯 Jüergen Habermas

Habermas was known for his work on the concept of modernity, particularly with respect to the discussions of rationalization originally set forth by Max Weber. He considers his major contribution to be the development of the concept and theory of communicative reason or communicative rationality, which distinguishes itself from the rationalist tradition, by locating rationality in structures of interpersonal linguistic communication rather than in the structure of the cosmos. His defence of modernity and civil society has been a source of inspiration to others, and is considered a major philosophical alternative to the varieties of post-structuralism. He has also offered an influential analysis of late capitalism.

哈贝马斯，生于 1929 年，曾先后在哥廷根大学（University of Göttingen）、苏黎世大学（University of Zurich）、伯恩大学（University of Bonn）学习哲学、心理学、历史学、经济学等，并获得哲学博士学位。1961 年，他完成教授资格论文《公共领域的结构转型》（"The Structural Transformation of the Public Sphere"），历任海德堡大学、法兰克福大学（Goethe University Frankfurt）教授、法兰克福大学社会研究所所长以及德国马普协会（Max Planck Society）生活世界研究所所长。1994 年退休。

The Max Planck Society for the Advancement of Science is a formally independent non-governmental and non-profit association of German research institutes. Founded in 1911 and was renamed to the Max Planck Society in 1948 in honor of its former president, theoretical physicist Max Planck. The society is funded by the federal and state governments of Germany.

哈贝马斯是西方马克思主义重要流派法兰克福学派（Frankfurt School）第二代的代表人物，著述丰富，迄今有数十部著作问世，主要代表作包括：《公共领域的结构转型》（*The Structural Transformation of the Public Sphere*，1962）、《认识与兴趣》（*Knowledge and Human Interests*，1968）、《作为意识形态的科学技术》（*Technology and Science as Ideology*，1968）、《合法化危机》（*Legitimation Crisis*，1975）、《重建历史唯物主义》（*Reconstruction of Historical Materialism*，1976）、《现代性的哲学话语》（*The Philosophical Discourse of Modernity*，1985）、《后形而上学思想》（*Post-Metaphysical Thinking*，1988）、《包容他者》（*The Inclusion of the Other*，1996）以及《真理与论证》（*Truth and Justification*，1998）等，广泛涉及社会科学和人文科学的不同领域。

哈贝马斯自进入法兰克福大学（Goethe University Frankfurt）社会研究所开始涉猎学术研究起，便以思想活跃、政治激进著称。他通过跨学科专业的研究方法，对不同的思想领域进行了深入的研究；通过历史分析和社会分析，对西方思想史、特别是法兰克福学派自身的历史进行了清理和批判，并在此基础上建立起了自成一说的交往行为理论。由于思想庞杂而深刻，体系宏大而完备，哈贝马斯被公认是当代最有影响力的思想家，甚至被誉为"当代的黑格尔"，在西方学术界占有举足轻重的地位。

进入 20 世纪 90 年代，哈贝马斯开始有意识地把交往行为理论向政治哲学和法哲学领域推进，通过对自由主义、社群主义政治理论的批判，主张建立一种新型的话语政治模式，提倡用程序主义来重建民主制度，因此他转向韦伯并视之为可替代观点的源泉。哈贝马斯认为，没有也不应该有代替资本主义的东西，因为资本主义已经证明有能力产生巨大的财富。虽然如此，马克思在资本主义经济中确认的一些根本问题仍然存在，例如资本主义倾向于产生经济危机。我们需要控制经济过程，而不是被经济过程所控制。哈贝马斯认为，强化控制的主要方式之一就是复兴公共领域。他认为公共领域就是民主的框架，通过民主程序的改革以及社区机构更一致地参与，公共领域能够被革新。

哈贝马斯的思想特色主要表现为以下几个方面：

（1）论战性。哈贝马斯进入学术领域后，便不断向各种不同的思想路线提出挑战，掀起了一场又一场学术论争。

（2）综合性。哈贝马斯是一位杰出的综合大师，他把不同的思想路线、理论范畴有机地结合起来，比如把马克思主义与精神路线、理论范畴有机地结合起来，比如对马克思主义与精神分析的综合、对于德国唯心主义哲学传统与美国实用主义哲学传统的综合、对于哲学先验主义与哲学经验主义的综合等。

（3）体系性。哈贝马斯十分重视自身理论体系的构建，长期以来，他逐步从方法论、认识论、语言哲学、社会学、美学、政治学、法学等角度，建立和完善了自己的交往行为理论体系，试图从规范的角度对马克思主义，特别是对法兰克福学派的批判理论加以系统重建。

（4）实践性。哈贝马斯虽然是一位学院派思想家，但十分看重自身思想的实践性。哈贝马斯于 2001 年 4 月访华，在北京和上海两地作了题为《全球化压力下的欧洲民族国家》等一系列的演讲，在中国学术界反响巨大。

2.4.2 安东尼·吉登斯 Anthony Giddens

Anthony Giddens is an English sociologist who is known for his theory of structuration and his holistic view of modern societies. Giddens has been highly influential in the USA, as well as many other parts of the world. His work has often been less well-received in his home country. He is considered to be one of the most prominent modern sociologists. In 2007, Giddens was listed as the fifth most-referenced author of books in the humanities.

安东尼·吉登斯，英国社会学家。他以结构理论（theory of structuration）与当代社会整体论（holistic view）而闻名。1959 年毕业于英国赫尔大学（the University of Hull），主修心理学与社会学。之后在伦敦政治经济学院（the London School of Economics and Political Science）获得社会学硕士，并于剑桥大学国王学院（King's College，Cambridge）获得博士学位。

在社会学研究领域，吉登斯是英语世界中最具有原创性的思想家之一。他从解读社会学经典开始他的学术生涯，同时广泛涉猎经济学、政治学、人类学、考古学、地理学、哲学、现象学等方面的最新成果，并不断从中汲取营养。在这一过程中，吉登斯逐渐找到了应对现代社会问题的独特思路，构建起自己的理论体系，提出了应对世界最新变化的全新对策。

根据吉登斯迄今为止的研究主题和思想发展脉络，我们可以将其思想发展分为四个阶段：

Four stages can be identified in his academic life. The first stage involved outlining a new vision of what sociology is, presenting a theoretical and methodological understanding of that field based on a critical reinterpretation of the classics, such as Marx, Weber, and Durkheim. In the second stage, Giddens developed the theory of structuration, an analysis of agency and structure in which primacy is granted to neither. The third stage was concerned with modernity, globalization and politics, especially the impact of modernity on social and personal life. In the most recent stage, Giddens has turned his attention to a more concrete range of problems relevant to the evolution of world society, namely environmental issues, focusing especially upon debates about climate change.

(1)第一个阶段:20世纪70年代。吉登斯从全面系统地解读、分析和梳理三大社会学经典作家(马克思、韦伯和迪尔凯姆)的著作入手,逐渐找准自己的问题与思路,创造出属于自己的思考方法。他在这期间取得的理论成就体现在几个方面:

首先,通过对马克思、韦伯和迪尔凯姆著作的详细解读与认真反思,梳理出社会学发展的基本脉络和内在逻辑,为自己思想体系的构建夯实了基础。

其次,在研究经典社会学思想家的过程中,提出了自己的社会理论思想,提出了自己的社会学观。他提出了"社会理论"这一新概念,并将社会学与社会理论严格地区分开来。他认为,社会理论问题源远流长,而社会学则是对社会之现代特征的理论反映。

最后,通过诠释经典社会学思想,提出了社会学研究的新规则,其中最核心的一条是"双重解释学"(double hermeneutic)的思想。他指出,在社会科学与自己的活动构成社会科学研究主题的人之间,存在着交互解释的作用。通过这种双重解释或交互解释过程,科学知识和由它决定的社会反思性既成为现代社会的重要后果,又构成了现代社会的基本条件。

(2)第二个阶段:20世纪80年代。吉登斯开始从解读经典转向体系构建,其标志是结构化理论体系的创立。

这一时期他的主要成果是结构化理论(theory of structuration)体系的构建。在被称为"结构化理论大纲"的《社会的构成》(*The Constitution of the Society*)一书中,吉登斯对自己的理论体系作了最为详尽的阐述。结构化理论的问题意识,来自二战后占据西方主流社会学的"二元"困局,即结构(structure)与行动(action/agency)的二元论,表现为功能主义/结构主义、解释学/现象学之间的对立。针对这一困局,吉登斯提出把这种二元论(dualism)建构为结构的二重性(duality of structure)。所谓结构的二重性,集中体现在"反复发生的社会实践"上。通过这种反复发生的社会实践,结构与行动的二元对立(binary opposition)得以内在化为社会生活的二重性(duality of social life)。吉登斯认为,以社会行动的生产和再生产为根基的规则和资源同时也是系统再生产的媒介,而结构化的过程就是行动者和结构之间的相互构成过程,是以实践意识为基础的例行化和制度化过程。因此,结构化理论关注的焦点,就是社会结构在人的日常生活中的形成过程。作为"虚拟秩序"的社会结构,只有在时间和空间的域化过程中才能获得真实的定位,对结构的理解不能脱离对行动者及其能动作用的分析。

结构化理论是吉登斯试图克服和消除客观主义(objectivism)与主观主义(subjectivism)、整体论(holism)与个体论(individualism)、决定论(determinism)与唯意志论(voluntarism)的二元对立而提出的,其主要手段是用结构二重性去说明个人与社会之间的互动关系。

第三个阶段：20 世纪 90 年代。20 世纪 90 年代吉登斯的理论旨趣发生了重大转变，开始从体系的构建转向对现实的观照，致力于用自己的理论去诊断和捕捉当代西方社会的重大问题和变化趋势，并在此基础上提出了一整套应对现实问题和社会转变的措施与方案。由此，吉登斯的社会理论开始对西方世界的政府决策和社会生活产生了强有力的影响。

吉登斯思想的第三期发展的主要理论成果是现代性（modernity）全球化理论的提出和构建。可以说，吉登斯的整个社会理论体系，都建立在对现代性的研究之上。根据他对现代性所进行的深入研究，他敏锐地发现我们生活的世界正在发生前所未有的巨变。基于这种判断，吉登斯得出这样一个结论：现代性已经进入激进化或全球化的新阶段，至少在西方发达国家如此。吉登斯明确反对后现代（post modernity）的说法，认为我们正进入一个激进现代化的阶段，我们生活于其中的世界是什么样的？它是怎么生成的？我们将如何"驯服""失控的世界"这个庞然大物（juggernaut）？对这些问题的回答，就构成了吉登斯的全球化理论（theories of globalization）。

吉登斯关于庞然大物的比喻有些抽象，他通过一些例证解释了这个比喻。如：切尔诺贝利核电站危机。在分析的过程中，吉登斯指出：在现代社会，我们都面临极大的不安全感，我们意识到这些危机的存在，然而即使连我们信任的专家也不能控制这个庞然大物。为什么这个庞然大物会随时失控呢？以切尔诺贝利核电站（Chernobyl Nuclear Power Plant）为例，吉登斯给出了四个理由。第一，设计者会犯错。第二，操控者会犯错。第三，我们无法预测改良的后果。第四，任何新知识都可能使这个庞然大物改变方向，而这会带来潜在的危机。

Anthony Giddens considers himself a modern social theorist, he has a very different view of the modern world than classical theorists of modernity like Marx and Weber. Giddens sees modernity as a juggernaut, a massive force that moves forward inexorably riding roughshod over everything in its path. People steer this juggernaut but, given its size and bulk, they can not totally control the path it takes and the speed at which it travels. The notion of a juggernaut is abstract. In what Giddens calls high modernity, we are all faced with great insecurity about life. We remain aware of the risks that surround us. The risks are global in nature. Why the risks? Why is the juggernaut always threatening to rush out of control? Giddens offers four reasons.

① Those who designed the juggernaut made mistakes. ② Those who run the juggernaut made mistakes. ③ We can't always foresee the consequences of modifying the juggernaut or creating new components for it. ④ People in general, and experts in particular, are constantly reflecting on the juggernaut and in the process, creating new knowledge about it.

第四个阶段：人类历史进入 21 世纪之后，吉登斯对现代国家的生态危机（ecological crisis）给予了高度关注。在他看来，生态问题（ecological problem）是社会关系的直观写照，反映出社会关系的不协调，某种程度上生态已逐步沦为人们建构社会关系的工具。因此，变革社会关系是解决生态危机的出路。

思考 Thinking it through：

对比马克思、韦伯和哈耶克三人对于资本主义的态度。

Hayek's Tragic Capitalism(Excerpt)

There's more to life than economics, even for economists.

Human Limitations

The deficiencies that he (Hayek) attributed to human nature are both cognitive and moral. First, human knowledge is severely limited. According to Hayek, a mind can only ever understand what is less complex than it. Hence, no human mind can ever understand itself, much less the vast aggregate of human minds—each with its own unique and ever-evolving needs, and each with its own idiosyncratic body of information concerning local economic circumstances—that constitutes an economic system. This is the deep reason why socialism is impossible in principle, and always leads to chaos when attempted. The central planner simply cannot have all the information required to allocate resources or direct economic activity rationally.

To remedy this problem, the planner has to dictate, rather than learn, what individual economic actors need and how they will behave. For the only sure way to know what they want and what they will do is to decide for them what they should want and what they should do. And the more closely the economic planner wants outcomes to conform to his plan, the more thorough this dictatorial control will have to be. Planners will have to increase control, if they are intent on realizing the plan.

... What Hayek was opposed to was governmental activity that would undermine the operation of the free-market price mechanism. In his view, prices generated in the market encapsulate the information that is unavailable to the central planner, and thereby enable rational economic activity. For example, the price of oranges in Omaha reflects the effects of blight on orange crops in Florida, a bumper crop of oranges in California, higher demand for oranges in New York City, lower demand in Fargo, increases in the price of fuel needed to transport oranges across the country, and so on. No human mind need gather and process all of this information, because the market price is generated in a way that already reflects all of it. Consumers in Omaha need only respond to the current price (by buying fewer oranges, say, because the price has gone up) in order to coordinate their activity with that of other economic agents elsewhere in the country.

Our Deepest Yearnings

... Hayek thought it unwise to defend capitalism by emphasizing the just rewards of hard work, because there simply is no necessary connection between virtue of any kind, on the one hand, and market success on the other. Moreover, the functioning of the market economy depends on adherence to rules of behavior that abstract from the personal qualities of individuals. In particular, it depends on treating most of one's fellow citizens not as members of the same tribe, religion, or the like, but as abstract economic actors—property owners, potential customers or clients, employers or employees, etc. It requires allowing these actors to pursue whatever ends they happen to have, rather than imposing someone overarching collective end, after the fashion of the central planner.

Hayek did not deny that all of this entailed an alienating individualism. On the contrary, he emphasized it, and warned that it was the deepest challenge to the stability of capitalism, against which defenders of the market must always be on guard. This brings us to his account of the moral defects inherent in human nature. To take seriously the thesis that human beings are the product of biological evolution is, for Hayek, to recognize that our natural state is to live in small tribal bands of the sort in which our ancestors were shaped by natural selection. Human psychology still reflects this primitive environment. We long for solidarity with a group that shares a common purpose and provides for its members based on their personal needs and merits. The impersonal, amoral, and self-interested nature of capitalist society repels us ...

In Hayek: *The Iron Cage of Liberty* (1996), one of the better books on Hayek, Andrew Gamble suggests that the economist was essentially committed to a variation on Max Weber's "iron cage" thesis. Like Weber, Hayek thinks that the prosperity and order of modern civilization has come at the cost of secular disenchantment and ennui. Unlike Weber, Hayek emphasizes capitalist individualism rather than bureaucratization as the "iron cage" that locks us into this bargain.

A Kind of Fusionism

Hayek developed these themes most fully in his later writings, especially his three-volume *Law, Legislation, and Liberty* (1973—1979)—perhaps his greatest work—and his last book, *The Fatal Conceit* (1988). It is also in these books that Hayek—who had, decades before, penned a famous essay titled "Why I Am Not a Conservative"—went in a strongly Burkean conservative direction. Just as market prices encapsulate economic information that is not available to any single mind, so too, the later Hayek argued, do traditional moral rules that have survived the winnowing process of cultural evolution encapsulate more information about human well-being than the individual can fathom ...

Hayek was committed, then, to a kind of fusionism—the project of marrying free market economics to social conservatism. Unlike the fusionism associated with modern American conservatism, though, Hayek's brand had a skeptical and tragic cast to it ... In his view, human psychology has been cobbled together by a contingent combination of biological and cultural evolutionary processes. The resulting aggregate of cognitive and affective tendencies does not entirely cohere, and never will.

Three Problems

For all its purported gritty realism, however, Hayek's fusionism is no more stable than the more familiar kind. Even putting aside his agnosticism and his materialist assumptions about human nature (neither of which I share), his position is seriously problematic in at least three respects. The first concerns a criticism of Hayek pressed by Irving Kristol, echoing an earlier and more general analysis of capitalism famously developed by Daniel Bell. The market price mechanism requires treating economic value as nothing more than the aggregate of individual preferences. There is, on this account, no fact of the matter about what something is worth over and above what people are, for whatever reason, willing to pay for it.

This subjectivism about value has great utility when our focus is merely on satisfying the material needs and wants people actually happen to have. Hayek's purely procedural conception of just action, however, effectively treats value subjectivism as a completely general principle of social organization. The rules that govern capitalist societies must not treat any of the diverse ends people happen to have as objectively better or worse than any other. To acknowledge that there is some objective fact of the matter about what people ought to want, or some standard of value independent of the market, would open the door to justifying interference with the choices of economic actors, and thereby destroy the price mechanism.

So, capitalist society, as Hayek understands it, must operate on the principle that what is good or bad for its citizens is whatever they take to be good or bad for them. And the problem is that this subjectivist principle is a universal acid that inevitably eats away at all morality—including the moral principles Hayek thinks essential to the preservation of capitalist society. If there is no standard of good apart from what people happen to want, how can Hayek complain if what they happen to want is an egalitarian redistribution of wealth, or freedom from religion and traditional family arrangements? ...

A second，related problem with Hayek's position is one emphasized by Roger Scruton. You first have to see yourself as part of a common society—defined by a shared language，territory，culture，and history—before you can see yourself as bound by the rules of that society. That includes the rules that govern the free market. But just as value subjectivism tends to undermine commitment to family and religion，so too does it eat away at national loyalties. Modern capitalist society has seen the rise of the cult of the sovereign individual，whose allegiances are only to those institutions he has chosen. And increasingly，he does not choose to give special allegiance to whatever capitalist nation he happens to have been born in. He may even take up an adversarial relationship toward that nation，castigating it for its real or imagined failings and pitting it against the "global community." The rise of multinational corporations and the free flow of populations across borders，often for the purposes of providing corporations with cheap labor，are other aspects of modern capitalist society that tend to undermine national loyalties.

That brings us to a third criticism of Hayek—leveled this time by Gamble—which is that he never adequately faced up to the dangers posed by corporate power. Most people cannot be entrepreneurs，and even those who can cannot match the tremendous advantages afforded by the deep pockets，legal resources，and other assets of a corporation. Vast numbers of citizens in actually existing capitalist societies simply must work for a corporation if they are going to work at all. But that entails an economic dependency of individuals on centralized authority，of a kind that is in some ways analogous to what Hayek warned of in his critique of central planning.

3 社会组织
Social Organizations

Social Organization — Meanings, Forms and Definitions

The structure of individual and group connections is referred to as social organization. The term "organization" refers to the overall technical arrangement of components, while "social" alludes to the fact that social structures emerge from individual and group interactions.

Thus, one of the key interests of sociology is to observe and evaluate human society's actions as they occur in their formal and ordered forms and ties. Individuals, groups, and institutions all contribute to the larger organization that is society. It is a vast network of social relationships that is structured like the parts of a watch. The organizations fit in with other organizations that influence society: the organizational process resembles a human body, a machine, a factory, an office, a bank, and human society. Sociologists are specifically concerned in the discovery and study of:

The individual and groups that impact individual conduct and social foundations;

In their organized behavior, what kinds of social relationships do they have;

How do individuals and groups interact with one another;

How these social ties are maintained, how they deteriorate or dissolve, and what factors influence them; and

How individuals, whether consciously or subconsciously, organize themselves in diverse social settings.

Meanings and Forms of Social Organization

Social organization consists of all the ways in which men live and work together, especially all of the participants of societies programmed, ordered and coordinated relationships. Social organizations arrange and communicate group actions at various levels. They organize and crystallize various individual and collective desires.

Definitions of Social Organization

A social organization, according to Duncan Mitchell, is "the interdependence of components, which is fundamental property of all long-lasting collective organizations such as groups or communities and societies."

Organizations, according to Ogburn & Nimkoff, are "groups of people who work together to accomplish a goal."

According to Nimkoff & Ogburn, "An organization is an articulation of various parts performing different functions, an active group device for doing something."

Duncan Mitchell says that, "Social organization means the interdependence of parts of all persistent collective entities, groups, communities and societies that are essential characteristics."

According to Broom and Selznick, an organization implies a specialized plan of parts. Social organization implies social relationship among gatherings. People and gatherings interrelated together make social organization. It is the consequence of social association among individuals. It is the organization of social relationship where people and gatherings partake. Every one of the social foundations are social organizations. Affiliations, clubs and any remaining proper gatherings are organizations. Social frameworks are additionally founded on social organizations. In a coordinated body; its individuals get into each other based on jobs and status. The collaboration among the individuals sets them into organizations. The method of such collaboration is called social organization.

Relationship of Social Organization, Status and Role

According to their social roles, called status, the participants in a social organization conduct their tasks. The tasks conducted in an organization are considered members' positions, and even people conduct their roles in accordance with their rank. Therefore, the basis of social involvement in an association is status and position. If official, an organized body has its duties and rank allocated to its representatives and office bearers. Like office-bearers. The President's, Vice-President's, and Secretary's responsibilities and ranks within an organization are defined by the rules and regulations of that entity. All trade unions and professional associations affiliated with the United Nations Organization (UNO) are social organizations in which participants' roles and status are specified. There are two broad categories of social organizations, namely, those that arise out of kinship and those that result from members' free and voluntary associations.

Relationship of Social Organization and Interaction

The product of social contact is social organization. Interaction between persons, between individuals，between organizations，between classes，between members of a family creates a social organization. Organization implies an association with participants or elements. By contact between them，the members of a family become an organized community. Likewise，the parts of a factory have reciprocal relation with each other. The components of one item travel from one segment to another section before it is finished and then it is translated into a whole by arranging its components. These factory parts communicate with each other and create components of a system，and then these components，organized together，make a machine as a whole complex. All is related to the relationship between sectors，groups and individuals. The outcome of social organization is this development.

Relationship of Social Organization and Social System

The social structure is an ongoing unit that is generated by the interdependence of its components. A structure assigns its components to various roles. Such modules have reciprocal interaction，assisting one another. With the support of each other，these distinct tasks done by separate parts make the entire structure and this interrelation between its parts is called organization. It says the functioning of the sections is a scheme. An individual still holds a social structure.

Social Interaction → Social Organization → Social System

All the three definitions above are interrelated. A family，by contact with its members，is an integrated structure. There is a greater degree of activity in a system than outside the system. By social contact，the members of a family establish an organized community. Although working as a whole，this community is a social system. On the basis of their rank and function，the members communicate. In the household，this fixes them in their respective positions. The family is an organized social entity today. If such an integrated family exists，it is a social structure in a certain situation.

（Reference：www.bookguideline.com/2021/07/social-organization-meanings-forms-and.html?）

3.1 概论 Introduction

组织(organization)指的是以公务关系为基础，为了完成特定目标的一群人的结合。组织作为社会权力(social power)的根源，在我们日常生活中的作用越来越重要。

3.1.1 社会组织的界定 Definition of Social Organization

社会组织(social organization)是一个历史范畴，是人类社会发展的产物，它的产生、变更和消亡服务于既定的目标,满足了一定时期内人们特定的社会需求和社会动机。社会组织存在于人类社会发展的经济、政治和文化等各个领域,在很大程度上增进了整个社会的联系和交往,从某种意义上,社会组织的兴盛和发展已经成为社会进步的标志。

关于社会组织的内涵,不同的组织学家、管理学家都提出了自己的定义,比较有代表性的有马克斯·韦伯的观点。马克斯·韦伯认为,社会组织是一个用规章制度限制外人进入的封闭性团体。

In sociology, a social organization is a pattern of relationships between and among individuals and social groups. It refers to the network of relationships in groups and how they interconnect. This network of relationships helps members of a group stay connected to one another in order to maintain a sense of community within a group. It is influenced by culture and other factors. These interactions come together to constitute common features in basic social units such as family, enterprises, clubs, states, etc. These are social organizations. Common examples of modern social organizations are government agencies, NGO's and corporations.

社会组织有广义和狭义之分。广义的社会组织是指社会上存在的一切人类活动共同体,包括一切社会群体,比如家庭、工厂、机关和学校等。狭义的社会组织则是指社会系统中一定的社会成员在一定时期内,依据特定的社会目标,具体执行一定的社会职能而有计划地组合起来的社会群体,是更高级、更复杂的社会组合方式;简单来说,狭义的社会组织指的是人们为了有效达成特定目标,按照一定的宗旨、制度或系统建立起来的活动集体。

3.1.2 社会组织的特征 Characteristics of Social Organization

社会组织可以由初级群体或非正式群体演化而来,同时与初级群体高度分离,具有鲜明的特点,主要表现在:

(1)社会组织具有特定的组织目标(organizational goals)。组织目标是社会组织形成的基本条件,是社会组织的灵魂。任何性质的社会组织都需要在运转中及时、准确地确立自己的组织目标。组织目标具有巨大的凝聚力和指向力,社会组织正是通过目标的设定和调整,控制了组织活动的性质、范围和进程。从本质上说,不同类型的社会组织具有不同的目标,而且同一社会组织在不同的历史时期也具有不同的组织目标。因此,从期限来看,组织目标可以分为长期目标(long-term goals)、中期目标(medium-term goals)和短期目标(short-term goals)。其中,长期目标从原则上规定了社会组织行动的方向;短期目标则立足于具体方案和行动步骤的安排;中期目标介于两者之间。

(2)社会组织由一定数量的相对固定的成员组成。社会组织是由至少两个或两个以上的人组成的系统。组织成员(organization members)是相对固定的,进入或退出组织都必须遵循既定的程序,尤其是组织成员资格(organization membership)的取得要经过严格的审核。

(3)社会组织是由众多相互关联的要素组成的权力结构体系。合法有效的权力结构体系是维持社会组织良好运作的必要手段。

(4)社会组织具有规范的组织章程(articles of association)。

(5)社会组织必须具备必要的物质基础(material basis)。任何社会组织都有一定的物质基础,这是社会组织有效运转的基本要求,又是社会组织结构的物质实体。

(6)社会组织是开放的系统。社会组织的存在和发展是社会进步的产物。伴随着社会的发展,社会组织也进行相应的新陈代谢(metabolism)。根据系统论的观点,社会系统可以分为开放系统(open system)、封闭系统(closed system)两种主要形式,开放系统不断的与外界进行物质、能量和信息的交换;封闭系统不与外界进行物质、能量和信息的交换。

3.1.3　社会组织的基本类型 Basic Types of Social Organization

(1)按照组织规模(size of organization)的大小,社会组织可以分为小型(small)的组织、中型(medium)的组织、大型(large)的组织和巨型(giant)的组织。

不论何种性质的社会组织都可以依据组织规模的大小进行划分,因此,这种划分方法具有普遍性和表层性。

(2)按照组织的形成方式,社会组织可以分为正式组织(formal organization)和非正式组织(informal organization)。正式组织是为了有效地实现组织目标,将组织成员之间的职责范围和相互关系予以明确规定,其组织制度和规范对成员具有正式约束力的社会组织。正式组织具有健全的组织制度和完善的组织管理模式。社会系统中的政府、军队、政党、学校、医院等都属于正式组织,它是社会组织的主要构成方式,是维持社会良性运转的主要力量。

A formal organization is a social system structured by clearly laid out rules, goals, and practices and that functions based on a division of labor and a clearly defined hierarchy of power.

非正式组织是人们在正式工作、共同生活过程中,由于性格、兴趣、爱好、价值观的相近或相似,自发形成的以亲密的感情为基础,以维护共同的利益和需要为目的社会组织。组织成员之间的关系比较自由、松散、沟通方式多为非正式渠道(informal communication channels),因此不可避免地会产生小道消息(grapevine)。非正式组织的存在很大程度上维护和加强了民间的社会关系,在特定的条件下,它可以发挥正式组织所不能发挥的作用,可以有效地配合正式组织的运作,因此非正式组织具有存在的必要性和合理性。

An informal organization is a group of people who share a common identity and are committed to achieving a common purpose. Informal organizations are created by the will and shared identity of their members.

Grapevine refers to an informal channel of communication separate from organization's formal, official communication channels.

（3）按照组织所具有的功能和目标，社会组织可以分为政治性组织（political organization）、经济性组织（economic organization）、文化性组织（cultural organization）和综合性组织（comprehensive organization）。

政治性组织是社会组织在政治领域的组合形式，是为政治服务的组织或者是执行政治功能的社会组织。它专门处理社会各种不同阶级、阶层和利益集团之间的利益关系。政治性组织，主要包括立法组织（legislative organization）、司法组织（judicial organization）、行政组织（administrative organization）、政党组织（party organization）、军事组织（military organization）等。

经济性组织是人们在经济关系的基础上建立起来的，服务于经济活动的社会组织。经济组织以追求社会物质财富为目的，存在于生产、交换、分配、消费等不同领域，主要包括生产组织（organization of production）、商业组织（commercial organization）、服务组织（service organization）、金融组织（financial organization）和交通组织（organization of transportation）等。

文化性组织是一种人们培养志趣、联络感情，传递知识和文化，丰富日常生活的社会组织。这里的文化组织是一个广义的概念，主要包括社会各级各类的教育组织（educational organization）、医疗组织（medical organization）、学术机构（academic institution）、科研单位、文艺组织（literary & artistic organization）和宗教组织（religious organization）等。

综合性组织指的是人们自愿组织而成，与政府之间不存在行政隶属关系，但在各种各样的社会事务中持有准政府身份的社会组织。它是指由各种社会关系交织而成的综合性社会组合形式，这种组织一般不以赢利为目的，由人们自愿组织，并且经民政部门批准成立的。在综合性组织中，中介组织（intermediary organization）是一种重要的类型。中介组织是市场经济对社会组织结构渗透的必然产物，它处于政府和经济主体之外的第三方，旨在沟通政府与经济主体之间、经济主体与经济主体之间的信息，协调双方的利益，为经济主体提供服务。中介组织承担了部分政府管理社会的职能，弥补了政府管理模式的不足，强化了社会管理功能。综合性组织主要包括行业协会、同业公会、商会、妇联、工会、个体劳动者协会、律师事务所、资产评估事务所等。

（4）按照组织目标和组织内部成员受惠程度，社会组织可分为互利性组织（mutual benefit organization）、服务性组织（service organization）、营利性组织（for-profit organization）和公益性组织（non-profit organization）。

互利性组织是指以组织成员为受益对象的社会组织，其成员可在组织中获得某种利益和方便。互利性组织主要包括各种类型的职业协会、会员制俱乐部、互助性团体等。

服务性组织是指旨在为社会提供服务的社会组织，它以服务为宗旨，为社会大众服务，使全体大众都得到益处。服务性组织主要包括学校、医院、福利机构等。

营利性组织是指以赢利为组织目标和宗旨的社会组织。在营利性组织中，组织的所有者能通过组织的运行得到实际利益。营利性组织主要包括各种类型的公司、企业等。

公益性组织是指以实现社会公众的利益为目标和行动指南的社会组织，它为社会所有人提供某一种类性质固定、正式而持续的服务。公益性组织主要包括政府机构、各种非营利机构等。

（5）按照组织对成员的控制关系，社会组织可以分为强制性组织（mandatory organization）、功利性组织（utilitarian organization）和规范性组织（normative organization）。

强制性组织是指以暴力为手段，强迫组织成员服从的社会组织。这类组织一般都是特殊管教机构，运作模式一般为行为正常的成员对行为异常的成员实施管制。强制性组织主要包括监狱、精神病院等。

功利性组织是指以金钱或物质为手段，控制组织成员服从组织目标的社会组织。功利性组织采用的手段一般包括工资、奖金、股息、各种福利和优厚待遇等，采用的形式一般包括奖励、惩罚、升级等。功利性组织主要包括各种各类的经济实体，比如公司、企业和经济性中介组织（economic intermediary organization）等。

规范性组织是指通过社会规范、价值观念等精神手段，将组织规范内化为成员的伦理观念或信仰来控制成员的社会组织。这类组织所采用的手段一般包括理论、思想观念、道德意识、信仰和价值观念等。规范性组织主要包括政府机构、军事组织、学校、科研机构、社会团体等。

3.1.4　社会组织的功能 Functions of Social Organization

Social organization provides a number of signposts for professionals involved in prevention, intervention, and program development activities. The primary elements of social organization, which are social networks, social capital, and community capacity, represent malleable aspects of individual and family life.

各种性质的社会组织在不同时期不同条件背景下发挥的功能有所差异，我们仅就社会组织的一般性功能做简要的分析（analysis）和归纳（induction）。

（1）维护社会安定（to maintain social stability）。社会组织承担着维护社会成员安全的职能。

（2）整合社会力量（to integrate social force）。社会组织通过各种方式把分散的、孤立的个体和家庭联系起来构成一定小规模的团体，再通过小团体之间的横向和纵向联系，构建整个社会。

（3）满足社会成员的社会需求（to meet social needs of people）。社会组织通过与组织成员建立一种相辅相成、平等交换的关系，在满足组织成员个体需求的基础上，发展组织自身特殊的功能以满足更广泛的社会成员的需求。

（4）促进社会效率（to promote social efficiency）。处于良好状态中的社会组织对汇集整合起来的力量有放大的作用，即整体大于各个部分的总和。

3.2 组织结构与组织过程
Organizational Structure and Process

3.2.1 组织结构 Organizational Structure

组织结构的概念有广义和狭义之分。狭义的组织结构，是指为了实现组织目标，在组织理论指导下，经过组织设计形成的组织内部各个部门、各个层次之间固定的排列方式，即组织内部的构成方式。广义的组织结构，除了包含狭义的组织结构内容外，还包括组织之间的相互关系类型，如专业化协作、经济联合体等。

1. 组织结构设计 Designing Organizational Structure

组织结构设计是社会组织的构成方式，它支撑着社会组织一系列工作的正常顺利开展。组织结构设计包括几项核心内容：组织规模（size of organization）与管理幅度（span of management）、专业化与部门化（specialization and departmentalization）、集权与分权（centralization and decentralization of authority）。

（1）组织规模与管理幅度。社会组织结构主要分为扁平结构（flat structure）和锥形结构（tall structure）两种形态，这主要是根据组织管理幅度和管理层次（layers of management）的不同所进行的分类。管理幅度即为能有效领导的直接下属的数量限度，它决定了社会组织要设置多少层次，配备多少管理人员，也就是说因为管理幅度的存在，才有了管理层次的设置和划分。社会组织规模与组织管理幅度、管理层次具有一定的关系，即在管理幅度一定的条件下，管理层次与组织规模成正比；而在组织规模一定的条件下，管理层次与管理幅度成反比。从成本角度分析，管理幅度越大，社会组织就高效，但这也不是绝对的，超过一定的度，组织成员的绩效（performance）会因管理者无法提供必要的指导和支持而受到影响。组织管理幅度主要跟工作能力、工作内容与性质、工作环境、工作条件四个因素相关。具体为：社会组织管理者和被管理者能力强，管理幅度可增大；管理者所处的管理层次高，下属（subordinates）工作相似性大，计划完善程度高，非管理性事务少，管理幅度可增大；管理者助手配备充分，信息手段完备，工作地点具有相近性，管理幅度可增大；社会组织处在稳定的环境之中，管理幅度可增大；反之亦然。

> Span of Management: The Span of Management refers to the number of subordinates who can be managed efficiently by a superior. Simply, the manager having the group of subordinates who report him directly is called as the span of management.

(2)专业化与部门化。社会组织职位的分解主要靠工作专业化来完成,它需要将社会组织的工作分解成若干步骤,再将其分配给组织成员,于是处于不同岗位的组织成员只需完成其分配的任务,通过这种分工和协作来共同达到组织目标。当工作专业化完成职位的确定、工作任务细分之后,就需要按照特定的类别对它们进行组合,以使共同的任务得以协调。部门化使职位之间的互动关系经常化、制度化,使社会组织成为由职位而连接成稳固的组合。部门化通常有四种方式,即:职能部门化(functional departmentalization)、地域部门化(geographical departmentalization)、产品部门化(product departmentalization)和顾客部门化(customer departmentalization)。职能部门化是社会组织依据工作的性质和执行的职能进行的组合方式;地域部门化是社会组织依据业务领域分布的地理区域进行的组合方式;产品部门化是社会组织依据开发经营的产品线进行的组合方式;顾客部门化是社会组织按为顾客提供服务为导向进行的组合方式。这四种方式反映了社会组织进行部门化改制过程中的历程,由职能部门化、地域部门化走向产品部门化、顾客部门化是社会组织进步和发展的标志。

> Specialization is an agreement within a community, organization, or larger group in which each of the members best suited for a specific activity assumes responsibility for its successful execution.
>
> Departmentalization refers to the process of grouping activities into departments.
>
> Functional Departmentalization: the grouping of jobs that perform similar functional activities, such as finance, manufacturing, marketing, and human resources.
>
> Geographical Departmentalization: the grouping of jobs according to geographic location, such as state, region, country, or continent.
>
> Product Departmentalization: the organization of jobs in relation to the products of the firm.
>
> Customer Departmentalization: the arrangement of jobs around the needs of various types of customers.

(3)集权与分权。集权与分权主要是指组织决策权集中于社会系统中何种层次,属高层还是低层。如果社会组织的高层管理者不考虑或较少考虑基层人员的意见,而自主决定组织的重要事务,则这个社会组织的集权化程度较高;如果社会组织中的决策权分散在组织各管理层甚至基层的工作人员。而组织成员普遍参与组织事务的积极性与热情较高,则这个社会组织便是一种分权化的结构模式。社会组织中集权倾向的产生受到社会组织发展历程和所处社会背景的影响,同组织管理者的性格、气质也有很大的关系。而分权的标志主要有四个:决策的频度、决策的幅度、决策的重要程度和对决策控制的程度。分权可以通过制度分权(institutional decentralization)和工作中的授权(delegation of authority)来实现。过分集权(excessive centralization)会产生降低决策质量、降低组织适应能力和降低组织成员工作热情的弊端；过分分权（excessive decentralization）会使组织松散、缺乏效率，相应的会降低决策质量。

> Centralization refers to the concentration of power or authority in a few hands only.
>
> In other words, Centralization structure can be defined as maximizing the power access to specialized personnel.
>
> Decentralization refers to the degree to which decision-making is spread throughout the organization, It simply means everyone has the right to speak. Decentralization can also be defined as promoting genuine cooperation and participative management among employees rather than independence maximizing individual institution initiatives.

2. 组织结构的类型 Types of Organizational Structure

组织结构主要包括纵、横两大系统，纵向是指社会组织垂直机构或人员之间的联系，主要强调领导隶属关系；横向是指社会组织职能机构或人员之间的联系，强调分工与协作关系。组织结构的基本类型有：U 形组织结构（U form organizational structure）、M 形组织结构（multi-divisional form）、矩阵制（the matrix organizational structure）、多维立体结构（the multidimensional organizational structure）、网络组织结构（network organizational structure）等。

（1）U 形组织结构，又称直线式结构（line structure），它有两套管理系统，即直线式领导管理系统和协助指导、监督的职能管理系统。直线职能制组织结构综合了直线制和职能制的优点，但它过于强调集权、统一，不利于提高灵活性，所以只适应于中型社会组织，在政府机构、事业单位和部分国有企业中比较常见。

> U form organizational structure is a type of business organization. It has its benefits and disadvantages, but it is an effective way to organize a company in the 21st century. The "u form organizational structure's advantages" are that it allows for better decision-making and planning. The U-form organization relies on a functional approach to departmentalization and is often used to implement a single-product strategy.

（2）M 形组织结构，又称事业部制，它是 1924 年由美国通用汽车公司副总裁小阿尔弗雷德·斯隆制定，所以又称斯隆模型（Sloan Model）。事业部制是在组织统一领导和指挥下，按照产品或服务、地域和顾客划分的进行生产经营活动的半独立经营组织。事业部制有利于组织高层管理者摆脱日常行政事务，专心致力于社会组织的战略决策；可以充分调动各事业部的积极性，提高组织经营的灵活性和适应能力；还便于发现人才、培养人才、使用人才和考核人才绩效。但事业部制由于整体性不强，组织中内部沟通和交流会产生一系列问题，所以主要适应于一些大规模经济组织，比如大型企业、跨国公司和实施多元化经营的企业。

> Multi-divisional form（also known as M-form）refers to an organizational structure by which the firm is separated into several semi-autonomous units which are guided and controlled by（financial）targets from the center.

（3）矩阵制，又称为目标—规划结构，它是在原有的纵向垂直领导系统的基础上，又建立一种横向的领导系统。各组织成员既同原有的职能部门保持组织、业务上的联系，又参加横向的项目协作。矩阵制兼具纵向的垂直领导和横向的项目协作的功能，可以集中优势解决问题，并且组织成员在参与项目工作时实现了资源共享和畅通交流，很好地克服了直线职能制的弊端。但正所谓"成也萧何、败也萧何"，这种双重领导在成就了矩阵制优点的同时，也造成了社会组织设计过于复杂，双向指挥，无所适从。矩阵制在社会组织中主要适应于高校、科研单位和一些重大工程项目、单项重大事务的临时性组织。

> The matrix organizational structure is a combination of two or more different kinds of organizational structures，such as project management or functional management. Additionally, the matrix structure is composed of both a traditional hierarchy of management，where employees are managed by a functional manager，as well as additional project managers who can manage employees across different departments. These two or more managerial systems intersect on a grid or matrix.

（4）多维立体结构由产品事业部、专业管理机构、经销区域管理机构三大管理系统组成。这种组织结构很好地兼具了事业部和矩阵制的优点，但是由于组织决策过程周期过长，费用过高，所以适应面也不宽，主要存在于跨国经营、跨地区经营的经济性组织中。

> A multidimensional organizational structure is an organization that pursues its objectives through multiple dimensions（product，region，account，market segment）.
>
> The multidimensional organization was discussed as early as the 1970s.It required the combination of the fall of costs of information，the development of dynamic multidimensional markets，and a new generation of workers and managers，to create this paradigm shift in organization forms.

3.2.2 网络型组织 Network Organizational Structure

网络型组织是日本学者山田荣作（Eisaku Yamada）在《全球方略：多国籍企业结构的动态变化》一书中通过对多国籍经济组织结构的研究而提出来的一种组织形式。在知识经济时代，传统的多层次的组织结构正在向着减少中间层次的方向发展，组织中原有的大单位划分成小单位，形成相互联结的网络型组织。西方国家中的大小企业之间开展研究开发、共同营销、互补生产等,以避免重复投资,加快资金回收,发挥独创精神,分散风险。日本的日本电气(Nippon Electric Company, Ltd.)、富士通公司(Fujitsu Ltd.)、东京新陶瓷公司(Kyocera Ltd.)和西武集团(Seibu Group)等,都以组织单纯化和单层化为目标,采用了网络组织。网络组织借助于现代通信技术、网络技术方便了组织的统一协调、分向活动,实现了组织的沟通与交流。

> The network organizational structure is a temporary or permanent arrangement of otherwise independent organizations or associates, forming an alliance to produce a product or service by sharing costs and core competencies. The network-based organizational structure opens in new window is built around alliances between organizations within the network. Each associate or organization of the network focuses on its core competency and performs some portion of the activities necessary to deliver the products and services of the network as a whole.

通常情况下,社会组织包括两种结构形态:以制度化、形式化的职能关系和职权关系为核心的正式结构(formal organizational structure)和以具体的人际交往关系为核心的非正式结构(informal organizational structure)。

(1)正式结构:具备明确的组织目标,其组织结构,组织成员的职权、职能均由管理部门规定,组织成员的行为要服从组织的规章制度和组织纪律。职权是依职位而具有,并正式设立于社会组织内部,严格规定组织成员活动范围和活动要求的权限范围。社会组织的正式结构一般以组织结构图的形式作为外在表现。

(2)非正式结构:伴随着正式结构的运转,在正式结构中产生,未经管理部门规定,由组织成员互动活动而自发形成的组织结构形式。在社会组织中,正式结构的制度化(institutionalization)、程序化(programmed)、非人格化(impersonalization)与组织成员的情感需要、人际交往的需要之间会产生一系列矛盾,于是非正式结构便应运而生。韦伯对于科层制的分析主要针对组织内部的正式关系,即组织的规章制度所强调的人与人之间的关系。韦伯很少讨论几乎在所有组织中都可能存在的非正式的小群体关系。但是在科层制中,做事情的方式经常会具有其他途径所无法获得的灵活性。彼得布劳在一项经典研究中分析了一个政府机构中的非正式关系。该机构规定:管理者遇到无法解决的问题时应该直接跟上司沟通而非互相商量。但管理者们害怕接触上司,因此他们经常违背规章制度在彼此间互相咨询。布劳得出结论:管理者们互相商议可能使问题得到更有效地处理。

非正式结构的存在对正式结构的正常运作有积极的作用。非正式结构可以满足组织成员心理上的需求,相互交往,相互尊重,融洽关系,增强合作,从而获得满足感和成就感,创造一种更加和谐、融洽的人际关系。在非正式结构里,共同的情感是维系组织的纽带,组织成员彼此间情感比较密切,互相依赖、相互信任,所以非正式结构的凝聚力往往超过正式结构的凝聚力。由于有自愿的结合基础,非正式结构的组织成员对某些问题的看法基本是一致的,因而感情融洽,行为协调,归属感较强。非正式结构成员之间感情密切、交往频繁,信息传播迅速,组织成员对信息反应往往具有很大的相似性。正是由于这些特点,非正式结构广泛渗透到正式结构的各个部分,成为正式结构非常重要的补充形式。

同时,非正式结构也具有消极的作用,尤其表现为:如果非正式结构与正式结构的目标发生冲突时,可以使正式结构的管理有效性降低,从而增大完成组织的工作目标的难度,可能产生极为不利的影响,甚至会引发正面的冲突,影响社会组织的生存和发展。非正式结构通过对其内部成员产生压力,使得非正式结构的组织成员在利益上保持一致性,从而在组织工作的责任、权力、利益分配上,对非组织成员产生不利的结果。由于感情的作用,使非正式结构的组织成员看问题容易出现片面性,信息的传输由于缺乏全面调查和了解,也容易失真,非正式结构容易成为传播小道消息和散布流言蜚语的源头,影响整个组织的凝聚力。非正式结构要求组织成员在价值观和感情倾向上保持一致,可能因此会束缚内部成员个人的发展。

3.2.3　组织管理 Organizational Management

> Organizational management describes the planning and managing of those individuals and resources to achieve that goal. Organizational management involves creating a plan, monitoring its progress and making changes based on results and feedback so the company can improve its performance.

社会组织活动的效果和效率,除受环境的影响和制约外,还依赖于对组织的管理,组织的管理伴随着社会组织的产生而产生。组织管理(organizational management)是指协调社会组织内部人力、物力、财力达成组织目标的过程,其中的关键是使组织成员的活动与组织目标相结合。以管理权力是否高度集中于最高领导者一人手中为标准,组织管理方式可以分为家长制(paternalism)管理方式和科层制(bureaucracy)管理方式。

1. 家长制管理方式

家长制的管理方式是建立在下级对上级的服从和效忠基础上的管理制度,它是小农经济的产物,它与初级社会关系密切相关。实行家长制管理方式的组织,其权力集中在最高领导者手中。最高领导者的权力既不划分、下放,也不受限制。组织的一切活动完全由领导者个人决定,领导者管理一切、决定一切。相应地,组织成员一般也没有职权划分,即使有也是由最高领导者任意安排,而且分工情况、责任大小根据领导者的意愿决定,没有明确而清晰的规章制度来确定权责,因此,组织领导者的个人情感和好恶对组织活动往往产生重大的影响。家长制的管理方式往往是家族式管理(family-run management),对组织成员的任用、奖惩多视个人关系的远近、感情亲疏而定,管理模式多为传统的方式和做法,管理没有严格的程序,命令的随意性很大。由于管理范围小,组织领导者处理问题、安排工作多凭个人的经验、惯例和感情,没有什么章程可以遵循,组织缺乏严格的工作程序和行为规范,即使存在组织规则,也是形同虚设。家长制的管理方式具有人治的典型特征,组织领导者始终处于领导地位,终生不变。在终身制(life tenure)的影响下,在组织内部强调对领导者的个人崇拜、个人效忠和绝对的服从。那么,对于大多数组织成员而言,他们只有执行的义务没有参与决策的权利,从而很大程度上不能发挥组织成员的优势和创造力。

Paternalism refers to attitude and practice that are commonly understood as an infringement on the personal freedom and autonomy of a person (or class of persons) with a beneficent or protective intent. Paternalism generally involves competing claims between individual liberty and authoritative social control. Questions concerning paternalism also may include both the claims of individual rights and social protections and the legal and socially legitimated means of satisfying those claims. The use of the term paternalism is almost exclusively negative, employed to diminish specific policies or practices by presenting them in opposition to individual freedom. The term paternalism first appeared in the late 19th century as an implied critique predicated on the inherent value of personal liberty and autonomy, positions elegantly outlined by Immanuel Kant in 1785 and John Stuart Mill in 1859. The etymology of paternalism, rooted in the Latin pater ("father"), reflects the implicit social hierarchies of patriarchal cultures, in which fathers or male heads of families were understood to be authority figures responsible for the welfare of subordinates and dependents. In this tradition, adult members of states, corporations, and communities functioned under the presumably benevolent authority of kings, presidents, and executives. Prior to industrialization, patronage systems informed the stratified economic, political, and social arrangements prevalent throughout Europe and the Americas. Paternalism, as it evolved through the industrial age of the 19th and 20th centuries, applied the model of family relations and practices of patronage (fatherly protection, tutelage, and control) to relationships between classes of people understood as unequal: employers and workers, the privileged and the underprivileged, the state and the masses.

Historically, paternalism is a critical term applied in the West to the system of beliefs and practices emerging in the transition from a social order of patriarchal class structures, including slavery in the United States, to a free society of autonomous and equal individuals. Although it is not defined by a single institution or set of institutions, paternalism was prevalent among the early industrial companies.

　　家长制的管理方式局限性很大,主要适合于组织规模较狭小、内部分工不发达的传统社会的社会组织。随着社会的发展和组织内部分工的精细化,社会组织规模出现了扩大化甚至垄断化。这种大规模的社会组织,分工细致,协作复杂,效率要求较高,完全依据个人经验的家长制的管理无法进行,家长制的管理方式不再适应现代社会组织管理的要求,而逐渐被新的更科学的管理方式所代替。

2. 科层制管理方式

科层制管理方式是指社会组织内部权力分工、职位分层等,各司其职的组织结构形式和管理方式。它往往与组织的正式结构相联系,按照规章制度对社会组织实行管理。科层制有一套为组织成员共同认可和严格执行的活动规则,它规定组织成员的权限、责任和活动程序等,要求每个成员必须按照规则行事,毫无例外。组织成员只可以拒绝不合乎规则的命令,但必须执行合乎规则的命令。科层制职能分工明确,根据组织目标和任务的不同,设立不同的职位和机构,各个职位和机构都有独立的管理范围、明确的任务权限,各司其职,各负其责,不得相互推诿或超越权限。

The term bureaucracy refers to a body of non-elected governing officials as well as to an administrative policy-making group. Historically, a bureaucracy was a government administration managed by departments staffed with non-elected officials. Today, bureaucracy is the administrative system governing any large institution, whether publicly owned or privately owned. There are two key dilemmas in bureaucracy. The first dilemma revolves around whether bureaucrats should be autonomous or directly accountable to their political masters. The second dilemma revolves around bureaucrats' behavior strictly following the law or whether they have leeway to determine appropriate solutions for varied circumstances.

实行科层制管理,最高领导者根据职能把权力下放,形成多层次的结构。每个权力层次管理每个层次的工作和活动,下级必须接受上级的领导和监督。

科层制的管理方式在现代社会组织中应用比较广泛,比较适合于行政性组织和大型常规组织的管理。科层制的优点就在于分工清楚,责任明朗,任人唯才,能够提高工作效率,保证组织活动的开展,这在很大程度上克服了家长制管理的主观随意性和无规则性。但是,科层制也有它的不足,它的最大缺点是带有明显的机械性,忽视人的主动性,只强调照章办事、约束行为,而缺乏灵活性和应变性,过于严格和刻板的规则会妨碍组织成员的创造力和积极性,从而影响组织绩效。

3.2.4 组织过程 Organizational Processes

1. 组织决策 Organizational Decision-Making

组织的决策是指社会组织为达到特定目标,进行方案择优,并加以实施的过程。组织的决策主要包括确立目标(setting goals)、规划方案(planning scheme)、方案择优(choosing scheme)几个阶段。

(1)确立目标。组织目标(organizational goals)是组织成员行动的导向。组织目标是为满足组织的需要,促进组织发展而确立的,因此,组织目标必须清晰而详细,具体是指组织目标概念正确、语意明确、表达清晰、目标的步骤与时间清楚、职权责任明确,而且尽量采用定量描述法(quantitative description),以方便具体的监督与考核。决策的目标往往是多个目标组成的目标丛（goals complex），这就需要分清主次，科学划分短期目标（short term goals）、中期目标（medium term goals）和长远目标（long term goals）。同时，设立目标必须考虑可行性（feasibility），不可脱离实际。

（2）规划方案。根据实现目标的途径，社会组织要尽可能的制定所有的施行方案。

（3）方案择优。方案的择优遵循满意原则，要经过严格的评定与分析。我们一般从方案的可行性和方案的可替代性（replaceability）两个方面给予考虑。首先，方案的可行性。执行方案需要资金、人员的支持，要对方案进行严格的会计预算（accounting budgets），寻找经济、投入与产出比相对较高的方案。当然，在选择方案时，既要坚持经济效益（economic benefits）又要考虑社会效益（social benefits），方案的实施不能损害其他组织甚至整个社会的利益，这是道德底线。其次，方案的可替代性。在评定方案时，要注意选择那些可替代的备选方案（alternatives）较多的方案，以防止客观环境的变化所导致的方案执行失败。

2. 组织的执行 Organizational Implementation

组织的执行体系主要包括：明确和分解组织目标（goal decomposition）、建立行为体系、制定执行的规则和保障以及建立执行监督体系（supervision system）这三个程序。

在明确和分解目标的基础上，社会组织需要通过建立行为体系，即组织行为程序、规则和制度来规范组织行为，保证组织目标的正确实施。

监督体系是指通过评价、激励和约束个体行为，修正、强化个体对目标和规则的深入理解。人的个体行为存在差异，而且组织成员在实施目标的过程中，不可避免的会带入个人的情感和好恶，这都是影响组织执行力的因素，特别是当组织成员的个体行为与组织目标出现分歧时，监督就显得尤为重要。这就需要建立监督与评估体系（supervision and evaluation system），通过组织的强制力使得组织成员的个体行为与组织的战略目标和行为规则相契合，并最终使组织规则和规章制度内化为组织成员的习惯和本能。如果达到这个层面，组织的执行力会非常强大。

3. 组织的协调 Organizational Coordination

组织的协调是指为了有效地提高社会组织整体的活动效能、实现设定的目标，采取灵活多样的措施进行调节与化解，使之相对稳定、相互配合、相互衔接的过程。

组织的协调主要是围绕和化解组织内外部关系的冲突。冲突是指两个或两个以上的社会单元在目标上互不相容或互相排斥，从而产生心理或行为上的矛盾，它包括社会组织内个人与个人之间的冲突，个人与组织之间的冲突，也包括群体间的冲突。冲突是组织发展过程中的一种临界状态，当组织内某种利益关系或价值观念出现不一致，而对方又不愿意妥协或让步时，就产生了冲突。适度的冲突能使组织保持旺盛的活力，在一定程度上激发组织成员的合作和创新精神，增强组织士气（organizational morale），甚至会促使组织变革（organizational change）和更新。

4. 组织的控制 Organizational Control

社会组织的控制是指为了保证社会组织正常运作，通过一定的媒介，对组织内部和外部实施的一系列管理活动。社会组织的控制活动主要包括建立社会组织反馈系统(organizational feedback system)和社会组织控制模型(organizational control model)。

社会组织反馈系统包括以咨询、监督等反馈调节形式为基础的系统,具有自我调节和整体效益最大化的功能。随着全球化的进程推进,社会分工更加精细化,甚至在决策内部也进行了分化,表现为咨询(counselling)与决策(decision making)分离的相对分离,从而产生了专司咨询的机构,快速、准确地收集信息,提供决策参考,这在一定程度上促进了决策的科学化,推进了组织的良性运行。同时,社会组织中还需建立一定的监督系统,具体是指建立检查机构和监察机构。监督系统可以使组织活动处于最广泛的监督之下,获得最大的透明度。

社会组织控制模型包括控制主体(control subject)、控制客体(control object)和控制手段(control means)。所谓控制主体是指控制行为的发出者,即施动者。在控制活动中,控制主体处于主动地位,可以积极地实施控制行为。控制客体,是控制活动指向的对象。就组织内部而言,是指对实现组织战略目标的组织结构与程序的控制。控制手段是实施控制行为的方式、方法和工具。对于组织自身的控制来说,层级控制是最为常用的控制手段,它通过权力链的级别设置来施行对组织活动、内容与程序的控制。

3.2.5　组织的变革 Organizational Change

1. 组织变革的原因和动力 Reason and Motivation for Organizational Change

社会组织的变革主要来自于两个方面的原因:外部的和内发的。社会组织是从属于社会大环境系统中的一个子系统,它必须适应外部条件的变化,否则就会被淘汰,所以外部条件(external conditions)发展变化是导致组织变革的外因。外部条件分为一般性条件和特殊条件。一般性条件主要包括政治制度、法律、产业政策和产业结构、科学技术、社会文化、自然环境等。特殊条件主要包括现有竞争者、潜在的竞争者、替代品生产厂商、供应商和用户。组织变革的内在动力(internal motivation)是组织变革的内因,主要有社会组织管理技术条件和方式,管理人员和管理水平,组织运行政策和目标,组织规模和业务,组织价值观念等。组织的外部条件和内在压力都会影响到组织的系统调整和组织变革,社会组织应该主动积极地去应对和适应。

社会组织变革的动力主要来自于高层决策、群体决策和组织成员自发进行这三种。

Organizational change refers to the actions in which a company or business alters a major component of its organization, such as its culture, the underlying technologies or infrastructure it uses to operate, or its internal processes. Organizational changes are those that have a significant impact on the organization as a whole. Major shifts to personnel, company goals, service offerings, and operations would all be considered forms of organizational change. It's a broad category.

2. 组织变革的过程 Organizational Change Processes

根据科特·勒温（Kurt Lewin）的"变革三步论"，组织的变革需要经历解冻现状、变革到新的状态、将新状态重新冻结并使之持久这三个过程。

Here are the three stages in Lewin's change model：

Stage 1 - Unfreeze

The first stage in Lewin's model deals with perception management and aims to prepare the affected stakeholders for the upcoming organizational change. Change leaders must look at ways to improve the company's preparedness for change and create a sense of urgency similar to Kotter's change model.

Stage 2 - Change

Once the status quo is disrupted，this stage deals with the implementation of change. In this stage，you must consider an agile and iterative approach that incorporates employee feedback to smoothen the transition.

Stage 3 - Refreeze

Employees move away from the transition phase towards stabilization or acceptance in the final "refreezing" stage. However，if change leaders fail to strengthen the change by reinforcing it into org culture，employees might revert to previous behaviors.

首先，组织变革需要对社会组织的现状进行解冻。其次，组织变革使社会组织变革到新的状态，创造和管理新的组织机制。最后，组织变革将组织的新状态重新冻结并使之持久，从而建立一个学习型组织（learning organization）。学习型组织是一种通过不间断地学习以达到不断充实自己、突破自己能力上限目的的组织。学习型组织可以适应复杂而多变的环境，将变革后的新状态维持好，并在条件再次改变时，为组织创造良好的内部环境来进行重新变革。

3.3 社会组织理论
Social Organization Theory

组织理论（organization theory）是指人类在社会组织活动中按一定形式安排事务的理论。人类社会的组织活动，随着社会分工日益复杂，组织种类愈加繁多，如行政组织、工商企业组织、文化教育组织等。

Organizational theory is the sociological study of the structures and operations of social organizations, including companies and bureaucratic institutions. Organizational theory includes the analysis of the productivity and performance of organizations and the actions of the employees and groups within them. Economists, business analysts and academic researchers who study organizational theory are interested in understanding the dynamics of a successful business.

古今中外有关组织管理的理论很多。中国悠久的组织发展历程也积累了丰富的组织管理思想,儒家的德治、仁治思想,法家的法治思想,道家的无为而治思想,墨家的兼爱非攻思想,以及孙子的谋略思想,这些传统管理理论对于中国乃至世界的组织管理理论具有深远的影响。在西方,组织管理理论按照时间的历程主要有古典管理理论(classical management theory)、新古典管理理论(neo classical management theory)以及当代的现代管理理论(modern management theory)。在此主要介绍西方的组织管理理论。

3.3.1　古典管理理论 Classical Management Theory

古典管理理论产生于 19 世纪末至 20 世纪初,它把为追求自我最大利益的理性经济人作为人性的主要假设,主要有泰勒的科学管理、法约尔的一般管理和韦伯的科层制管理。

Classical theory can address the primary aspects of a business's formal organizational structure. This theory discusses how to divide up professional tasks in the most efficient and effective way.

Classical theorists pay particular attention to the professional dynamics and relationships within an organization and how these relationships may impact the company's function and production. The underlying purpose of this theory is to help businesses create the most beneficial structures within a company that can then help the organization accomplish its goals.

1. 行政理论 Administrative Theory

古典理论的一个重要流派是行政理论或万能管理原则学派,目前关于组织结构的理论多数来源于行政理论学派,该学派的著名代表是法国工业学家亨利·法约尔(Henri Fayol,1841—1925)。

亨利·法约尔:古典管理理论的主要代表人之一,亦为管理过程学派的创始人。他出身于一个法国资产阶级家庭。19 岁毕业时他取得了矿业工程师资格。1860 年他被任命为科芒特里矿井组工程师。在他漫长而成绩卓著的经营生涯中,他一直从事这项事业。1918 年,他退休时的职务是公司总经理,然后他继续在公司里担任一名董事,直到 1925 年 12 月去世，其代表作是《一般管理与工业管理》（*General and Industrial Management*，1949）。法约尔的一般管理理论在现代管理中已作为普遍遵循的准则，这使他的理论成为管理史上的一个重要里程碑，由此他被称为"组织管理之父"（the father of modern management theory）。

Fayol's work was one of the first comprehensive statements of a general theory of management. He proposed that there were six types of organizational activity, five primary functions of management and fourteen principles of management.

Fayol divided the range of activities undertaken within an industrial undertaking into six types: technical activities, commercial activities, financial activities, security activities, accounting activities, and managerial activities.

法约尔认为，企业的全部活动可分为六类：技术性活动（technical activities）（生产、制造、加工）；商业性活动（commercial activities）（购买、销售、交换）；财务性活动（financial activities）（资金筹集和运用）；安全性活动（security activities）（设备和人员的保护）；会计性活动（accounting activities）（存货盘点、资产负债表制作、成本核算、统计）；管理性活动（managerial activities），包括计划（planning）、组织（organizing）、指挥（commanding）、协调（co-ordinating）、控制（controlling）。在这六类活动中，法约尔主要集中研究了管理活动。

法约尔把管理活动分为计划、组织、指挥、协调与控制五大职能，并对这五大职能进行了详细的分析和讨论。他认为：计划就是探索未来、指定行动方向和制定行动方案，计划是管理的首要因素，具有普遍的适用性，而且是一切组织活动的基础；组织就是建立企业的物质和社会双重结构，即为企业的经营提供所有必要的原料、设备、资金、人员；指挥就是使其人员发挥作用；协调就连接、联合、调和所有的活动和力量，使各职能的社会组织机构和物资设备机构之间保持一定比例，在工作中做到先后有序，有条不紊；控制就是注意一切是否按已制定的规章和下达的命令进行，以证实各项工作是否都与已定计划相符合，是否与下达的缺点和错误，以便加以纠正并避免重犯。法约尔的管理职能理论适用于各种类型的组织。

法约尔担当了创立管理理论的重任。他提出了他的理论依据：管理是一种可应用于一切机构的独立的活动；一个人在某机构内地位愈高，其管理活动愈加重要；管理是可以教授的。法约尔创立的管理理论的核心是对管理的原则和管理的要素的论述。在法约尔的笔下，"原则"一词不是一个固定不变的、僵化的概念，因为他认为：在管理方面，没有什么死板和绝对的东西，只有尺度问题，因而原则是灵活的、可以适用于一切需要的；原则的有效把握依赖于使用它的人的智慧、经验、判断和掌握的尺度。法约尔提出的 14 项著名的管理原则，包括：劳动分工（division of work）；权力与责任（authority and responsibility）；纪律（discipline）；统一指挥（unity of command）；统一领导（unity of direction）；个别利益服从整体利益（subordination of individual interest to general interest）；合理的报酬（remuneration）；集权与分权（centralization and decentralization）；等级链（scalar chain）；

秩序(order);公平(equity);保持人员稳定(stability of tenure of personnel);首创精神(initiative);团结精神(esprit de corps)。虽然他提出的 14 项管理内容涵盖相当广泛,但绝大部分与组织相关联,其中有几项属于组织原则,比如劳动分工原则、统一指挥原则、适当的集权与分权原则和等级链原则等。

Principles of Management

1. Division of work: In practice, employees are specialized in different areas and they have different skills. Different levels of expertise can be distinguished within the knowledge areas (from generalist to specialist). Personal and professional developments support this. According to Henri Fayol specialization promotes efficiency of the workforce and increases productivity.

2. Authority and Responsibility: the accompanying power or authority gives the management the right to give orders to the subordinates.

3. Discipline: This principle is about obedience. It is often a part of the core values of a mission and vision in the form of good conduct and respectful interactions.

4. Unity of command: Every employee should receive orders from only one superior or behalf of the superior.

5. Unity of direction: Each group of organizational activities that have the same objective should be directed by one manager using one plan for achievement of one common goal.

6. Subordination of Individual Interest to General Interest - The interests of any one employee or group of employees should not take precedence over the interests of the organization as a whole.

7. Remuneration: All workers must be paid a fair wage for their services. The wages paid must be as per a certain standard of living to the employee at the same time it is within the paying capacity of the company.

8. Centralization and Decentralization: This refers to the degree to which subordinates are involved in decision making.

9. Scalar chain: The line of authority from top management to the lowest ranks represents the scalar chain. Communications should follow this chain. However if someone needs to communicate some other person in emergency he/she might use "Gang Plank".

10. Order: this principle is concerned with systematic arrangement of men, machines, materials, etc. There should be a specific place for every employee in an organization. That is "a place for everything (people) and everything has a place".

11. Equity: All the employees in the organization must be treated equally with respect to the justice and kindliness.

12. Stability of tenure of personnel: High employee turnover is inefficient. Management should provide orderly personnel planning and ensure that replacements are available to fill vacancies.

13. Initiative: Employees who are allowed to originate and carry out plans will exert high levels of effort.

14. Esprit de Corps: Promoting team spirit will build harmony and unity within the organization.

在法约尔之后,其他学者吸取了法约尔 14 条原则的精华,集中强调了组织的 5 个基本方面:组织结构(organizational structure)(用组织图表来代表组织形式);组织分工(division of labor)(将工作分为个人与团体能做的各个部分);组织协调(organizational coordination)(调节组织各部分以达到组织目标);等级关系(hierarchical relations)(规定指挥的等级链条并为协调提供条件,同级链条上的横向联系只有在各自主管人允许的前提下才能进行);组织功能(organizational functions)(根据组织中各种不同的功能分配工作)。

2. 科学管理理论 Theory of Scientific Management

科学管理(scientific management)是通过重新设计工作流程(work procedure),对员工与工作任务之间的关系进行系统性研究,并且通过标准化(standardization)与客观分析等方式,促使效率与生产量极大化(maximation)。与行政理论强调组织和管理的原则不同,科学管理理论强调计量和工作结构本身,目的在于创造出完成工作任务更有效的方法,这种理论的著名代表是美国学者泰勒。

弗雷德里克·温斯洛·泰勒(Frederick Winslow Taylor,1856—1915),美国人,西方古典经济管理理论的主要代表,科学管理理论的创始人。他自幼酷爱研究,先后当过一般工人、车间管理员、技师、小组长、工长、制图部主任、总经理。泰勒的经历从实践上为他积累了丰富的经验,为他形成科学管理理论打下坚实的基础,其代表作为《科学管理的原理》(*The Principles of Scientific Management*),由于他在科学管理方面所作的特殊贡献,被誉为"科学管理之父"。他详细记录每个工作的步骤及所需时间,设计出最有效的工作方法,并对每个工作制定一定的工作标准量,归划为一个标准的工作流程;将人的动作与时间,以最经济的方式达成最高的生产量,因此又被称为机械模式。泰勒作为古典组织理论的奠基人,以自己在工厂的经验为基础,致力于宣传与推广科学管理原理,尝试用科学化的管理模式代替传统组织的管理模式。泰勒致力于提高劳动生产率,把重点放在计划、标准化和在作业层改进的努力方向上,以便用最小的投入取得最大的产出。通过最大限度地提高每个工人的生产效率,使劳资双方都能获得最大的效益。泰勒把管理描述为一个完成组织目标的过程,即按照所谓合理化的公式约束工作人员的外在行为。

Frederick Winslow Taylor was an American mechanical engineer. He was widely known for his methods to improve industrial efficiency. He was one of the first management consultants. In 1911, Taylor summed up his efficiency techniques in his book *The Principles of Scientific Management* which, in 2001, Fellows of the Academy of Management voted the most influential management book of the twentieth century. His pioneering work in applying engineering principles to the work done on the factory floor was instrumental in the creation and development of the branch of engineering that is now known as industrial engineering. Taylor made his name, and was most proud of his work, in scientific management; however, he made his fortune patenting steel-process improvements. As a result, scientific management is sometimes referred to as Taylorism.

泰勒的科学管理理论,从其内容上看,可以划分为作业管理(job management)和组织管理(organizational management)两大方面:

(1)作业管理主要是针对工厂工人的劳动作业方法进行科学的管理。泰勒认为,要用科学的方法,进行试验研究,制定合理的日工作量;要科学选择、合理安排、计划,培训工人,使工人的能力与工作相适应;要确定标准化作业方法,形成一套标准化作业方法、规则和制度,使工人尽快、熟练地掌握生产作业方法;要把工人工作任务完成情况与工人工资收入相联系,实行刺激性的工资制度。泰勒认为,只有这样,才有助于鼓励工人个人生产积极性,迅速提高劳动生产率。

(2)组织管理。泰勒认为,劳动生产率(labor productivity),不仅受工人的劳动态度、工作定额、作业方法和工资制度等因素的影响,同时它还受管理人员的组织、指挥的影响。泰勒主张,把计划管理工作与工人的实际操作相分离,预先为工人科学、合理地规定生产过程、操作规程以及加工速度、方法,实行科学管理;实行职能管理,每个管理人员的管理工作专门化(specialization),并在自己的工作范围内,直接指挥调度工人;考虑到企业的机构和规模,较大的企业要实行例外原则,高层管理人员(senior management)把日常管理的权限下放,只保留企业重大事项的决策、指挥权。泰勒认为,摆脱日常事务、减轻负担,可以使高层管理高效化。德鲁克对泰勒给予很高的评价。

According to Peter Drucker, Frederick W. Taylor was the first man in recorded history who deemed work deserving of systematic observation and study. On Taylor's "scientific management" rests, above all, the tremendous surge of affluence in the last seventy-five years which has lifted the working masses in the developed countries well above any level recorded before, even for the well-to-do. Taylor, though the Isaac Newton (or perhaps the Archimedes) of the science of work, laid only first foundations, however. Not much has been added to them since—even though he has been dead all of sixty years.

　　另外,泰勒强调组织变革的过程是渐进式而并非暴风骤雨式的,组织的变革需要人才的保障、规章和法律的制约,这使传统组织的专断特权和专制命令被取代。泰勒的组织理念与管理科学发展后期的一些思想不谋而合,表现出了极大的超前性(advancement)与实用性(practicability)。科学管理思想在管理思想发展史上占有重要地位,对管理实践的发展有着巨大作用。

3. 结构主义学派 Structuralism School

　　结构主义(structuralism)是一种科学流派,侧重对结构的认识,不追究对本质的了解,提倡学科之间互通有无,以及一种整体的科学,要透过表面的现象,寻求底层的关系,以期获得放诸四海而皆准的结构。"结构主义"并不是一个被清楚界定的"流派",通常将索绪尔(Saussure)的作品当作一个起点。结构主义是 20 世纪下半叶分析研究语言、文化与社会的流行方法。结构主义导源于 1915—1930 年俄国学者的形式主义(formalism),其后以法国为根据地加以发展。

　　结构主义学派在组织研究中运用了归纳法。它是在考察各种不同组织的基础上确定有效控制组织实际运行的共同因素,而不是创造一种组织结构的概念模型,而后推广到所有组织中。结构主义方法(structuralism methodology)的主要奠基人是德国社会学家马克斯·韦伯,他提出了科层组织体系理论。

Structuralism refers to different schools of thought in different contexts. Emile Durkheim based his sociological concept on "structure" and "function". From his work emerged the sociological approach of structural functionalism. Apart from Durkheim's use of the term structure, the semiological concept of Ferdinand de Saussure became fundamental for structuralism. Saussure conceived language and society as a system of relations. His linguistic approach was also a refutation of evolutionary linguistics. In sociology, structuralism is a general theory of culture and methodology that implies that elements of human culture must be understood by way of their relationship to a broader system. It works to uncover the structures that underlie all the things that humans do, think, perceive, and feel.

Simon Blackburnas summarized structuralism as the belief that phenomena of human life are not intelligible except through their interrelations. These relations constitute a structure, and behind local variations in the surface phenomena there are constant laws of abstract structure.

Structuralism in Europe developed in the early 20th century, mainly in France and the Russian Empire, in the structural linguistics of Ferdinand de Saussure and the subsequent Prague, Moscow, and Copenhagen schools of linguistics.

　　马克斯·韦伯,德国著名学者,古典行政组织理论的代表人物,其代表作有《经济史》、《新教伦理与资本主义精神》等。他提出了理想的行政组织体系、并对古典组织理论做出杰出贡献,因而被誉为"组织理论之父"。

韦伯研究了理想的（ideal）行政组织体系。所谓"理想的"，是指这种组织体系并不是最合乎需要的，而是组织的"纯粹的"形态，是一种标准模式（standard mode）。韦伯的理论主要关注理想化组织（idealistic organization）的建立，他认为任何一种组织都是以某种形式的权力为基础的，由此他将影响组织建立的权力分为三种：传统性的权力是以古老传统的不可侵犯性和执行这种权力的人的地位的合法性为基础的；合理合法的权力是以正式规范、法则及在此规则下实施权力为依据的，之所以能服从这种权力，是由于存在着依法建立的等级制度；神授的权力是指个体特别的神性、英雄主义或魅力特征的感染力。韦伯认为，只有合理合法的权力才是行政组织体系的基础，因为它保证了组织长期稳定的发展，而合理合法的权力的最高发展形式则是理想的科层制组织。这种理论是适应环境的需要而出现的，被认为是对工业社会中大型而复杂的组织进行行政管理的最有效手段。韦伯理想的行政组织体系的思想是根据对教会、政府、军队和企业的经验的分析而得出的，他确信等级、权力和行政体系是一切社会组织的基础。韦伯据此提出了劳动分工、层级节制、职业训练、法制等理想化组织的系统原则。

古典理论是以等级规则和非人格因素为基础建立的，它是现代理论的基石，这些理论之所以被称为科学管理理论，是因为作为组织成员必须遵守组织规则，而不带个人情感因素，并能因此提高组织机构的效率。古典理论为西方管理理论奠定了基础，完成了使管理从经验到科学的转变，是西方管理理论第一个发展时期的重要标志。但是，古典学派强调物质因素（material factors）的作用，却忽视了人的主观能动作用（subjective initiation）；强调物质鼓励（material incentives），却忽视了人的社会需要（social needs）；强调正式组织，却忽视了非正式组织，从而大大限制了它的价值。

3.3.2　新古典管理理论 Neo-Classical Management Theory

到了 20 世纪 20 年代，新古典管理理论替代了古典理论。古典与新古典理论的关键区别在于，古典理论认为工人的满意仅仅是基于物质和经济需要，而新古典理论在考虑了物质和经济需求的同时也考虑到工作满意度（job satisfaction）和其他社会需求。新古典管理理论为了克服古典学派对人与人之间关系忽略的弊端，把行为科学引入了组织管理领域，管理研究的中心是人与人之间的关系。其代表主要有乔治·埃尔顿·梅奥（George Elton Mayo）的人际关系理论和切斯特·巴纳德（Chester Barnard）的行为主义学派（behaviorism）。

1. 人际关系理论 Human Relations Theory

人际关系理论产生于 20 世纪 20 年代至 30 年代初期，以"霍桑实验"（Hawthorne Studies）研究而闻名，这些实验是以古典理论传统为基础的，目的在于评价工作环境对生产力的影响。

Human Relations Theory came as a reaction to the classical approach, which stressed on formal structure. The classical school neglected the human side and under emphasized on the socio-psychological aspect of organization. According to Human Relations Approach, management is the Study of behaviour of people at work. This approach had its origin in a series of experiments conducted by Professor Elton Mayo and his associates at the Harvard School of Business at the Western Electric Company's Hawthorne Works, near Chicago.

"霍桑实验"是指 1924—1932 年在美国芝加哥郊外的西方电器公司的霍桑工厂(Hawthorne Plant of the Western Electric Company)中进行的一系列试验。该研究小组在美国社会学家梅奥的领导下,由一些人类学家、生理学家、统计学家和西方电气公司劳动人事部门管理人员组成。霍桑工厂具有完善的娱乐设施、医疗制度和养老金制度,但工人仍然有很强的不满情绪,生产效率很低。为了探究原因,美国国家研究委员会组织了一个包括多方面专家的研究小组进驻霍桑工厂,开始进行试验。实验分为四个阶段:照明试验、继电器装配工人小组试验、大规模访问交谈和对接线板接线工作室的研究。

霍桑实验历时八年,获得了大量的一手资料,为人际关系理论的形成以及后来行为科学的发展打下了基础,它由美国行为科学家梅奥主持。

George Elton Mayo (1880—1949) was an Australian born psychologist, industrial researcher, and organizational theorist. Elton Mayo and a team of researchers from Harvard University wanted to determine what physical conditions in the workplace—such as light and noise levels — would stimulate employees to be most productive. From 1924 to 1932, Mayo's team carried out a number of "experiments" to look at ways of improving productivity. The research involved manipulating length of rest and lunch periods and piecework payment plans. Mayo concluded that productivity partly depended on the informal social patterns of interaction in the work group.

Mayo, in communicating to business leaders, advanced the idea that managers who understand the nature of informal ties among workers can make decisions for management's benefit. Mayo concluded that people's work performance is dependent on both social relationships and job content. He suggested a tension between workers' "logic of sentiment" and managers' "logic of cost and efficiency" which could lead to conflict within organizations.

乔治·埃尔顿·梅奥,美籍澳大利亚人,行为科学家,他曾亲身参与了霍桑实验。他在代表作《工业文明的人类问题》(*The Human Problems of an Industrialized Civilization*)中总结了霍桑实验及其他几个实验的初步成果,并阐述了他的人群关系论的主要思想。

梅奥的人群关系理论的内容主要包括:工人是社会人(social man)而不是经济人(economic man);企业中存在着非正式组织;企业的领导者应注重通过提高员工的满意度

（satisfaction）来激发士气（morale），从而达到提高生产率（increase productivity）的目的。

梅奥在霍桑工厂的车间里演示了劳动条件的改善对工人的生产效率所起的直接和积极的影响，但实验结果却使他发现，不管工作条件（working conditions）是好是坏，实验组（experimental group）的生产效率总是提高的。由于工作条件不足以说明产量的变化，研究者就不得不把目光转向工作的其他因素上。他们观察到，这个工作团体的成员在实验期间形成了对工作的进行有积极影响的强烈信念。也就是说主要影响生产效率的并非劳动条件本身，而是工人的强烈组织信念。

经过进一步的分析，他们揭示出了形成强烈组织信念的三个基本因素：即自觉（awareness）（工人认识到自己的职责和重要性）；人际关系（human relations）（实验组织人员和管理者之间良好的人与人之间的关系）；工作环境（团体中创造了一种轻松愉快的工作环境）。基于这些初步的研究成果，研究者提出了工作团体成员间、雇员和他们的管理者间的社会关系性质，是完成生产任务和工作质量的潜在动力的假定。

按照霍桑效应（Hawthorn Effect），创造企业内的条件：社会关系（social relations）（小组互动、非正式关系）与社会条件（social environment）（企业养老机构、膳食机构、体育设施）可提升员工的满意度进而提高工作业绩（job performance）（劳动生产率）。其中，耶鲁大学社会学家斯坦利·米尔格拉姆（Stanley Milgram）曾经提出过一个相当有趣的理论，称之为"六度分离"（Six Degrees of Separation）理论。简单的说，对于任何你不认识、没有关系的人，通常不需要超过六个人的关系，就能够联结在一起。

> The Hawthorne Effect is used to describe a change in the behavior of an individual that results from their awareness of being observed. The effect suggests that workers tend to change their behavior at work in response to the attention they receive from their supervisor.
>
> The Hawthorne Effect derives its name from industrial experiments that were carried out in the Hawthorne suburb（now called Cicero）of Chicago in the 1920s and 1930s. The research comprised several productivity studies that tested the impact of changes in lighting and work structures，such as break times and working hours，on employee productivity.

梅奥在许多领域做出了重大贡献，包括商业管理（business administration）、工业社会学（industrial sociology）、哲学（philosophy）和社会心理学（social psychology）。他在工业领域的现场研究（field study）对工业和组织心理学产生了重大影响。梅奥在密切关注工业文明的人类、社会和政治问题时，就已经建立了对当今所谓的组织行为的科学研究，这让他闻名于世。梅奥的工作为人类关系运动奠定了基础。他强调指出，除了工业场所的正式组织外，还存在非正式的组织结构。梅奥认识到工业组织的"现有科学管理方法的不足"，并强调了为这些组织工作的人们之间的关系的重要性。他关于群体关系的思想在他1933年出版的《工业文明的人类问题》中得到了发展,该书部分基于他对霍桑的研究。人际关系学说的观点加强了正在形成的组织信念,认为在影响效率的诸多因素中,人是最重要的,从而使组织管理理论开始转向对人际关系和非正式组织的研究。

2. 行为主义学派 Behaviorism

行为主义是20世纪初起源于美国的心理学流派,主张心理学应该研究可以被观察和直接测量的行为,反对研究没有科学根据的意识。其主要特色为以系统方法理解人类和动物行为,并假设所有行为的产生皆是由环境中的刺激(stimuli)所产生的反应(reflexes);特别是个体在环境及生命史中所受到的惩罚、激励、刺激与行为结果所造成的强化(reinforcement)。虽然行为主义者(behaviorist)通常接受遗传因子是决定行为的重要因素,但他们主要仍较重视环境因素所带来的影响。

约翰·华生(John B. Watson,1878—1958)在20世纪上半叶开创了方法学的行为主义(methodological behaviorism),他反对内省的研究方法(introspective methods),主张研究可测量可观察的行为(measuring observable behaviors)。伯尔赫斯·弗雷德里克·斯金纳(B. F. Skinner,1904—1990)则对传统的心理学研究提出了道德上的问题,主张运用实用主义研究心理学。华生与伊万·巴甫洛夫(Ivan Pavlov,1849—1936)探讨了古典制约的刺激与反应过程,斯金纳则探讨了操作制约,指出结果会产生后效强化,并且能够产生控制性以及作为行为的前因。行为主义的观点一直在发展,当今它仍是各种管理理论的基础之一。行为主义学派可看成是连接传统的古典理论和分析当代各种管理理论的桥梁。行为科学理论(behavior science)的代表人物有很多,例如马斯洛(Abraham Maslow,1908—1970)、赫茨伯格(Frederick Herzberg,1923—2000)、麦格雷戈(Douglas McGregor,1906—1964)等。

In 1913, Watson published the article "Psychology as the Behaviorist Views It". In this article, Watson outlines the major features of his new philosophy of psychology, behaviorism: Psychology as the behaviorist views it is a purely objective experimental branch of natural science. Its theoretical goal is the prediction and control of behavior. Introspection forms no essential part of its methods, nor is the scientific value of its data dependent upon the readiness with which they lend themselves to interpretation in terms of consciousness. The behaviorist, in his efforts to get a unitary scheme of animal response, recognizes no dividing line between man and brute. The behavior of man, with all of its refinement and complexity, forms only a part of the behaviorist's total scheme of investigation.

马斯洛的"需要层次理论"(Maslow's hierarchy of needs)把需要分为五个层次:生理需要(physiological needs)、安全需要(safety needs)、社交需要(love and social belonging needs)、尊重需要(esteem needs)、自我实现需要(self-actualization),认为只有尚未满足的需要才能够影响行为,而且只有排在前面的需要得到了满足,才能产生更高一级的需要。

Maslow's hierarchy of needs is an idea in psychology proposed by Abraham Maslow in his paper "A Theory of Human Motivation" in the journal *Psychological Review*（1943）. Maslow subsequently extended the idea to include his observations of humans' innate curiosity. His theories parallel many other theories of human developmental psychology, some of which focus on describing the stages of growth in humans. The theory is a classification system intended to reflect the universal needs of society as its base, then proceeding to more acquired emotions. The hierarchy of needs is split between deficiency needs and growth needs, with two key themes involved within the theory being individualism and the prioritization of needs. While the theory is usually shown as a pyramid in illustrations, Maslow himself never created a pyramid to represent the hierarchy of needs.

赫茨伯格在《工作与激励》(*The Motivation to Work*，1959)一书中提出了激励的双因素理论(two-factor theory)，即激励因素和保健因素(motivation-hygiene theory)。20 世纪年代末，赫茨伯格在匹兹堡发现：属于工作本身或工作内容方面的因素(例如：挑战性的工作、认可、责任)使职工感到觉得满意；属于工作环境或工作关系方面的因素(例如，地位、工作安全感、薪水、福利)使职工感到觉得不满意。前者被赫茨伯格称作激励因素(motivational factors)，后者被称作保健因素(hygiene factors)。该理论认为：激励因子有生涯发展、工作特性、责任、成就、赏识。保健因素有工资、改善人际关系、工作条件、地位、福利。该理论认为：满意的对立面不是不满意，而是没有满意；不满意的对立面不是满意，而是没有不满意。和马斯洛的层次需求理论不同，赫茨伯格认为低层次需求的满足，并不会产生激励效果(motivational effect)，而只会导致不满意感的消失。

麦格雷戈提出 X 理论(theory X)、Y 理论(theory Y)和 Z 理论(theory Z)。X 理论对员工人性的基本判断为：人天性好逸恶劳、以自我为中心、缺乏进取心，并且通常容易受骗。Y 理论对员工的人性的基本判断为：人天性不是好逸恶劳，外来的控制与惩罚并不是促使人们为实现组织目标而工作的唯一方法，一般人是主动承担责任的，大多数人都具有一定的想象力、独创性和创造力，人的智慧和潜能只是部分地得到了发挥。Z 理论认为企业与职工的利益是一致的，两者的积极性可融为一体。

Theory X and Theory Y are theories of human work motivation and management. They were created by Douglas McGregor in the 1950s, and developed further in the 1960s. McGregor's work was rooted in motivation theory alongside the works of Abraham Maslow. Theory X style managers believe their employees are less intelligent, lazier, and work solely for a sustainable income. Theory Y managers assume employees are internally motivated, enjoy their job, and work to better themselves without a direct reward in return. These managers view their employees as one of the most valuable assets to the company, driving the internal workings of the corporation. Unlike Theories X and Y, Theory Z recognizes a transcendent dimension to worker's motivation. An optimal managerial style would help cultivate worker's creativity, insight, meaning and moral excellence.

行为学派认为构成人类行为基础的基本假设是自身的成熟、成就和内在发展,重视民主、非集权的组织形式,强调权力均等,反对非人格化的科层制。他们认为,如果管理者想真正有所作为,他们必须设法使组织成员认识到自己的重要性。为了使组织的运行富有成效,管理者应当提供机会提高工人的能力和实现自身发展的各种需求。

总之,新古典理论认为组织的实现要满足人的需求,注重组织内个人和团体的行为。但是他们在强调组织管理中人的因素的同时,却忽略了规章制度(rules and regulations)和物质的因素。

3.3.3 现代组织管理理论 Modern Organizational Management Theory

现代组织管理理论产生于第二次世界大战之后,是一种全面系统研究社会组织各方面内容的理论体系,它试图在总体上分析组织,试图对影响整个组织的各种因素进行一体化考察。其基本思想是:社会组织是一个系统,它由若干相互区别、相互联系又相互依存的要素组成。现代组织理论流派很多,其主要流派有管理科学(management science)、系统理论(systems theory)和权变理论(contingency theory)这几种。切斯特·巴纳德(Cheseter I. Barnard)是西方现代管理理论社会系统学派的创始人。

Chester Irving Barnard was an American business executive, public administrator, and the author of pioneering work in management theory and organizational studies. Barnard's classic 1938 book, *The Functions of the Executive discusses*, as the title suggests, the functions of the executive, but not from a merely intuitive point of view, but instead deriving them from his conception of cooperative systems.

Barnard was a great admirer of Talcott Parsons (1902—1979) and he and Parsons corresponded persistently. The two scholars would send manuscripts for commentary to each other and they would write long letters where they engage in a common theoretical discussion. Barnard formulated two interesting theories: one of authority and the other of incentives. Both are seen in the context of a communication system grounded in seven essential rules:

The channels of communication should be definite；

Everyone should know of the channels of communication；

Everyone should have access to the formal channels of communication；

Lines of communication should be as short and as direct as possible；

Competence of persons serving as communication centers should be adequate；

The line of communication should not be interrupted when the organization is functioning；

Every communication should be authenticated.

Thus，what makes a communication authoritative，rests with the subordinate，rather than with his superior.

管理学界几乎一致认为：巴纳德关于组织理论的探讨，至今无人超越，西方管理学界称他是现代管理理论的奠基人（founder）。1938 年，巴纳德出版了著名的《经理人员的职能》（*The Functions of Executives*）一书，此书自出版以来一直是"专业经理人员写出的有关组织和管理的最能启发人的思想的著作"，被誉为美国现代管理科学的经典作品。1948 年，巴纳德又出版了另一部重要的管理学著作《组织与管理》（*Organization and Management*），巴纳德的这些学术成果为现代管理学的建立和发展做出了非常突出的贡献。

研究管理必须从研究组织开始，巴纳德以前的组织理论，受古典经济学影响，偏重于专业分工和结构效率，对组织中的人员（personnel）没有足够的重视。这种组织理论的缺陷，直到巴纳德时才有了根本性的改观。巴纳德以社会科学家的宽广视野看待组织，以物理学家的细致态度来分析组织。他把社会学概念应用于分析经理人员的职能和工作过程，并把研究重点放在组织结构的逻辑分析上，提出了一套协作和组织的理论体系。巴纳德的理论贡献（theoretical contribution）在于：他从最简单的协作（cooperation）入手，揭示了组织的本质及其最一般的规律。

巴纳德在组织管理理论方面的开创性研究，奠定了现代组织理论的基础。后来的许多学者如德鲁克（Peter Drucker）等人都极大地受益于巴纳德。

1. 管理科学学派 Management Science

管理科学学派又称数量学派，或计量学派，也称数量管理科学学派，是现代管理理论中的一个主要学派。该学派将数学引入管理领域，用电子计算机作为工具，把科学的原理、方法和工具应用于管理的各种活动，使管理问题的研究由定性分析（qualitative analysis）发展为定量分析（qualitative analysis），制定用于管理决策的数学统计模型（mathematical statistics model），并进行求解，以减低管理的不确定性（uncertainty），使投入的资源发挥最大的作用，得到最大的经济效果。管理科学学派以定量模型、计算机模拟（computer imitation）为基础，来推进以前几乎靠个人的判断和经验进行的决策。该学派所依据的信念是：只要管理、组织、计划或决策是一个逻辑过程（logical process），那就一定能够用数学符号和数学关系来表示。他们区别于其他学派的主要特点不是着重利用数学方法和电子计算机技术研究管理问题,而是几乎把注意力全部放在建立数学模型(set up mathematical model),进行模拟和求解上。

管理科学学派可以追溯到 20 世纪初泰勒的"科学管理"(scientific management),然而正式成立于 1939 年由英国曼切斯特大学(University of Manchester)教授布莱克特(Blackett)领导的运筹学(operational research)小组,该小组运用运筹学解决英国雷达系统的合理布置问题。第二次世界大战结束后,由于战后恢复和经济建设需要,英美对运筹学的研究逐步从军事转入民用企业的应用。管理科学学派是对泰勒科学管理理论的发展和升华,其重要特点是将数学模型广泛应用于经营管理。管理科学学派由著名的运筹学专家组成,把定量方法运用到管理中并试图解决组织管理的一些问题,把全局的计划和预测与实现组织目标的管理结合起来。尽管在高层组织中已比较早地运用了统计学和计量方法,但大多数学者把第二次世界大战作为管理科学的起点。管理科学学派对组织的基本看法是:组织是由"经济人"(economic man)组成的一个追求经济利益的系统,同时又是由物质技术和决策网络组成的系统。

2. 系统理论 System Management Theory

系统管理理论是运用系统论(system theory)、信息论(theory of information)、控制论(cybernetics)原理,把管理视为一个系统,以实现管理优化的理论。

> Systems theory seeks to explain and develop hypotheses around characteristics that arise within complex systems that seemingly could not arise in any single system within the whole, a system is "more than the sum of its parts". The systems management theory proposes that businesses, like the human body, consists of multiple components that work harmoniously so that the larger system can function optimally. According to the theory, the success of an organization depends on several key elements: synergy, interdependence, and interrelations between various subsystems.

美国社会学家巴纳德最早把系统理论和社会学知识用于管理领域,创立了社会系统学派,并采用社会学系统观点来研究组织问题奠定了现代组织理论的基石。他认为传统组织理论满足于从技术上去分析组织的结构和特征,却没有从人与人之间的协作关系去考察组织。巴纳德认为,个人是社会组织的重要构成要素,是有自由意志(free will)的决定者,个人具有决策的能力与选择的自由,甚至可以改变环境因素,达到社会组织预设的目标。

3. 权变理论 Contingency Theory

权变理论,又称情境理论。20 世纪 60 年代以后关于领导有效性研究转入权变理论。权变理论认为,领导的有效性不是取决于领导者不变的品质和行为,而是取决于领导者、被领导者和情境条件三者的配合关系,即领导有效性是领导者、被领导者和领导情境三个变量的函数。这是因为:社会组织系统是由各个分系统和子系统构成,而且组织具有多变量性,因此管理不存在不加改变就可以应用于各种情况的万能原则。各个不同种类的社会组织,其管理和组织方法都是不同的,因此,管理模式应该随着社会组织所处的独特的环境条件和每个社会组织所固有的内在因素的变化而变化。权变理论试图了解社会组织在变化的条件下和特殊的环境中实际运行的情况,寻求和掌握其规律,以期提出适应于不同具体情况的社会组织结构设计和组织管理模式。

> A contingency theory is an organizational theory that claims that there is no best way to organize a corporation, to lead a company, or to make decisions. Instead, the optimal course of action is contingent (dependent) upon the internal and external situation. Contingent leaders are flexible in choosing and adapting to succinct strategies to suit change in situation at a particular period in time in the running of the organization.

权变理论强调组织管理没有固定的模式和原则,组织管理的方式必须根据组织各要素及内外条件的变化而变化。

3.3.4 组织理论的发展 Development of Organizational Theory

20 世纪 80 年代末至 90 年代初,随着经济全球化的逐步深化,传统组织的设计已经不再符合时代的要求,知识和信息成为现代组织运行的重要内容。1990 年,美国麻省理工学院(Massachusetts Institute of Technology)的彼得·圣吉(Peter M. Senge,1947—)出版的《第五项修炼:学习型组织的艺术与实务》(*The Fifth Discipline*:*The Art & Practice of the Learning Organization*)一书,提出了组织学习与学习型组织的理论。

> *The Fifth Discipline*:*The Art and Practice of the Learning Organization* is a book by Peter Senge, focusing on group problem solving using the systems thinking method in order to convert companies into learning organizations. The five disciplines represent approaches (theories and methods) for developing three core learning capabilities: fostering aspiration, developing reflective conversation, and understanding complexity. The five disciplines of a "learning organization" discussed in the book are:
>
> "Personal mastery is a discipline of continually clarifying and deepening our personal vision, of focusing our energies, of developing patience, and of seeing reality objectively."
>
> "Mental models are deeply ingrained assumptions, generalizations, or even pictures of images that influence how we understand the world and how we take action."
>
> "Building shared vision — a practice of unearthing shared pictures of the future that foster genuine commitment and enrollment rather than compliance."

"Team learning starts with 'dialogue', the capacity of members of a team to suspend assumptions and enter into genuine 'thinking together'."

"Systems thinking — The Fifth Discipline that integrates the other four."

Senge describes extensively the role of what he refers to as "mental models," which he says are integral in order to "focus on the openness needed to unearth shortcomings" in perceptions. The book also focuses on "team learning" with the goal of developing "the skills of groups of people to look for the larger picture beyond individual perspectives". In addition to these principles, the author stresses the importance of "personal mastery" to foster "the personal motivation to continually learn how actions affect the world."

他通过提出自我超越(personal mastery)、改善心智模式(mental models)、建立共同愿景(shared vision)、团体学习(team learning)和系统思考(systems thinking)这五项修炼,把学习型组织定位于在组织中,人们可以通过不断地一起学习以达到不断提高自己能力的目的,保持持续的创造力,突破各种发展瓶颈,以实现组织与个人的共同目标,并以此作为企业立身的一个基本原则的组织形式。它能认识环境、适应环境,进而能动地作用于环境。这里的"学习"是指组织成员对环境、竞争者和组织本身的各种情况分析、探索和交流过程。与传统的学习意义不同,不仅是指知识、信息的获取,更重要的是指提高自身能力以对变化的环境做出有效的应变。

学习型组织具备以下特征:人性是善良的,但并不是一成不变的;成员之间的交流既是垂直指令式的,又是横向协商式的;组织的战略是先导型的,思考问题的方式是系统的;领导方式一般是民主参与式的;组织分工强调扩大每个员工的工作范畴使其灵活丰富,组织利用经济、非经济两类因素激励实现组织目标,保证成员目标的一致性。

延伸阅读 Further Reading

思考 Thinking it through:

彼得·德鲁克对组织理论的发展。

The Coming of the New Organization(Excerpt)

The typical large business 20 years hence will have fewer than half the levels of management of its counterpart today, and no more than a third of the managers. In its structure, and in its management problems and concerns, it will bear little resemblance to the typical manufacturing company, circa 1950, which our textbooks still consider the norm. Instead, it is far more likely to resemble organizations that neither the practicing manager nor the management scholar pays much attention to today: the hospital, the university, the symphony orchestra. For like them, the typical business will be knowledge-based, an organization composed largely of specialists who direct and discipline their own performance through organized feedback from colleagues, customers, and headquarters. For this reason, it will be what I call an information-based organization.

Businesses, especially large ones, have little choice but to become information-based. Demographics, for one, demands the shift. The center of gravity in employment is moving fast from manual and clerical workers to knowledge workers who resist the command-and-control model that business took from the military 100 years ago. Economics also dictates change, especially the need for large businesses to innovate and to be entrepreneurs. But above all, information technology demands the shift.

Advanced data-processing technology isn't necessary to create an information-based organization, of course. As we shall see, the British built just such an organization in India when "information technology" meant the quill pen, and barefoot runners were the "telecommunications" systems. But as advanced technology becomes more and more prevalent, we have to engage in analysis and diagnosis—that is, in "information"—even more intensively or risk being swamped by the data we generate.

So far most computer users still use the new technology only to do faster what they have always done before, crunch conventional numbers. But as soon as a company takes the first tentative steps from data to information, its decision processes, management structure, and even the way its work gets done begin to be transformed. In fact, this is already happening, quite fast, in a number of companies throughout the world.

We can readily see the first step in this transformation process when we consider the impact of computer technology on capital-investment decisions. We have known for a long time that there is no one right way to analyze a proposed capital investment. To understand it we need at least six analyses: the expected rate of return; the payout period and the investment's expected productive life; the discounted present value of all returns through the productive lifetime of the investment; the risk in not making the investment or deferring it; the cost and risk in case of failure; and finally, the opportunity cost. Every accounting student is taught these concepts. But before the advent of data-processing capacity, the actual analyses would have taken man-years of clerical toil to complete. Now anyone with a spreadsheet should be able to do them in a few hours.

The availability of this information transforms the capital-investment analysis from opinion into diagnosis, that is, into the rational weighing of alternative assumptions. Then the information transforms the capital-investment decision from an opportunistic, financial decision governed by the numbers into a business decision based on the probability of alternative strategic assumptions. So the decision both presupposes a business strategy and challenges that strategy and its assumptions.

The second area that is affected when a company focuses its data-processing capacity on producing information is its organization structure. Almost immediately, it becomes clear that both the number of management levels and the number of managers can be sharply cut. The reason is straightforward: it turns out that whole layers of management neither make decisions nor lead. Instead, their main, if not their only, function is to serve as "relays"—human boosters for the faint, unfocused signals that pass for communication in the traditional pre-information organization.

One of America's largest defense contractors made this discovery when it asked what information its top corporate and operating managers needed to do their jobs. Where did it come from? What form was it in? How did it flow? The search for answers soon revealed that whole layers of management—perhaps as many as 6 out of a total of 14— existed only because these questions had not been asked before. The company had had data galore. But it had always used its copious data for control rather than for information.

Information is data endowed with relevance and purpose. Converting data into information thus requires knowledge. And knowledge, by definition, is specialized. (In fact, truly knowledgeable people tend toward overspecialization, whatever their field, precisely because there is always so much more to know.)

The information-based organization requires far more specialists overall than the command-and-control companies we are accustomed to. Moreover, the specialists are found in operations, not at corporate headquarters. Indeed, the operating organization tends to become an organization of specialists of all kinds.

Information-based organizations need central operating work such as legal counsel, public relations, and labor relations as much as ever. But the need for service staffs—that is, for people without operating responsibilities who only advise, counsel, or coordinate—shrinks drastically. In its central management, the information-based organization needs few, if any, specialists.

Because of its flatter structure, the large, information-based organization will more closely resemble the businesses of a century ago than today's big companies. Back then, however, all the knowledge, such as it was, lay with the very top people. The rest were helpers or hands, who mostly did the same work and did as they were told. In the information-based organization, the knowledge will be primarily at the bottom, in the minds of the specialists who do different work and direct themselves. So today's typical organization in which knowledge tends to be concentrated in service staffs, perched rather insecurely between top management and the operating people, will likely be labeled a phase, an attempt to infuse knowledge from the top rather than obtain information from below.

Finally, a good deal of work will be done differently in the information-based organization. Traditional departments will serve as guardians of standards, as centers for training and the assignment of specialists; they won't be where the work gets done. That will happen largely in task-focused teams.

This change is already underway in what used to be the most clearly defined of all departments—research. In pharmaceuticals, in telecommunications, in papermaking, the traditional sequence of research, development, manufacturing, and marketing is being replaced by synchrony: specialists from all these functions work together as a team, from the inception of research to a product's establishment in the market.

How task forces will develop to tackle other business opportunities and problems remains to be seen. I suspect, however, that the need for a task force, its assignment, its composition, and its leadership will have to be decided on case by case. So the organization that will be developed will go beyond the matrix and may indeed be quite different from it. One thing is clear, though: it will require greater self-discipline and even greater emphasis on individual responsibility for relationships and for communications.

To say that information technology is transforming business enterprises is simple. What this transformation will require of companies and top managements is much harder to decipher. That is why I find it helpful to look for clues in other kinds of information-based organizations, such as the hospital, the symphony orchestra, and the British administration in India.

A fair-sized hospital of about 400 beds will have a staff of several hundred physicians and 1,200 to 1,500 paramedics divided among some 60 medical and paramedical specialties. Each specialty has its own knowledge, its own training, its own language. In each specialty, especially the paramedical ones like the clinical lab and physical therapy, there is a head person who is a working specialist rather than a full-time manager. The head of each specialty reports directly to the top, and there is little middle management. A good deal of the work is done in ad hoc teams as required by an individual patient's diagnosis and condition.

(Reference: hbr.org/1988/01/the-coming-of-the-new-organization)

4 文 化
Culture

Culture and Society

Culture is what differentiates one group or society from the next; different societies have different cultures.

Key Points

Different societies have different cultures; a culture represents the beliefs and practices of a group, while society represents the people who share those beliefs and practices.

Material culture refers to the objects or belongings of a group of people, such as automobiles, stores, and the physical structures where people worship. Nonmaterial culture, in contrast, consists of the ideas, attitudes, and beliefs of a society.

In 18th and 19th century Europe, the term "culture" was equated with civilization and considered a unique aspect of Western society. Remnants of that colonial definition of culture can be seen today in the idea of " high culture ".

During the Romantic Era, culture became equated with nationalism and gave rise to the idea of multiple national cultures.

Today, social scientists understand culture as a society's norms, values, and beliefs; as well as its objects and symbols, and the meaning given to those objects and symbols.

Key Terms

Civilization: An organized culture encompassing many communities, often on the scale of a nation or a people; a stage or system of social, political or technical development.

High culture: The artistic entertainment and material artifacts associated with a society's aristocracy or most learned members, usually requiring significant education to be appreciated or highly skilled labor to be produced.

Popular culture: The prevailing vernacular culture in any given society, including art, cooking, clothing, entertainment, films, mass media, music, sports, and style.

Nationalism: The idea of supporting one's country and culture; patriotism.

Culture encompasses human elements beyond biology: for example, our norms and values, the stories we tell, learned or acquired behaviors, religious beliefs, art and fashion, and so on. Culture is what differentiates one group or society from the next.

Different societies have different cultures; however, it is important not to confuse the idea of culture with society. A culture represents the beliefs and practices of a group, while society represents the people who share those beliefs and practices. Neither society nor culture could exist without the other.

Defining Culture

Almost every human behavior, from shopping to marriage to expressions of feelings, is learned. Behavior based on learned customs is not necessarily a bad thing — being familiar with unwritten rules helps people feel secure and confident that their behaviors will not be challenged or disrupted. However even the simplest actions — such as commuting to work, ordering food from a restaurant, and greeting someone on the street — evidence a great deal of cultural propriety.

Material culture refers to the objects or belongings of a group of people (such as automobiles, stores, and the physical structures where people worship). Nonmaterial culture, in contrast, consists of the ideas, attitudes, and beliefs of a society. Material and nonmaterial aspects of culture are linked, and physical objects often symbolize cultural ideas. A metro pass is a material object, but it represents a form of nonmaterial culture (namely capitalism, and the acceptance of paying for transportation). Clothing, hairstyles, and jewelry are part of material culture, but the appropriateness of wearing certain clothing for specific events reflects nonmaterial culture. A school building belongs to material culture, but the teaching methods and educational standards are part of education's nonmaterial culture.

These material and nonmaterial aspects of culture can vary subtly from region to region. As people travel farther afield, moving from different regions to entirely different parts of the world, certain material and nonmaterial aspects of culture become dramatically unfamiliar. As we interact with cultures other than our own, we become more aware of our own culture — which might otherwise be invisible to us — and to the differences and commonalities between our culture and others.

The History of "Culture"

Some people think of culture in the singular, in the way that it was thought of in Europe during the 18th and early 19th centuries: as something achieved through evolution and progress. This concept of culture reflected inequalities within European societies and their colonies around the world; in short, it equates culture with civilization and contrasts both with nature or non-civilization. According to this understanding of culture, some countries are more "civilized" than others, and some people are therefore more "cultured" than others.

When people talk about culture in the sense of civilization or refinement, they are really talking about "high culture," which is different from the sociological concept of culture. High culture refers to elite goods and activities, such as haute cuisine, high fashion or couture, museum-caliber art, and classical music. In common parlance, people may refer to others as being "cultured" if they know about and take part in these activities. Someone who uses culture in this sense might argue that classical music is more refined than music by working-class people, such as jazz or the indigenous music traditions of aboriginal peoples. Popular (or "pop") culture, by contrast, is more mainstream and influenced by mass media and the common opinion. Popular culture tends to change as tastes and opinions change over time, whereas high culture generally stays the same throughout the years. For example, Mozart is considered high culture, whereas Britney Spears is considered pop culture; Mozart is likely to still be popular in 100 years, but Britney Spears will likely be forgotten by all but a few.

[Reference: socialsci. libretexts. org/Bookshelves/Sociology/Introduction _ to _ Sociology/Book%3A_Sociology_(Boundless)/03%3A_Culture/3.01%3A_Culture_and_Society/3.1 B%3A_Culture_and_Society]

4.1　文化的内涵 Meanings of Culture

文化(culture)是社会学中最为广泛使用的概念之一。当我们在日常生活中使用"文化"这个词的时候,我们通常将文化视为人类精神活动(mental activity)的产物,如文学、艺术、音乐、建筑等等。社会学家在使用文化这个词的时候,也包括此类活动,但又不止于此。文化与社会紧密相关,指的是社会成员及其群体的生活方式(way of life)。从某种程度上说,人们的社会活动(social activities)就是文化生活(cultural life),人们的文化生活就是社会活动。从微观层面(micro level)来看,文化体现和渗透于人们的衣食住行(basic necessities of life)中,不了解文化就不能真正了解社会。从宏观层面(macro level)来看,每个国家、民族都有自己独特的生活方式,每个国家都有自己不同的情况,每个民族都有属于自己的生活方式，这就是文化。

随着全球化进程的展开，了解文化的多样性（cultural diversity）已经是人与人之间交流与沟通的重要前提和基础，因此，不可不重视文化。

4.1.1 "文化"概说 Overview of Culture

什么是文化？"文化"是个有着丰富内涵和宽泛外延的概念。研究文化的学者们从多角度、多侧面定义了"文化"，在丰富了"文化"内涵（connotation）的同时，也扩展或限定了"文化"的外延（extension）。

According to *Cambridge Dictionary*, culture is the way of life, especially the general customs and beliefs, of a particular group of people at a particular time; the attitudes, behavior, opinions, etc. of a particular group of people within society; the way of life of a particular people, esp. as shown in their ordinary behavior and habits, their attitudes toward each other, and their moral and religious beliefs; and the arts of describing, showing, or performing that represent the traditions or the way of life of a particular people or group; literature, art, music, dance, theater, etc.

在中国，文化是"人文教化"的简称；这意味着有人才有文化，文化是讨论人类社会的专属语，文是语言文字，教化是文化的真正重心所在。在古汉语中，"文化"指的是以伦理道德教导世人，使人们成为在思想、观念、言行和举止上合乎特定礼仪规范的人；此意在现代汉语中仍沿用。总括起来，我们今天汉语中的"文化"概念有两种含义：一是指历代统治者所施行的文治教化的总和；二是指文物典章、朝政纲纪、道德伦序，以及成为礼俗日用的一整套观念（notion）和习俗（convention）。

近代"人类学"（anthropology）、"文化学"（culturology）意义上的"文化"（culture），是一个外来语，它是20世纪初由欧洲经日本传入中国的。culture来源于拉丁语colere，原指种植、耕耘、农作，后转义为对人的培养、教育、发展、尊重。前一义是人对土地的耕作（cultivation），是对外在自然的人化（humanization）；后一义是通过教育与培养提高人的素质，是对人自身的教化（educate），是内在自然的人化。因此文化的涵义不仅耕耘土地，还指照料土地、饲养动物；照料人们的生活，如穿衣、装饰身体的风俗；还意味着居住在城镇或市区，以及培养正确的道德和心智等。在中世纪晚期，文化开始指道德完美与心智、艺术成就。

文化的构成包含三个层次：器物（物质文化）（material culture）、制度（制度文化）（institutional culture）和观念（精神文化）（spiritual culture）。器物（implements）层次，指的是人们为了适应自然、与自然和谐相处而创造的物质文化；制度层次，指的是人们为了与他人和谐相处而创造的制度，包括道德伦理、社会规范、社会制度、风俗习惯等；观念层次，人们为了寻找生命的价值意义，去除内心焦虑，发展出来的精神文化，如艺术、文学、音乐、戏剧等。

文化是社会价值系统（social value system）的总和。但是，不同学科对文化有不同的理解。哲学认为文化从本质上讲是哲学思想表现形式。例如：从存在主义（existentialism）的角度来看，文化是对个体或群体的存在方式的描述。

According to *Stanford Encyclopedia of Philosophy*, "existentialism" is a term that belongs to intellectual history. Its definition is thus to some extent one of historical convenience. existentialism became identified with a cultural movement that flourished in Europe in the 1940s and 1950s. On the existential view, to understand what a human being, is it is not enough to know all the truths that natural science—including the science of psychology—could tell us. The dualist who holds that human beings are composed of independent substances — "mind" and "body"—is no better off in this regard than is the physicalist who holds that human existence can be adequately explained in terms of the fundamental physical constituents of the universe. Existentialism does not deny the validity of the basic categories of physics, biology, psychology, and the other sciences (categories such as matter, causality, force, function, organism, development, motivation, and so on). It claims only that human beings cannot be fully understood in terms of them. Nor can such an understanding be gained by supplementing our scientific picture with a moral one. Categories of moral theory such as intention, blame, responsibility, character, duty, virtue, and the like *do* capture important aspects of the human condition, but neither moral thinking (governed by the norms of the good and the right) nor scientific thinking (governed by the norm of truth) suffices. "Existentialism", therefore, may be defined as the philosophical theory which holds that a further set of categories, governed by the norm of authenticity, is necessary to grasp human existence.

功能主义学派认为，文化包括物质（substance）和精神（spirit）两个方面，不论是具体的（specific）物质现象，如手杖、工具、器皿等，还是抽象的（abstract）社会现象，如风俗习惯、思想意识、社会制度等，都具有满足人类实际生活需要的作用。

在社会学和文化人类学（cultural anthropology）中，"文化"也可以作为符号体系尤其是象征性符号体系来把握。文化的核心是其符号系统（symbol system），如文字。各文字体系有相应的认知心理。

目前，关于文化的定义，都是一个早已超越了本义和引申义的、分歧颇多的概念。1952年，美国人类学家阿尔弗雷德·克罗依伯（Alfred Kroeber）和克莱德·克拉克洪（Clyde Kluckhohn）在《文化：概念和定义的批判性回顾》（*Culture：A Critical Review of Concepts and Definitions*）一书中，对1871—1951年理论界存在的164种"文化"定义进行了综合性介绍。他们认为，这些定义可分为描述性（descriptive）、历史性（historic）、规范性（normative）、心理性（mental）、结构性（constitutive）、遗传性（genetic）六大类。诸如此类的总结在国内外研究中很多。也有人统计认为，文化的定义有上千种之多。每个学者都从本学科、本专业、本研究领域及要说明的问题角度揭示了文化的丰富内涵。

中国学者关于文化的界定取得了丰硕成果,从概念的内涵方面来看,国内较有影响的是"人化说"。坚持"人化说"的学者认为,文化的本质就是"人化",即人的本质力量的对象化。他们认为:凡人化了的东西,就是文化。人化说把人与文化及实践紧密联系在一起,从人的角度理解文化,从文化的角度理解人,从实践中理解人与文化的统一,从而包容了物质财富与精神财富,实现了文化界定的动与静(dynamic and static)、有与无(being and not being)的统一。

美国人类学家赫斯科维茨(Melville Jean Herskovits,1895—1963)曾指出:①文化是学而知之的(learned);②文化是由构成人类存在的生物学成分、环境科学成分、心理学成分以及历史学成分衍生而来的;③文化具有结构;④文化分为各个方面;⑤文化是动态的(dynamic);⑥文化是可变的(alterable);⑦文化显示出规律性(regularity),它可借助科学方法加以分析;⑧文化是个人适应其整个环境的工具,是表达其创造性的手段。这些主张从多方面对文化进行了描述,也得到了大多数美国人类学家的赞同。

> Herskovits was very active in professional organizations, and the list of his awards and honors is long. He contributed summary articles on the state of anthropology to various publications, edited *The American Anthropologist* from 1949 through 1952, and served as editor of the *International Directory of Anthropologists* in 1950. In addition to his presidency of the African Studies Association in 1957—1958, he was president of the American Folklore Society (1945), vice-president of the American Association for the Advancement of Science (1934), a member of the executive board of the American Anthropological Association (1947), and a member of the permanent council of the International Anthropology Congress. He was a pivotal figure in the organization of the First International Congress of Africanists, held in Ghana in 1962.

4.1.2 文化的特性 Characteristics of Culture

通过对不同文化的比较研究,才能了解文化的特点。文化有如下特性:

(1)习得性。文化是学习得来的,而不是通过遗传而天生具有的。文化不仅是现实的存在,也是正在生成的存在。它既需要静态的表征(static representation),也需要动态的描述(dynamic description)。因此,我们既要看到文化作为人的实践成果而存在,又要看到文化将随实践而发展的动态性。

(2)设计性。康德给文化下的定义是:有理性的实体(rational entity)为了一定的目的而进行的能力之创造。这里表达了文化是一种有设计的活动的思想。

(3)共有性。文化是一系列共有的概念、价值观和行为准则,它是使个人行为能力为集体所接受的共同标准。文化不是出自个体,而是来自群体生活。

（4）多样性。人类行为和习俗的多样性是显而易见的。

综上所述,文化是一定社会历史条件下人的实践活动及其成果的总和,它既是对人存在方式的表征,又是指引人发展的设计。

4.2　文化的类型与结构 Types and Structures of Culture

文化现象(cultural phenomenon)纷繁复杂,包罗万象,如科学、技术、知识、房屋、器皿、机械、社会组织、制度、政治和法律形式、伦理、道德、风俗、习惯、语言、教育、宗教、信仰、审美意识、文学、艺术等都属于文化现象。为更好地把握文化诸现象,有必要了解文化的分类以及文化的内部及外部结构,这是我们在这一节要讨论的问题。

4.2.1　文化的类型 Types of Culture

在社会学史上,由于分类标准(taxonomy)的差别,人们对文化的分类是有很大差别的。美籍苏格兰学者罗伯特·莫里森·麦基弗(Robert Morrison MaClver,1882—1970)认为文化由两部分构成,即文明体系(civilizational system)和文化体系(cultural system)。文明体系更强调工具性(instrumentality),文化体系具有更突出的目的性(intentionality)。文明体系是由社会体系中有实用性的(practical)元素组合而成的,这些元素具有高度的工具性(instrumental),是人类达到某些目的的工具和手段,其本身并无自我价值,如科学技术、经济、政治等。而文化体系是由社会中具有"目的价值"的元素组合而成的,对人类来讲它们本身就有价值,是人类追求的目的。

英国马林诺夫斯基(Bronislaw Malinowski,1884—1942)根据文化的功能,把文化现象分为四类:①物质设备;②精神文化;③语言;④社会组织。美国的威廉·菲尔丁·奥格本(William Fielding Ogburn)把文化的功能与产生(起源)结合起来,首先把文化现象划分为物质文化和非物质文化(intangible culture),物质文化指的是工具、机器、房屋之类具体的人工的产物;非物质文化指的是两个方面:①知识、艺术、宗教之类所反映的不可见的精神文化;②在非物质文化中又划分出的宗教、艺术一类精神文化和规范人类行为的制度、习惯一类调适文化。

目前,因内的文化学或文化哲学研究者大多能同意把文化的构成最粗略地划分为物质文化、精神文化和制度文化(institutional culture),这种划分能够最大限度地涵盖整个文化世界。

1. 物质文化 Material Culture

研究物质文化意味着研究人与人造物之间的关系,例如物体的制造、保存等等。诸如艺术史、考古学、人类学等科目都会研究到物质文化。对物质文化的研究缘起于人类学,最初关注的是非西方的物质文化,由此来阐释社会的演进与衰退。

Material culture is the aspect of social reality grounded in the objects and architecture that surround people. It includes the usage, consumption, creation, and trade of objects as well as the behaviors, norms, and rituals that the objects create or take part in. The term is most commonly used in archaeological studies. Material culture can be described as any object that humans use to survive, define social relationships, represent facets of identity, or benefit peoples' state of mind, social, or economic standing. Material culture is contrasting to symbolic culture, which includes nonmaterial symbols, beliefs, and social constructs. Material culture studies as an academic field grew along the field of anthropology and so began by studying non-Western material culture.

物质文化又称器物文化，是指能够满足人的基本生存需要的文化产品。物质文化是一个非常丰富多样的领域。马林诺夫斯基曾经把人的基本需要概括成七个方面：新陈代谢（metabolism）、生殖（reproduction）、舒适（comfort）、安全（safety）、运动（exercise）、发育（development）和健康（health）。

物质文化具有人工物质性。第一，物质文化与制度文化、精神文化的最根本区别在于它的物质性。物质文化是有形的、具体可见的，而制度文化、精神文化更多地以无形的方式存在。物质文化同时还体现人的主观能动性和创造性，它不同于一般的自然物，是一种比自然物质性更高的物质性。第二，物质文化具有人工创造性，这是它与自然物质的最根本区别。物质文化产品必须是经过人的加工，体现了人的思想，能够维持个体生命的再生产和社会的再生产的文化产品。

物质文化具有较强的共通性。物质文化与制度文化、精神文化不同，物质文化更容易为大家共享，特别是先进的物质文化。

物质文化直接反映生产力的发展水平，随着生产力的发展而不断提升。物质文化是人类财富和能力的化身与体现，其中生产工具（instrument of production）则是一定社会的生产力水平（level of productivity）的标志。因此，人们对历史的时代划分往往以生产工具为标准。如石器时代（The Stone Age）、青铜器时代（The Bronze Age）、铁器时代（The Iron Age）、机器时代、电器时代等。

2. 制度文化 Institutional Culture

制度文化是人类处理个人所面对的各种社会关系的产物，它是人类智慧在制度或规范中的凝结。它包括社会的经济制度、婚姻制度、家族制度、政治法律制度、商品交换制度、企业制度、公共管理制度、教育制度、婚姻家庭制度等，以及实行上述制度的各种具有物质载体的机构设施、个体对社会事物的参与形式、反映在各种制度中的人的主观心态等。制度文化不仅为人们提供了若干行为模式，调节人与人之间的关系，而且还以制度的形式规定了各种社会组织的职能，使整个社会按一定秩序运行。

Institutional culture is defined as the collective, mutual shaping patterns of norms, values, practices, beliefs and assumptions that guide the behavior of individuals and groups in high education and provide a frame of reference within which to interpret the meaning of events and actions.

与物质文化相比,制度文化在整个文化世界中是深一层次的文化。它以一定物质文化为基础,主要满足人的交往需求,以更合理地处理个人之间、个人与群体之间的关系。人在社会交往中所结成的交往关系需要制度化、组织化,这就形成了制度文化,人的交往实践活动是制度文化产生的源泉和动力。

制度文化具有阶级性(class character)。制度文化包容着个体对社会事务的参与形式,而这种参与形式在阶级社会中无疑是具有阶级性的,因此制度文化具有阶级性。每个社会中的统治阶级(ruling class)总在通过制度文化为自己的合法性(legality)进行论证。

制度文化也具有一定程度的普适性(universality)。在某些方面,制度文化可以超越地域的限制,形成一些共性的东西,如政治文化,有地域型的政治文化、臣民型的政治文化、公民型的政治文化等。自由、民主、平等是人类的普遍追求,千百年来,人们前仆后继为之进行了孜孜探索。自由、民主、平等已经成为公认的政治文化,其核心思想应该说是有共通之处的。

制度文化具有时代性和民族性。制度文化具有明显的时代色彩,特定时代总有其特定的制度文化,而且带有鲜明的民族特点,特定的民族总有其特定的制度文化。

在制度文化诸要素中,经济制度(economic system)是基础,政治法律制度是核心。经济制度即生产关系,包括生产资料的所有制形式,生产过程中的人际关系或劳动组合方式、管理方式,劳动产品的分配形式等等。经济制度作为社会生产方式的内容,构成了社会的经济基础;作为国家对经济活动进行管理的体制,又具有上层建筑的属性。政治法律制度(political & legal system)是社会的上层建筑,它要把社会的经济制度、婚姻制度、家庭制度等以法的形式确立并固定下来。政治法律制度反映着特定时代物质文化的要求,并给予物质文化尤其是生产力以重大的影响,而生产力又是通过制度化了的社会关系的各种形式给予人们的衣食住行以影响。

3. 精神文化 Spiritual Culture

Spiritual Culture is a bridge between old and new stages of the world development, guaranteeing the positive development and coexistence of the humanity in a harmonic unity with Nature.

精神文化是人类的文化心态及其在观念形态上的对象化。它是文化的核心部分,是人类智慧在观念中的凝结。在文化的所有层面中,最具有内在性、最集中地体现出人与动物及其他存在物本质差别、最能体现文化的超越性和创造性本质特征的是精神文化。正如著名法国哲学家帕斯卡尔(Blaise Pascal,1623—1662)所断言的那样,"思想形成人的伟大"。他指出,很难想象人若没有思想,那就成了一块顽石或者一头畜牲了。精神文化包括两个部分,一是存在于人心中的文化心态、文化心理、文化观念、文化思想等。二是已经理论化、对象化的思想理论体系,如政治法律思想、艺术、道德学说、美学、宗教、哲学、科学等。

精神文化与制度文化一样,具有明显的时代特色(era characteristics)。例如,中世纪的欧洲,信奉上帝是一种普遍性的社会文化心理,人们不是从人的现实存在而是从神的意志那里引申出社会与国家制度,以"君权神授"(divine right of kings)为核心的社会政治学说是那时普遍状态的反映。

精神文化同样具有民族特色(national features)。这种差异不仅是形式的,而且是内容的。精神文化的民族特色在民族文学艺术作品的内容、形式和艺术风格所体现出来的文化心理上,也表现得十分鲜明。此外,宗教和哲学也无不体现出精神文化的民族特色。

物质文化与制度文化、精神文化的区分是相对的。物质文化中包含有满足人的精神需求的成分,而且随着社会的发展和进步,这些因素显得越发重要起来。在物质文化的成果中,人们不仅要让物质文化满足人生存的需要,而且还要尽可能地满足人的审美需要。制度文化也以一定的物质文化为基础,不能离开物质文化而独立发展,精神文化有时也需要依托一定的物质载体而体现,真正的精神文化不应是外在于物质文化和制度文化的独立的东西,而是内在于物质文化和制度文化、内在于人所有活动深层机理性的东西。文化的这三个层面不是彼此分离、互相对立的,而是水乳交融、内在结合的关系。制度文化、精神文化的发展离不开物质文化的发展与繁荣。同时,制度文化、精神文化的发展与繁荣又必然会推进物质文化的发展。

4.2.2 文化的结构 Structure of Culture

任何一个社会的文化均有其特定的文化体系,而不是一盘散沙。文化所结成的这种系统体系所表现出的不同层次就是文化的结构。下面将从内部结构和外部结构这两个层次对文化的结构进行分析。

1. 文化的内部结构 Internal Structure of Culture

从内部结构来看,文化是由文化特质(cultural trait)、文化丛(cultural complex)和文化模式(cultural model)这三个层次组成的综合体。

(1)文化特质是指一种文化区别于其他文化的最小单位。一个社会的文化内容就是各种文化特质的总和。文化特质可以是物质的,可以是社会的,也可以是精神的;可以是具体的,也可以是抽象的。

> A cultural trait is a single identifiable material or non-material element within a culture, and is conceivable as an object in itself. Similar traits can be grouped together as components, or subsystems of culture.

文化特质可以独立存在,只是呈显出它的特殊历史和特殊形式,而不会与其他特质相混淆。当然,这种界限是相对的,常根据研究者的目标而设定界限。

(2)文化丛亦称文化集丛、文化特质丛,它是许多文化特质的聚合。指功能上互相整合的一组文化特质。它存在于一定的时空之中并作为一个文化单位发挥功用。文化丛通常是以某一个文化特质为中心,结合一些在功能上有连带关系的特质而组成的,其中每个特质都围绕中心特质而对于整体发挥功用。

> Culture complex is a group of culture traits all interrelated and dominated by one essential trait. It is also called culture pattern, a distinctive pattern of activities, beliefs, rites, and traditions associated with one central feature of life in a particular culture. An example is the cluster of activities, ceremonies, folklore, songs, and stories.

文化丛的概念最初是美国学者克拉克·威斯勒(Clark Wissler,1870—1947)等人在研究物质文化的产生和发展,研究各民族物质文化的传播、采用及其交互影响的历史过程时提出来的。文化丛与人们的某种特定活动有关,而且往往是物质文化与非物质文化的特殊结合。文化丛表示着人类依据一定的自然生态环境进行创造的能力,首先显示了人与自然的契合。如中国南方的竹文化,人们的衣食住行无不与竹子有关。

文化丛并不是一些文化特质或文化要素机械地堆积成毫无联系的任意分布,而常常是围绕一种中心文化内聚起来的。例如,马文化丛是围绕驯马文化内聚起来的,畜牧文化丛是围绕牲畜饲养文化内聚起来的。不仅物质文化丛是这样的,精神文化丛也是这样。由此可见,文化丛可以看作一个功能上相互整合的文化特质群,即文化群。

(3)文化模式是不同文化的构成方式及其稳定特征。它是一个社会中所有文化内容(包括文化特质与文化丛)组合在一起的特殊形式和结构,是许多不同文化丛有机联结而成的某个民族的生活环境、生活方式和生活习俗的总和。由于生态环境不同,不同人类群体的文化特质是千差万别的。这些不同文化的构成方式及其特征,我们就称之为"文化模式"。

> Cultural models (CM) are mental structures and patterns of behavior that distinguish one culture from another. CM are based on joint experience and are shared by the majority of the members of a certain ethnic or social culture; they are connected with the system of values of these cultures.

我们可以从不同的角度对文化模式进行分类。从文化模式的共性与个性上(universality and individuality)划分,可分为普遍文化模式与特殊文化模式。人类正因为有普遍文化模式,才可以进行文化交流、借鉴和相互吸收。

特殊的文化模式(specific cultural models)指不同国家或民族,甚至是不同地区或社会群体的多样的文化结构和文化内容。

从文化模式的结构成分上划分,可以依据文化特质的多少及方式的繁简程度,把文化模式分为简单文化模式（simple cultural model）与复杂文化模式（complex cultural model）。简单文化模式的文化特质一般很少，其结构也比较简单。复杂文化模式的文化特质则较为或相当复杂。

从文化模式的区域划分，又可划分为西方文化模式（Western cultural model）和东方文化模式（Eastern cultural model）。东方文化模式又可划分为印度文化模式、中国文化模式、日本文化模式等。中国文化模式又可划分为山西文化模式、广东文化模式、江苏文化模式等。

此外，我们还可以从文化模式的整体性上划分，将之区分为全文化模式与基本文化模式。从文化模式的内容及其不同性质划分，可将之分为不同系统的文化模式。

每一种文化模式都是历史的产物，是各种文化特质交互作用的结果。文化模式并不是人们计划的结果，而是在一定的文化生态环境中长时间形成的。文化模式不是可以任意构成的。虽然文化创造是人类的一种有意识的行为，但是，要任意设计一种文化模式，让人们去遵照它生活，是行不通的。文化模式是长时间形成的，是城市文化见之于生活习惯和社会心理的一种需要。

理解文化模式更应该注意研究不同文化模式的历史个性和特殊的价值取向。文化模式的历史个性是指人们长期适应一种文化模式所表现出来的心理、性格和行为特征。所谓风格模式，就是指文化模式个性而言的。

文化模式的历史个性又与其价值取向（value orientation）相关。物质文化是如此，精神文化也是如此。在东西方传统文化中，西方人所追求的"逻各斯、道"（logos，the Word），与中国人追求的"道"（Tao）、印度人追求的"梵"（Buddhist），各有不同的旨趣。它们在价值理念上也大相径庭。因此可以说，任何文化模式都含有一套价值体系。文化模式不同，人们的价值观念及其价值取向也各不相同。

由于文化模式有不同的历史个性和价值取向，所以各民族的文化交往必须相互尊重，一切社会的改革必须考虑民族文化的需要。尽管传统的文化模式有保守、束缚人的一面，但是如果你不尊重它、顺应它，无论办什么事情，注定是要失败的。

文化模式具有相对稳定性（relative stability）。一种文化的历史愈悠久，时间延续愈长，它的模式就愈稳定，其个性就愈突出，价值取向也就愈明确。文化模式也不是一成不变的，而是随着历史的发展、科学的进步及外来文化的传播和影响，而不断发展、变化的。

2. 文化的外部结构 External Structure of Culture

文化的外部结构又称文化的空间结构或区域结构，是指文化分散在一定的地域内的情形，或指文化的空间分布状态。

（1）文化区（cultural area）是指有着类似文化特质的区域。它是由文化背景相同的人们聚居的地区，在这一文化区内聚居的人们，有着相同的生活环境、生活方式和生活习俗。

A cultural area refers to a geography with one relatively homogeneous human activity or culture. Such activities are often associated with an ethnolinguistic group and with the territory it inhabits. Specific cultures often do not limit their geographic coverage to the borders of a nation state, or to smaller subdivisions of a state. Cultural "spheres of influence" may also overlap or form concentric structures of macro-cultures encompassing smaller local cultures. Different boundaries may also be drawn depending on the particular aspect of interest, such as religion and folklore, dress and architecture, or language.

文化区不同于行政区(administrative region)。行政区只是一个行政管理的区域单位，而文化区则是不同文化特质的空间载体。前者是人为地划分的，后者是在一定地理环境中形成的，有些行政区由于长久的历史划分，可能本身就具有文化区的性质。

文化区具有相对稳定性(stability)。最初，人类依据不同的生态环境创造了各种文化特质(cultural trait)，其中有些文化特质因不适合人们的需要而被淘汰了，有的则被代代传递、积累、保留了下来。一般地说，凡被传递、保留下来的文化特质，都是比较适合人们生活需要的，具有一定的生命力(vitality)。而且这些文化一旦被保留下来，作为一种历史的文化遗产就具有相对的稳定性。就世界而言，无论是东方文化区，还是西方文化区，从古到今都保留着它们各自不同的民族性格(national character)。这种民族性格一旦形成，就具有相对的稳定性。

文化区具有时代特征(characteristics of the times)。作为一种文化共同体是不断发展、变化的。在整个社会经济发展的过程中，文化区不断地自我发展，正是这种不断发展，使它具有时代特征。特别是现代化经济的发展以及文化的传播和交流，不仅打破了传统文化区域封闭性的体系，而且正在形成和造就与传统文化区域性质和面貌完全不同的新的文化区域。

(2)文化中心(cultural center)是指在文化区域中占有重要地位的社区。它是文化区域中某种文化的典型代表，是文化区域中起支配作用的文化模式的发源地或传播中心。任何文化区域都有一个文化中心。文化中心的存在和发展，决定着文化区域的存在和发展。在古代，黄河流域物产丰富，山河壮丽，是当时的文化中心。在今天，首都北京是我国的文化中心。纽约是美国的主要文化中心。从地理和区域来看，大多数国家的首都都是主要的文化中心。从另一方面来讲，文化在一个大的文化区域内是多中心的，而不是单一的。例如，在中国这个大文化区中，由于地域的广泛，各省会、县、市、城镇都是特定区域内的大小文化中心。文化中心对于团体生活有一种控制力量，不但在这个中心生活的人行为上要受其约束，在此中心外的，无论远近都受其文化传播的影响。它从吃、穿、住、行到思想行为，无一不对周围的社会产生影响。诚然，历史在发展，社会在前进，文化中心也必随条件的变化而转移。

A cultural center is an organization, building or complex that promotes culture and arts. Cultural centers can be neighborhood communities, arts organizations, private facilities, government-sponsored, or activist-run.

（3）文化边界（cultural boundary）是指两种及两种以上文化模式以比较直接的方式互动的社区。任何文化模式，都有其文化边界。在边界的人兼受多种不同文化模式的影响，原有的文化特征影响弱化，外来文化的影响较中心强。文化边界的现象在我国的边疆地区表现尤为明显，如新疆地区，受中东阿拉伯世界影响较大，而东北地区则兼有俄罗斯和东洋文化的影响。文化边界的存在和发展，也影响着文化模式的存在和发展。如深圳经济特区是一个开放型的新兴城市，是各个文化模式的汇集地区，是中国的文化边界。随着时代的推移和社会的发展，文化必将出现无明显边界的世界性趋势。

A cultural boundary (also called cultural border) in ethnology is a geographical boundary between two identifiable ethnic or ethnolinguistic cultures. It is a boundary line that runs along differences in ethnicity such as language and religion.

4.3　文化的功能 Functions of Culture

文化总能在一定程度上满足人的需要，解决人面临的多种问题。今天，文化已经成为推动个人、群体和社会发展的软力量。

4.3.1　文化推动人的社会化 Culture Promotes the Socialization of Man

许多文化学家都认为，文化的功能在于直接或间接地满足人的需要。文化为生活所必需的物品和服务的生产及分配提供保证，能够满足人的多重需要。正因为文化成功地处理了人所面对的基本问题，文化才可能持续存在下去。

文化的个人功能实质上就是文化的个人社会化功能，它是指文化对个人起着塑造人格、实现社会化、提升境界的作用。

第一，文化影响人的行为规范。一个人要想成为社会的成员，要想在社会中生存和活动，就必须使自己的行为符合社会规范，而这只有经过社会文化的教化才能够达到。人刚生下来时还只是一个生物的人（biological man），没有思想和知识。人通过教化演变成一个社会人（social man）。中华民族"卧如弓，坐如钟，站如松，行如风"的说法，也是人们常说的"坐有坐相，站有站相，吃有吃相"。这种仪态举止不是天然生成的（nature），它是后天文化教化的（nurture）结果。

第二，文化培养人们对自身身份、地位的认同，即文化认同（cultural identity）。文化认同是一个人对于自身属于某个社会群体的认同感。文化认同是文化社会学的一个课题,也与心理学密切相关,是一个人的自我概念及自我认知(self-perception)。这种认同感的对象往往与国籍、民族、宗教、社会阶层、世代、定居地方或者任何类型具有其独特文化的社会群体有关。文化认同不但是个人的特征,也是具有相同的文化认同或教养的人所组成的群体的特征。

Cultural identity is a part of a person's identity, or their self-conception and self-perception, and is related to nationality, ethnicity, religion, social class, generation, locality or any kind of social group that has its own distinct culture. Cultural identity is both characteristic of the individual but also of the culturally identical group of members sharing the same cultural identity. Cultural knowledge, category label and social connection make up a person's cultural identity. Cultural knowledge is when a person connects to their identity through understanding their culture's core characteristics. Category label is where a person connects with their identity through indirect membership of said culture. Social connects is where a person connects with their identity through social relationships In recent decades, a new form of identification has emerged which breaks down the understanding of the individual as a coherent whole subject into a collection of various cultural identifiers. These cultural identifiers may be the result of various conditions including: location, sex, race, history, nationality, language, sexuality, religious beliefs, ethnicity, aesthetics, and even food.

文化认同是身份认同的其中一个层面,代表着认同某个具有独特文化的群体及他们对文化的理解方式。文化认同与民族认同(national identity)相似并有重叠,但两者意义并不相同。当一个人可以接纳并且认同某个民族具有的文化,并不代表自身属于某个民族。又例如文化基督徒,指对基督教的文化认同,而非其信仰价值观认同。

文化认同是身份传播理论(communication theory of identity)的一个子集。文化认同是一个人的身份的中心点,意味着他们怎样看待自己,也意味他们怎样理解自身和世界的关系。

人们怎样与生活中的文化现实进行互动是由一连串的文化复杂性共同建立而成的。国家是文化复杂性的一个很大的因素。文化认同有很多种影响因素,例如一个人的宗教、血统、肤色、语言、社会阶级、教育、职业、技能、家庭和政治主张。这些因素影响着人们对文化的理解,为一个人的身份认同发展做出或大或小的贡献。美国人类学家林顿(Ralph Linton,1893—1953)在《人的研究》(*The Study of Man*,1936)一书中,曾用"身份"(identity)一词指代个人在群体中所占据的地位或职位;用"角色"(role)一词指代对占据这一位置的人所期望的行为。林顿认为,所有"身份"和"角色"都来自社会模式,并成为社会模式的整合部分。一个人只有接受社会文化的教化,才能成为真正的社会人和文化人,才能在社会中确立自己的身份和地位,才能扮演好一定的社会群体角色。

第三，文化可以造就人的心理和人格（personality）。人类的正义感、是非感、审美感、羞耻感、罪感以及认知、情绪等诸如此类的心理、道德与良心，伟大与崇高，鄙俗与渺小等所谓人格，究竟是从哪里来的？人类的所有这些心理、性格、行为，都不是天生的，都不是生物的人原有的东西，而是社会教化的结果。

第四，文化还带给人以经验、知识和技能。正是因为传授（impart）和教化（educate），一个生物性的孩子（biological child）才成长为有一定经验、知识和技能的人，从而在社会中真正成为一个独立的人（independent man），一个聪明的、有才智的人。

第五，文化提升人的境界。人不是生活在真空中的，人要过现实而世俗的生活，但这种生活不同于动物的生存，而恰恰相反，人离动物的生存状态越远，离人的文化的存在就越近。人充分发挥人的主体作用（the dominant role），不断改进和提升人的存在状态，促进人的发展，特别是人的全面发展（all-round development of human being）。人的全面发展首先是一种自由的发展，不是强迫或被动的发展。

由此可见，社会文化是人的社会化（socialization）的重要变量（significant quantity），它不仅使生物的人变为社会的合格成员，而且通过人的社会文化教化造就了伟大的人格。

4.3.2 文化的群体功能 The Functions of Culture for Groups

文化的群体功能是指文化对社会群体（团体、组织、民族、国家等）起着目标指向、规范约束和价值整合的作用。任何一个社会群体，都有自己特定的目标、规范和价值观念，这些本身就是文化。正是这些文化规范，维系着社会群体的存在和发展。这也是我们所说的广义的组织文化。

组织文化（organizational culture）是指一个组织由其共有的价值观（value）、仪式（rite）、符号（symbol）、信念（faith）等内化认同表现出其特有的行为模式，包括组织人员的行为规律、工作的团体规范、组织信奉的主要价值（chief value）、指导组织决策的哲学观念等。

Organizational culture is the collection of values, expectations, and practices that guide and inform the actions of all group members. Organizational culture includes an organization's expectations, experiences, philosophy, as well as the values that guide member behavior, and is expressed in member self-image, inner workings, interactions with the outside world, and future expectations. Culture is based on shared attitudes, beliefs, customs, and written and unwritten rules that have been developed over time and are considered valid. Organizational culture transformation takes place when the organization starts a process to pull together its core values, and vision to obtain its cultural goals.

组织文化通过培育组织成员的认同感（sense of identity）、归属感（sense of belonging）和价值观，建立起成员与组织之间的相互依存关系，使个人的行为、思想、感情、信念、习惯与整个组织有机地统一起来，形成相对稳固的文化氛围，凝聚成一种无形的合力与整体趋向,以此激发出组织成员的主观能动性(subjective initiative),为组织的共同目标而努力。

例如,世界 500 强公司胜出其他公司的重要原因之一,就在于这些公司不断给他们的企业文化(enterprise culture)注入活力,这些一流公司的企业文化同普通公司的企业文化有着显著的不同。

一般来讲,"组织文化"不容易被改变;因为改变"组织文化",等于改变众人的"性格"和"习惯"。尽管组织成员具有多样化的特征,但他们仍然会用相似的术语描述组织文化,这就是文化的共有方面。

4.3.3　文化调整社会生活秩序 Culture Adjusts Social Orders

文化的社会功能(social function)是指文化对整个社会起着整合的作用(functions of integration)。

一个社会共同的价值观念(common values)使其成员感到自己存在的价值,以此增强社会成员的自我认同(self-identification)与社会认同(social identification)。文化作为一定的价值体系使人形成十分明确的价值需求和取向。规范整合使价值内化(internalization)为个人的行为准则,从而维持一定的社会秩序(social order)。文化的整合功能是维持社会秩序的基础。

文化的推动功能是指文化推动社会进步(social progress)的功能,它包括提供知识、协调社会工程管理和巩固社会进步的成果这三个方面的功能。社会进步必须以新的知识为动力,而新的知识,包括新的科学、技术、理论,必须依赖于文化创新(cultural innovation)。有计划地推动社会进步,是一项巨大的社会系统工程(social system engineering),各系统之间的协调,有赖于文化调适。此外,每一次社会改革和社会进步所取得的新成果,都必须以新的文化巩固起来,以维持新制度的秩序和稳定。文化作为一种复杂的符号系统,是能够储存社会经验并把它们从上一代传到下一代,从上一个时代传到下一个时代,从一个国家传到另一个国家的唯一机制。文化的主要载体(carrier)是语言,文化离开语言,就无文化可言。除了文化,人类不再拥有其他任何储存和传递人类积累的极其丰富的经验的机制,因此文化被称之为人类的记忆,决非偶然。

文化不仅具有上述的正向功能,而且也具有反功能。这种认识是受美国功能派社会学家默顿的启发而提出来的。默顿认为,社会并非总是处于整合状态,非整合状态也兼而有之。这种非整合状态,也是文化功能的一种表现。文化的正向功能维持社会体系的均衡,而反向功能则破坏社会体系的均衡。文化的反向功能一般在两种情形下发生:①发生于负文化(counter-culture)团体之中。在文化整体中存在着许多与社会主体文化相对应的次属文化,即亚文化。有些亚文化是正文化,如科技发明小组的文化,但也有些亚文化是负文化,如吸毒团伙的文化、青少年犯罪团伙的文化等,这些负文化所发挥的功能,对于整个文化而言,是反方向、非整合的。如反动文化、法西斯文化在反动阶级或法西斯执政时期称霸一时,助纣为虐。②发生于文化滞后（cultural lag）时。文化滞后是指在文化变迁（cultural change）过程中，精神文化的发展落后于物质文化发展的现象。当这种情形出现时，文化滞后部分对于整个社会而言是非整合的反向功能。

文化反映了人的存在状态，与人的发展息息相关，人的发展又体现于社会群体中，人的发展也构成了社会发展的基本内容。文化给人与社会的发展提供了材料，推进人的社会化，影响群体的效力，调整社会的秩序，文化使一个社会的规范、观念更为系统化、秩序化。一个人不能没有文化，一个社会也同样不能没有文化。

延伸阅读 Further Reading

思考 Thinking it through：
文化有怎样的功能？

Zigawei

Xujiahui means "Xu family junction" — more precisely, "property of Xu family at the junction of two rivers". The "Xu family" refers to the family of Xu Guangqi（Hsü Kuang-ch'i；1562 – 1633）.

Most of what is now Xujiahui was once the ancestral home of the Xu family. Pronounced in the Shanghainese dialect of Wu Chinese，it is called "zi-ga-wei". During the 18th century it was known by Shanghai's western residents as "Ziccawei" or "Siccawei"（English）or "Zikawei" or "Zi-ka-wei"（French）. The area is still listed in a number of contemporary guidebooks and literature as "Zikawei" or some variant thereof those acquired by other means. Zikaweian is an entirely one square mile complex that covers most of present-day Xujiahui. Including orphanages，schools，libraries and the Xujiahui observatory（now the Shanghai Bureau of Meteorology）.

The Tou-Se-We Orphanage（Mandarin：Tushanwan）is half a mile to the south of Xujiahui junction；T'ou Sè Wè was a Chinese orphanage，vocational school，printing house active in Xujiahui District. It is considered to be the birthplace of modern Chinese creative arts. The orphanage was founded in 1864 and specialized in teaching their orphan charges practical vocations such as carpentry，painting，wood carving，and printing. The publishing work of the T'ou-Sè-Wè printing house included numerous works both in French and Chinese. Their works received accolade at world exhibitions in 1900，1915，1935 and 1939. The orphanage closed in 1960. The sole surviving building of the orphanage is now the Tou-Se-We Museum，which is opened in June of 2010.

Up until the late 1990s，the area was predominantly an industrial area. During the late 1990s，many of the state-owned factories were sold off and torn down. Xujiahui is now mainly a retail district of downtown Shanghai.

5 社会化
Socialization

Understanding Socialization in Sociology

Overview and Discussion of a Key Sociological Concept

By Nicki Lisa Cole，Ph.D.

Socialization is a process that introduces people to social norms and customs. This process helps individuals function well in society, and, in turn, helps society run smoothly. Family members, teachers, religious leaders, and peers all play roles in a person's socialization.

This process typically occurs in two stages: primary socialization takes place from birth through adolescence, and secondary socialization continues throughout one's life. Adult socialization may occur whenever people find themselves in new circumstances, especially those in which they interact with individuals whose norms or customs differ from theirs.

The Purpose of Socialization

During socialization, a person learns to become a member of a group, community, or society. This process not only accustoms people to social groups but also results in such groups sustaining themselves. For example, a new sorority member gets an insider's look at the customs and traditions of a Greek organization. As the years pass, the member can apply the information she's learned about the sorority when newcomers join, allowing the group to carry on its traditions.

On a macro level, socialization ensures that we have a process through which the norms and customs of society are transmitted. Socialization teaches people what is expected of them in a particular group or situation; it is a form of social control.

Socialization has numerous goals for youth and adults alike. It teaches children to control their biological impulses, such as using a toilet instead of wetting their pants or bed. The socialization process also helps individuals develop a conscience aligned with social norms and prepares them to perform various roles.

The Socialization Process in Three Parts

Socialization involves both social structure and interpersonal relations. It contains three key parts: context, content and process, and results. Context, perhaps, defines socialization the most, as it refers to culture, language, social structures and one's rank within them. It also includes history and the roles people and institutions played in the past. One's life context will significantly affect the socialization process. For example, a family's economic class may have a huge impact on how parents socialize their children.

Research has found that parents emphasize the values and behaviors most likely to help children succeed given their station in life. Parents who expect their children to work blue-collar jobs are more likely to emphasize conformity and respect for authority, while those who expect their children to pursue artistic, managerial, or entrepreneurial professions are more likely to emphasize creativity and independence.

Gender stereotypes also exert a strong influence on socialization processes. Cultural expectations for gender roles and gendered behavior are imparted to children through color-coded clothes and types of play. Girls usually receive toys that emphasize physical appearance and domesticity such as dolls or dollhouses, while boys receive playthings that involve thinking skills or call to mind traditionally male professions such as Legos, toy soldiers, or race cars. Additionally, research has shown that girls with brothers are socialized to understand that household labor is expected of them but not of their male siblings.

Race also plays a factor in socialization. Since White people don't disproportionately experience police violence, they can encourage their children to know their rights and defend them when the authorities try to violate them. In contrast, parents of color must have what's known as "the talk" with their children, instructing them to remain calm, compliant, and safe in the presence of law enforcement.

While context sets the stage for socialization, the content and process constitute the work of this undertaking. How parents assign chores or tell their kids to interact with police are examples of content and process, which are also defined by the duration of socialization, those involved, the methods used, and the type of experience.

School is an important source of socialization for students of all ages. In class, young people receive guidelines related to behavior, authority, schedules, tasks, and deadlines. Teaching this content requires social interaction between educators and students. Typically, rules and expectations are both written and spoken, and student conduct is either rewarded or penalized. As this occurs, students learn behavioral norms suitable for school.

In the classroom, students also learn what sociologists describe as "hidden curricula." In her book *Dude*, *You're a Fag*, sociologist C. J. Pascoe revealed the hidden curriculum of gender and sexuality in U. S. high schools. Through in-depth research at a large California school, Pascoe revealed how faculty members and events like pep rallies and dances reinforce rigid gender roles and heterosexism. In particular, the school sent the message that aggressive and hypersexual behaviors are generally acceptable in White boys but threatening in Black ones. Though not an "official" part of the schooling experience, this hidden curriculum tells students what society expects of them based on their gender, race, or class background.

Results are the outcome of socialization and refer to the way a person thinks and behaves after undergoing this process. For example, with small children, socialization tends to focus on control of biological and emotional impulses, such as drinking from a cup rather than from a bottle or asking permission before picking something up. As children mature, the results of socialization include knowing how to wait their turn, obey rules, or organize their days around a school or work schedule. We can see the results of socialization in just about everything, from men shaving their faces to women shaving their legs and armpits.

Stages and Forms of Socialization

Sociologists recognize two stages of socialization: primary and secondary.

Primary socialization occurs from birth through adolescence. Caregivers, teachers, coaches, religious figures, and peers guide this process.

Secondary socialization occurs throughout our lives as we encounter groups and situations that were not part of our primary socialization experience. This might include a college experience, where many people interact with members of different populations and learn new norms, values, and behaviors. Secondary socialization also takes place in the workplace or while traveling somewhere new. As we learn about unfamiliar places and adapt to them, we experience secondary socialization.

Meanwhile, group socialization occurs throughout all stages of life. For example, peer groups influence how one speaks and dresses. During childhood and adolescence, this tends to break down along gender lines. It is common to see groups of children of either gender wearing the same hair and clothing styles.

Organizational socialization occurs within an institution or organization to familiarize a person with its norms, values, and practices. This process often unfolds in nonprofits and companies. New employees in a workplace have to learn how to collaborate, meet management's goals, and take breaks in a manner suitable for the company. At a nonprofit, individuals may learn how to speak about social causes in a way that reflects the organization's mission.

Many people also experience anticipatory socialization at some point. This form of socialization is largely self-directed and refers to the steps one takes to prepare for a new role, position, or occupation. This may involve seeking guidance from people who've previously served in the role, observing others currently in these roles, or training for the new position during an apprenticeship. In short, anticipatory socialization transitions people into new roles so they know what to expect when they officially step into them.

Finally, forced socialization takes place in institutions such as prisons, mental hospitals, military units, and some boarding schools. In these settings, coercion is used to re-socialize people into individuals who behave in a manner fitting of the norms, values, and customs of the institution. In prisons and psychiatric hospitals, this process may be framed as rehabilitation. In the military, however, forced socialization aims to create an entirely new identity for the individual.

Criticism of Socialization

While socialization is a necessary part of society, it also has drawbacks. Since dominant cultural norms, values, assumptions, and beliefs guide the process, it is not a neutral endeavor. This means that socialization may reproduce the prejudices that lead to forms of social injustice and inequality.

Representations of racial minorities in film, television, and advertising tend to be rooted in harmful stereotypes. These portrayals socialize viewers to perceive racial minorities in certain ways and expect particular behaviors and attitudes from them. Race and racism influence socialization processes in other ways too. Research has shown that racial prejudices affect treatment and discipline of students. Tainted by racism, the behavior of teachers socializes all students to have low expectations for youth of color. This kind of socialization results in an over-representation of minority students in remedial classes and an under-representation of them in gifted class. It may also result in these students being punished more harshly for the same kinds of offenses that White students commit, such as talking back to teachers or coming to class unprepared.

While socialization is necessary, it's important to recognize the values, norms, and behaviors this process reproduces. As society's ideas about race, class, and gender evolve, so will the forms of socialization that involve these identity markers.

(Reference: www.thoughtco.com/socialization-in-sociology-4104466)

5.1 社会化概述 Introduction to Socialization

人类与动物的本质区别之一在于，人类具有自我意识。据说，人类是唯一知道他们存在并会死亡的生物。但是，我们如何理解个体区别于他人的自我意识？它产生于哪里？它是与生俱来的还是后天习得的？为什么社会学家也对此感兴趣？这一切，都要从社会化说起。

> In sociology, socialization is the process of internalizing the norms and ideologies of society. Socialization essentially represents the whole process of learning throughout the life course and is a central influence on the behavior, beliefs, and actions of adults as well as of children.
>
> Socialization is strongly connected to developmental psychology. Individual views are influenced by the society's consensus and usually tend toward what that society finds acceptable or "normal". Socialization provides only a partial explanation for human beliefs and behaviors, maintaining that agents are not blank slates predetermined by their environment; scientific research provides evidence that people are shaped by both social influences and genes.

5.1.1 什么是社会化 What Is Socialization

早在 1895 年，德国社会学家齐美尔（Georg Simmel，1858—1918）在其《社会学的根本问题》一文中，首先用"社会化"一词来表示群体形成的过程，这是社会化的最初含义。个体从自然人向社会人转变是一个系统的过程，它要求人必须在社会认可的行为标准中形成自身的行为模式，使之成为符合社会要求的社会一员，这就是社会化。

社会化是一个广泛应用于社会学、社会心理学、人类学、政治学与教育学范畴的名词，指的是人类学习、继承各种社会规范、传统、意识形态等社会文化元素，并逐渐适应于其中的过程。社会化本质上代表了整个生命过程中的整个学习过程，对成人和儿童的行为、信念和行动产生了核心影响。在社会学中，该概念是指社会规范（social norms）和意识形态内化的过程。对个人来说，社会化是学习同时扮演不同角色的过程。个人的社会化常受到地区文化的影响，且因个人的成长背景，社会化的过程、内容也会随之改变。社会化既让个体学习成为与其他社会成员一样的人，也在培育着独特的自我。

社会化对社会和个体的发展具有双重重要性，因此，它不仅是社会学的研究问题，也是其他学科，如：人类学（anthropology）以及教育学（pedagogy）的研究话题，但每个学科各有侧重。社会学对社会化的理解侧重人与社会的互动和社会对人的规范作用。社会学对社会化的关注集中在社会规范的内化和社会角色的形成。文化人类学的社会化侧重文化继承，把社会化看作文化的延续和传递的过程,关注民族文化(ethnic culture)模式对其成员人格和社会行为的影响。教育学对社会化的理解侧重社会系统化教育过程对人的影响,关注个体特点、学习经验和人格差异在社会化中的作用以及社会心理经验在自我形成中的影响。

社会化是在特定的社会与文化环境中,个体形成适应于该社会与文化的人格,掌握该社会所公认的行为方式的过程。人与动物有本质的差别,人类的社会化历程相当长,乃至人的一生;因此社会化与发展心理学(developmental psychology)紧密相关。

个体的成长与发展是一系列的社会化过程,是一个学习社会角色和道德规范的过程。许多事实证明,儿童要能健康地成长,不仅需要在身体上受到照顾,还需要与社会成员进行交往,发生感情上的联系,获得社会化。据相关科学史料记载,历史上约一百个小孩是野兽哺育的。这些孩子被称为野孩子(feral child),他们在很小的年龄就开始与世隔绝,不懂得人类社会行为和语言。在这些案例中,大部分是人为禁锢的情况;有部分被确定为是由野生动物养育的例子:其中有由熊哺育大的"熊孩",由羊哺育大的"羊孩",由豹哺育大的"豹孩",由猴哺育大的"猴孩"。这些儿童即使重回人类社会,也难以正常生活,其根本原因就在于他们自幼脱离了人类社会,未经历社会化的过程。因为人类的语言、规范、行为等不是与生俱来的(native),而是个体在后天生活中习得的(learned)。

A feral child (also called wild child) is a young individual who has lived isolated from human contact from a very young age, with little or no experience of human care, social behavior, or language. Feral children lack the basic social skills that are normally learned in the process of socialization. For example, they may be unable to learn to use a toilet, have trouble learning to walk upright after walking on fours all their lives, or display a complete lack of interest in the human activity around them. They often seem mentally impaired and have almost insurmountable trouble learning a human language. The impaired ability to learn a natural language after having been isolated for so many years is often attributed to the existence of a critical period for language learning, and taken as evidence in favor of the critical period hypothesis.

可见,人类只有学习一定的知识和生活经验才能获得适应社会的社会特征,形成人类的心理结构和行为动力系统,获得明确的自我概念(self-concept)。但这里牵涉的理论问题比较多,诸如,社会化主要在人发展的哪个阶段,社会化的内容是什么,从什么角度研究等。对这些问题,学界都存在着分歧。分歧主要集中在以下几方面:

(1)在社会化的时间上:在20世纪50年代以前,社会学所研究的社会化主要是针对儿童和青少年来说的,因而,许多人认为青少年时期就实现了由"生物人"向"社会人"的转变,实现了人的社会化。现代社会学研究认为,由于社会不断变化发展,很多东西需要人不断学习,即"活到老,学到老",因此,由"生物人"向"社会人"的转化只是社会化的起点,社会化还包括个人成年后与社会之间发生的教化(education)、内化和调适的全部内容,所以,人类的社会化是一个毕生的过程（life-long process）。

（2）在社会化的内容上：社会化就是教会人做事，如美籍德国犹太人人本主义哲学家和精神分析心理学家埃里希·弗罗姆（Erich Fromm，1900—1980）所认为的社会化诱导社会的成员去做那些要想使社会正常延续就必须做的事。

（3）在社会化的过程上：传统观点认为，社会化仅仅是社会对个人的教化、作用，正如奥地利精神病医师、心理学家、精神分析学派创始人西格蒙德·弗洛伊德（Sigmund Freud，1856—1939）所认为的，青少年是学习时期，是社会对个人教化的时期。现在多数学者认为，社会化是社会与个人双向（bidirectional）作用的过程，既包括个人"内化"了社会文化价值观，接受了教化，使社会文化得以延续，又包括个人根据自己的需要，积极反作用于（react upon）社会，在与社会互动的过程中，对社会发生影响。

5.1.2 社会化的基本内容 The Basic Content of Socialization

社会化的内容很丰富。具体说来，个人社会化的基本内容可以概括为四个方面，这四个方面都关乎身份和角色。

1. 性别社会化 Gender Socialization

社会性别指与男性气质和女性气质有关或用于区别两者的一系列特征。社会性别一词的意思因语境而异，它所包含的可能是生物性别（即男性、女性、双性人所拥有的状态）、基于生物性别的社会结构（即性别角色）、性别认同（gender identity）。大多文化采取性别二元论（dualist）的观点，即认为社会仅有两种性别（男性/男孩及女性/女孩）。性别社会化（gender socialization）是指人们将其所在社会的性别规范内化的过程。性别社会化的内容涉及性别期望、性别角色和性别认同。社会通过各种手段教化个体有关性别规范和相关的象征意义，个体同样加入到这一过程中，学习和使用性别规范及其象征。性别社会化是贯穿人一生的性别认同过程。

> Gender socialization refers to the learning of behavior and attitudes considered appropriate for a given sex. Boys learn to be boys and girls learn to be girls. This "learning" happens by way of many different agents of socialization. The behavior that is seen to be appropriate for each gender is largely determined by societal, cultural, and economic values in a given society. Gender socialization can therefore vary considerably among societies with different values. The family is certainly important in reinforcing gender roles, but so are groups including friends, peers, school, work, and the mass media. Gender roles are reinforced through "countless subtle and not so subtle ways".

在儿童习得性别角色的过程中，社会化的中介家庭和媒体扮演了重要的角色。亲子互动的研究显示了父母对待男女孩的不同，尽管父母自认为对男孩女孩的反应是一样的。孩子们接触的玩具、图书、电视节目等，都强调了男性与女性的差别。

2. 种族（民族）社会化 Racial-Ethnic Socialization

一般来说，民族与种族社会化是少数民族（ethnic minority）家庭教养的核心成分，是父母向子女传递种族和民族特征等信息、促进子女社会适应的过程。子女的年龄、性别、父母与子女的受歧视经历等影响着父母对子女传递民族与种族社会化的内容和时机。种族（民族）社会化的具体内容有文化教化、平等教育、预备接受偏见教育、提升不信任感等。

Racial-ethnic socialization is the developmental processes by which children acquire the behaviors, perceptions, values, and attitudes of an ethnic group, and come to see themselves and others as members of the group. The existing literature conceptualizes racial socialization as having multiple dimensions. Researchers have identified five dimensions that commonly appear in the racial socialization literature: cultural socialization, preparation for bias, promotion of mistrust, egalitarianism, and the other.

3. 政治社会化 Political Socialization

政治社会化是个人逐渐学习、接受和内化现有社会所认可的政治信念、政治立场和政治态度的过程。在这一过程中，个人逐渐认识自己所处社会的政治制度与占主导地位的政治主张，并逐渐把这种政治主张与政治规范内化为自己的政治信念与政治立场。政治社会化是人的社会化过程最困难、最复杂的一环，有时需要人一生的努力，但一旦人们接受并内化了某种政治信念和立场，就会产生一种顽强的定势，很难改变。政治社会化甚至会塑造一个人的自我认知和自我意识，使得个体将全人发展与政治体系捆绑起来。促成政治社会化的主要媒介是学校、家庭、媒体、政府。

Political socialization refers to a learning process by which norms and behaviors acceptable to a well running political system are transmitted from one generation to another. It is through the performance of this function that individuals are inducted into the political culture and their orientations towards political objects are formed. Schools, families, media, and the state have a major influence in this process.

4. 组织社会化 Organizational Socialization

所谓组织社会化是指员工为了适应所在组织的价值体系、组织目标和行为规范而调整自己态度、获取相应的知识技能的过程；是个体进入职场后，为适应组织角色、完成组织目标所需要学习的内容和经历的过程。在这个过程中，个体需要了解岗位角色，接受组织文化、组织价值观；这也是一个获得有关组织信息的调适过程，期望其行为以及能力能够符合组织的要求。组织社会化的内容包括新员工从进入组织到成为该组织既定成员过程中涉及社会和文化方面的所有学习。

> Organizational socialization is the process by which employees learn the knowledge and skills, the organization and its history, values, jargon, culture, and procedures. They also learn about their work team, the specific people they work with, their own role in the organization, the skills needed to do their job, and both formal procedures and informal norms. Socialization functions as a control system to help newcomers learn to internalize and obey organizational values and practices.

社会化的内容非常丰富,以上只是最基本的四种。

5.2 社会化的相关理论 Related Theories of Socialization

人与动物的本质区别在于:人类有自我意识(self-awareness),即自我区别于他人的独特身份认同。这种身份认同的来源是哪里? 先天还是后天,遗传还是环境? 这一直是儿童发展理论要研究的重要问题,学者们对此一直争论不休。不过,学者们基本上达成了一个共识:对于儿童发展过程而言,遗传和环境不可或缺,人的社会化既受到先天遗传因素(genetic factor)的影响,同时又被后天环境因素(environmental factor)塑造。

5.2.1 皮亚杰与儿童认知发展阶段理论
Piaget and the Stage Theory of Children's Cognitive Development

让·皮亚杰(Jean Piage,1896—1980),瑞士人,近代最有名的发展心理学家(developmental psychologist)。皮亚杰从事关于儿童发展方面的许多研究,但是他最出名的著作是关于认知的,他的认知发展理论(cognitive development theory)成为了这个学科的典范。皮亚杰早年接受生物学的训练,但他在大学读书时就已经开始对心理学有兴趣,并涉猎心理学早期发展的各个学派如病理心理学(psychopathology)、精神分析学(psychoanalysis)、荣格(Carl Gustav Jung,1875—1961)的潜意识心理学(subconscious psychology)和弗洛伊德的学说(Freudian theory)。皮亚杰从 1929—1975 年在日内瓦大学(University of Geneva)担任心理学教授。截至 20 世纪末期,皮亚杰在心理学领域的著作被引用量仅次于斯金纳。

Jean Piaget（1896—1980）was a Swiss psychologist known for his work on child development. Piaget placed great importance on the education of children. Before Piaget became a psychologist, he was trained in natural history and philosophy. His theory of child development is studied in pre-service education programs. Educators continue to incorporate constructivist-based strategies. However, his ideas did not become widely popularized until the 1960s. This then led to the emergence of the study of development as a major sub-discipline in psychology. By the end of the 20th century, Piaget was second only to B. F. Skinner as the most-cited psychologist of that era.

皮亚杰认为,儿童并不是被动接受信息的,而是会对他们所看到的事物进行选择和解释;换言之,皮亚杰强调儿童积极理解世界的能力。皮亚杰最著名的学说,就是他的儿童认知发展阶段理论:

The four development stages are described in Piaget's theory as:

（1）Sensorimotor stage is from birth to age two. The children experience the world through movement and their senses. During the sensorimotor stage children are extremely egocentric, meaning they cannot perceive the world from others' viewpoints.

（2）Preoperational stage starts when the child begins to learn to speak at age two and lasts up until the age of seven. During this stage of cognitive development, Piaget noted that children do not yet understand concrete logic and cannot mentally manipulate information. The child still has trouble seeing things from different points of view.

（3）Concrete operational stage is from age seven to eleven. In this stage, children can converse and think logically but are limited to what they can physically manipulate. They are no longer egocentric, they become more aware of logic and conservation, topics previously foreign to them. Children also improve drastically with their classification skills.

（4）Formal operational stage is from age eleven to sixteen and onwards. Children develop abstract thought and can easily conserve and think logically in their mind. Abstract thought is newly present during this stage of development. Children are able to think abstractly.

第一个阶段:皮亚杰称之为感知运动阶段(感觉—动作期,sensorimotor stage,0—2岁),因为婴儿在这个阶段的学习主要依靠接触物体、摆弄物体以及探索他们周围的环境。直到大约四个月大,婴儿才能将自己与周围的环境区分开来。婴儿逐渐认识到,人与物体都是独立于自己感知的存在。1岁时发展出物体恒存(object permanence)。皮亚杰认为,物体恒存是思维发展的起点。

Object permanence is the understanding that objects continue to exist even when they cannot be sensed. This is a fundamental concept studied in the field of developmental psychology, the sub-field of psychology that addresses the development of young children's social and mental capacities.

第二个阶段：皮亚杰称之为前运算阶段（前运算思维期，pre-operational stage，2—7岁）。在这个阶段，儿童获得了语言能力，并且能够以符号方式使用词语来描述事物。例如：一个4岁的孩子可以用手比划一个物体的形状。皮亚杰之所以称这一阶段为前运算，是因为儿童还不具备系统使用他们心智的能力。处于这一阶段的儿童是以自我为中心的，他们对世界的解释是基于自己的立场。因此，他们无法理解他人与自己理解方式的不同。他们也无法理解因果、重量、速度等概念。总之，这个阶段的儿童能使用语言与符号等表征外在事物，具有推理能力但不符逻辑，未形成保留概念，缺乏可逆性，以自我为中心去直接推理。

第三个阶段：皮亚杰称之为具体运算阶段（具体运算思维期，concrete operational stage，7—11岁）。在这一阶段，儿童掌握了抽象的逻辑概念，能处理因果性这样的观念。他们开始学习处理数学中的加减乘除运算，逐渐减少以自我为中心的倾向；能通过对具体物的操作来协助思考。

第四个阶段：皮亚杰称之为形式运算阶段（形式运算思维期，formal operational stage，11—16岁）。在这个阶段，成长中的孩子开始有能力把握高度抽象的概念。当他们面临一个特殊的处境时，他们有能力评估所有的解决方法，并且有能力预演，以便找到解决问题的方法。皮亚杰根据自己的观察指出，前三个发展阶段具有普遍性，但并不是所有的成年人都会经历第四个时期。形式运算（formal operation）思维的发展依赖于学校教育。教育受限的成年人倾向于从更加具体的角度思考，并且继续保留许多自我中心的痕迹。

皮亚杰认为，以上四个阶段有如下特点：发展顺序不变，但具有个别差异。依赖认知发展，但可普遍化为其它功能。各发展阶段都是在逻辑上有组织的整体。各阶段的顺序是自然的阶层（所有成功发展的阶段都会有前面阶段的元素参与合作，但后一阶段比起前面的阶段，更加不同，而且更加统整）。每个阶段，在思考模式上会表现出质的不同，而不仅仅是量的差异。

皮亚杰的理论有部分跟苏联心理学家列维·维果茨基（L. S. Vygotsky，1896—1934）的理论相似。维果茨基曾对皮亚杰的理论提出过一个有益的批评：儿童从不同的社会群体获得不同的学习机会；这些机会强烈影响了儿童与社会互动过程中的学习能力。简言之，学习与认知的发展无法避免地受到他们嵌入其中的社会结构的影响。恰恰是这些结构，限制了部分儿童的发展，但又推动了另一些儿童的发展。

皮亚杰的发展心理学理论广泛流传。例如，哲学家，也是社会理论家的哈贝马斯将皮亚杰的理论结合到他的研究中，以沟通行动论而闻名。

5.2.2 社会学习理论 Social Learning Theory

社会学习理论是美国心理学家阿尔波特·班杜拉（Albert Bandura，1925—2021）提出的社会心理学基础理论，是在强化学习理论（theory of reinforcement learning）的基础上发展起来的。20世纪60年代，班杜拉突破行为主义（behaviorism）理论框架，从认知和行为联合起作用的观点看待社会学习。既强调社会环境，也强调认知因素（cognitive factors）对学习的影响，他不仅注意个体的行为表现，还关心行为的社会习得过程（acquisition process），认为自我调节在行为改变中起着关键作用。20世纪80年代中期，班杜拉在社会学习理论的基础上，提出了社会认知理论（social cognitive theory）。

Albert Bandura（1925—2021）was a Canadian-American psychologist who was a professor in psychology at Stanford University. Bandura is known as the originator of social learning theory and the theoretical constructor of self-efficacy. A 2002 survey ranked Bandura as the fourth most-frequently cited psychologist of all time, behind B. F. Skinner, Sigmund Freud, and Jean Piaget. Bandura was widely described as one of the most influential psychologists of all time.

强化学习理论（reinforcement theory）认为：学习，从本质上来说，是因为受到增强与惩罚的影响而改变了行为的发生概率。社会学习理论还认为：不仅加诸于个体本身的刺激物可以让其获得或消退某种行为，观察他人的行为及结果也可以获得同样的效果。由此，行为主义学派的强化理论被用来解释许多社会心理学问题。例如，榜样的教育意义被空前重视起来。

Reinforcement theory is the theory generally states that people seek out and remember information that provides cognitive support for their pre-existing attitudes and beliefs. The main assumption guides this theory is that people do not like to be wrong and often feel uncomfortable when their beliefs are challenged. This theory focuses on the behavior to consequence connection, noting that a behavior will continue frequency based on pleasant or unpleasant results.

社会学习论认为儿童的社会化是学习其所处群体的共享知识，该理论强调外部环境对儿童社会化养成的重要作用。成功的社会化需要儿童获得大量周遭世界的信息。他们必须学会用语言与周边的人交流达成自己的需要，必须识别周边的人的类型，知道什么样的行为是被周围的人期待的。

Social learning theory states that learning is a cognitive process that takes place in a social context. Learning also occurs through the observation of rewards and punishments. When a particular behavior is rewarded regularly, it will most likely persist; conversely, if a particular behavior is constantly punished, it will most likely desist. The theory expands on traditional behavioral theories, in which behavior is governed only by reinforcements, by placing emphasis on the important roles of various internal processes in the learning individual.

依据社会学习的观点,社会化是儿童学会来自养育群体的共享文化的过程。正是文化赋予了不同的群体以不同的意义。尽管文化各有千秋,但儿童习得文化的过程是相同的。

总之,社会学习论强调的是儿童从环境中获得的认知和行为的能力,行为的内容取决于社会学习——文化的影响。

5.3 社会化的中介 Agents of Socialization

社会化仅对人类的信仰和行为提供了部分解释,认为社会化的中介(agents)不是由环境预先确定的白板;科学研究表明,人们是由社会影响和基因共同塑造的。促进社会化的社会组织(中介)包括家庭、同辈群体、学校、职业群体、媒体、民间团体、青少年中心等。

Socialization agents are a combination of social groups and social institutions that provide the first experiences of socialization. Primary agents of socialization include people such as parents, and usually occur when people are very young. Agents of secondary socialization include secondary relationship (not close, personal or intimate) and function to "Liberate the individual from a dependence upon the primary attachments and relationships formed within the family group". The family is usually considered the primary agent of socialization, and schools, peer groups, and the mass media are considered secondary socialization agencies.

Agents of socialization teach people what society expects of them. They tell them what is right and wrong, and they give them the skills they need to function as members of their culture.

人的社会化,不仅受人类遗传因素(genetic factor)的影响,而且也与环境因素直接相关。外在环境中有许多社会化的中介;本书主要论及家庭、学校与同辈和媒体三个方面。环境因素有自然环境、社会环境之分,这里主要讨论社会环境对个体社会化(individual socialization)的影响。

5.3.1 家庭 Families

在一个社会的全部制度中,家庭的定位不尽相同。在绝大部分传统社会中,一个人的原生家庭(protogenetic family)决定着今后生活的社会地位。在现代社会中,社会地位并不是以出身(family background)衡量。但是,家庭所在区域和所处阶层相当显著地影响着个体的社会化。儿童会在潜移默化中学会父母、家人、邻里的行为方式。值得注意的是,由于家庭体制变化万千,婴儿所体验到的家庭亲密关系(affinity),在各个文化中并不一样。在现代社会中,个体会在自己的核心家庭度过童年。而在世界上许多其他的文化中,许多儿童也被他们的祖父母、叔叔、阿姨照料。当然,有些孩子也会在单亲家庭(single parent family)或重新组合的家庭(recombinational family)中成长。

关于家庭关系对儿童社会化的影响,学者们有许多讨论。这里主要讨论母亲的角色在儿童社会化过程中的功能。

众所周知,婴儿与照料者(care giver)之间的关系很重要,但是,母亲是必须的吗？精神分析学派(psychoanalytic school)认定婴儿和照料者(通常是母亲)之间的密切情感联系是健康人格(healthy personality)发展的基本条件。因为育儿是一个互动的过程。

婴儿一出生就能意识到自己的身体,知道饥、渴、痛,并能产生不愉快的情绪,甚至是全身性的紧张。他们首先要排除身体紧张和满足身体的需要。为了满足婴儿的需要,成人必须学会弄明白婴儿符号的意义;同时婴儿也渐渐知道主要照料者是满足自己需要的来源。婴儿早期的这些交流是真正意义上的互动,成人学习如何有效地照顾婴儿,婴儿也形成了对成人强烈的情感依恋。

近来的研究表明,有情绪反应的照料者对婴儿社会化有着重要影响。或许只有母亲才能够产生这样强烈的情绪,建立温暖的关系,给予儿童安全感(sense of security)。这是其他有可能照顾儿童的照料者所无法替代的。安全的母子依恋关系会产生正向的结果。多年来,社会赋予母亲的主要责任是养育子女,父亲的主要责任是外出工作打拼事业,大多数家庭都遵从这种劳动分工模式。因此正常的儿童发展是与母亲建立亲密、持续的依恋关系。母亲的工作、家庭冲突的焦虑会影响儿童的问题行为(problem behavior)和焦虑水平(anxiety level)。

5.3.2　学校与同辈群体 School and Peer Group

学校是另一个重要的社会化中介。学校给予儿童社会化的影响是社会结构赋予的。社会有组织地、有计划地对儿童进行系统的教育。学校教会学生阅读、写作、计算等能力,但事实上学校的功能远不止此。教师通过奖惩措施(reward and punishment)强化了学生的人格特征,如准时、毅力等。学校教会学生那些被期待的特征,并保留这些特征,在今后的社会生活中能够促进社会交互作用。

教师的期待(expectation)作用影响着学生的学习动机(learning motivation)、对成功的期待以及自我评价。正如大家所知道的,教师的期望效应(expectation effect)非常有效。如果教师对学生抱有良好的期待,一段时间后,这种期望就会成为现实,学生真的如期望的那样获得了良性发展。这种效应也被称为"罗森塔尔效应"(the Rosenthal effect)。

The Rosenthal effect, or Pygmalion effect, is a psychological phenomenon in which high expectations lead to improved performance in a given area. The effect is named for the Greek myth of Pygmalion, the sculptor who fell in love with the perfectly beautiful statue he created. The psychologists Robert Rosenthal borrowed something of the myth by advancing the idea that teachers' expectations of their students affect the students' performance. The idea behind the Rosenthal effect is that increasing the leader's expectation of the follower's performance will result in better follower performance.

总之,学校承担了教育孩子的功能,并且为孩子们将来的生命历程阶段做准备。同时,学校也以相当微妙的(subtle)方式对学生产生影响。他们被要求在课堂上保持安静、遵守学校的规章、正确回应学校教职人员的权威,并通过教师期待产生了自我期待。当他们毕业离开学校后,这些又会成为影响他们职业生涯规划(career planning)的因素。

不仅如此,孩子们还在学校中形成了同辈群体,依据年龄分班的体制强化了同龄群体的影响。

同辈群体又称同龄群体,是指由年龄、家庭背景、爱好、志趣等方面相近的人结合而成的关系较为密切的群体。与家庭不同的是,在同辈群体中,儿童是自发地组织到一起,没有必要一方服从另外一方,他们的身份是平等的。

The term peer group refers to a group of individuals that share similar characteristics with one another. These characteristics may be age, education, ethnic background, etc. In sociology, a peer group is both a social group and a primary group of people who have similar interests, age, background, or social status. The members of this group are likely to influence the person's beliefs, attitudes, and behavior.

同辈群体内儿童之间的相互作用是自愿的,他们有了第一次选择关系人的机会。这种选择使儿童有了社会胜任感和发展自我认同的机会。儿童知道了朋友的作用,了解了自己与他人的不同。自己与同辈群体的关系是建立在家庭之外的,为今后的独立提供了一定的基础。这时,非家庭身份认同使儿童开始反抗父母对其社会化影响。

随着儿童年龄的增长,同辈群体的影响也会越来越大,甚至超过了家庭与家长、学校和老师的影响。研究表明,同辈群体可能具有超越儿童期和青春期的显著影响。在职场和其他领域,相似年龄人群组成的非正式团体(informal group)在塑造个人的态度和行为方面具有重要影响。可见,同辈群体对个体的社会化起着重要、特殊的作用,主要表现在:

(1)在宽松的条件下进行充分社会化。同辈群体本来就是按照自己的兴趣和需要自由选择或形成的交往群体,因而它不像在学校和家庭中受到那么多的限制与禁忌,而是在相互交往中突破"禁忌",无所顾忌地相互交流、玩耍、游戏,在相互信赖和随意的交流中完成社会化。

（2）在潜移默化中实现无意社会化。家庭和学校的社会化都是家长和老师经过认真思考、精心策划而有目的、有步骤地进行的，而在同辈群体中，不需要规划与思考，他们对各种社会规范的认识、对相互交往的默契以及独特的价值观，都往往是在共同的兴趣、爱好驱使下，在游戏或玩乐中形成的。

（3）在共同的志趣联结下形成共同的价值观。家庭和学校所进行的社会化往往是按照社会公认的规范和价值观进行的。而同辈群体的成员往往是志趣相投、背景相仿，在所受教育、智力水平、对外界事物的感受与认识等方面都有着极大的相近性，他们在玩乐、交流中相互影响，形成自己独特的价值标准，这种价值标准可能被社会所认可，但也有可能不被社会认可，甚至是对立的。并且，在这种共同的独特价值观下，同辈群体有自己的生活方式与处世方式。由此可见同辈群体对人的社会化有着重要的影响。在同辈文化中的社会化是个体从儿童向青少年角色过渡的一个基本条件。

At an early age, the peer group becomes an important part of socialization. Unlike other agents of socialization, such as family and school, peer groups allow children to escape the direct supervision of adults. Among peers, children learn to form relationships on their own, and have the chance to discuss interests that adults may not share with them, such as clothing and popular music, or drugs and sex. Peer groups can have great influence or peer pressure on each other's behavior. However, currently more than 23 percent of children globally lack enough connections with their age group, and their cognitive, emotional and social development are delayed than other kids.

5.3.3 大众传媒 Media

从 19 世纪早期开始，大众传媒开始影响人类生活。传媒从印刷品开始，很快就以收音机、电视机、录音机、录像机等开始了电子传播。这些传媒方式，对人们的意见、态度和行为产生了巨大的影响力。功能主义认为，传媒促进了社会整合（social integration）和社会团结（social solidarity）。在现代生活中，媒体已经与人密不可分，影响着人的生活方式。大众传媒包括报纸、书籍、电视、广播、网络等，为个体提供了一个广泛的社会化途径。

媒体对个体社会化的影响通常被区分为正负两个方面：

一方面，通过各种传媒，个人能接受大量信息。特别是网络，其信息量巨大，并且形式多样，涉及了社会生活的方方面面。个体可以主动获取大量可以支持自己价值观的信息，开阔眼界，分享社会的经验，接受普通大众的价值观和生活方式。在多元文化价值（multicultural values）下，个体面临纷繁的选项，要比以前花费更多的时间和精力对选项进行比较，对自己的选择给予充足的理由肯定。这一过程，使得个体社会化有增强作用（reinforcement），个体在区别和选择中对自我有一个更加清晰的认识。

另一方面，大众媒体为了经济利益也会产生一些低俗的、不值得赞赏的价值观，在某些媒体上，充斥着各种暴力（violence）、色情（eroticism）和权钱交易（power-for-money deal）内容，对没有辨识力的个体产生负面影响，尤其是对青少年的社会化产生不利影响。

5.4　社会化的结果 Results of Socialization

人们通过社会化获得新技能、知识和行为方式。本节内容主要讨论社会化的一些特定结果，包括性别角色、语言和认知能力、道德发展以及工作定向。

5.4.1　性别角色 Gender Roles

1. 父母亲的影响 Parental Influence

不同社会对女性和男性的性格特征（traits of character）和行为方式（way of act）有着不同的期待。传统上认为男性要有能力、竞争、有逻辑、有雄心壮志和果敢。女性则是温暖的、善于表达、温柔、敏感、圆通。婴儿自出生后，父母就会根据婴儿不同的性别给其穿不同的衣服、做不同的游戏、买不同的玩具以及给予不同的人生期待和性格上的要求。

父母在照看孩子的时候，与孩子互动是有区别的。母亲常常以孩子的生理需要和情感需要为导向，父亲则常陪同与孩子进行一些剧烈的身体活动。母亲和父亲与孩子的对话也是不同的，母亲具有社会情绪性（emotionality）特征（支持或否定），父亲的谈话却常是具有事实性（factuality）。因此婴儿从一出生就在有区别地进行着男性和女性角色的学习。

父母的期待对儿童的性别角色的学习影响最大。孩子们从观察父母互动的不同来学习恰当的行为。他们会从学习恰当的角色行为中得到奖赏（rewards）；相反，从学习异性的角色行为中得到惩罚。儿童获得的早期与异性交往的经验来自他们与自己母亲或父亲交往的行为模式。例如，一个女孩子与一个男孩子拥有温暖、亲密的关系，她很有可能与自己的父亲是这样亲密的关系。当然，孩子的性别角色期待不仅来自核心家庭（nuclear family），也可能来自祖父母、叔叔、阿姨，这取决于儿童成长的背景和文化。不同文化对儿童性别角色的期待是不同的。

2. 学校的影响 Influence of School

儿童在学校中学习性别角色的资源是方方面面的，有教师教育的，也有向同伴学习以及受课本上知识潜移默化的影响形成的。

举例来说，在中美这两种不同的文化类型中，男孩子们都趋于参与那些活泼性的活动，而女孩子们则更喜爱从事文静的或室内的活动。在中国和美国儿童的故事里，男性从事职业的范围比女性从事职业的范围要广得多。学校教材中对男女性从事的活动、活动类型以及职业类型有着明确的性别角色划分。可见，性别角色是一个跨文化的（cross-cultural）普遍现象（universal phenomenon），是个体社会化的结果，甚至已完全内化，达到了无意识的（automatically）程度。

3. 大众媒体 Mass Media

性别角色社会化（gender role socialization）的一个主要影响因素是大众媒体（mass media）。有研究对 175 个故事场景进行分析发现，男性更多地被刻画成独立、勇敢和有进取心的，而女性则被更多地描述为依赖、情感丰富和浪漫的。故事中男性的职业主要是医生、律师和银行家，而女性是护士、社工和秘书。这也许是对男女性别角色的刻板印象，但儿童正是从不同的媒体中学习不同的性别角色，最终形成自己身为男性或女性的社会角色。

5.4.2　语言与认知图式 Language and Cognitive Schemata

成为一个社会人的前提是使用语言与他人交流。儿童语言的习得以他们的知觉和动作技能为必备条件，受到社会学习的影响。语言有三个主要成分：语音、语词以及赋予意义规则。年幼的儿童获得语言技能是一个循序渐进的过程，他们首先掌握有意义的语音，然后是学习词汇，最后学会句子。

从认知层面来讲，儿童必须发展在头脑中表征这个世界的能力。这种能力的获得与语言密切相关。世界上有无穷多的事物需要儿童去记忆，这是一个庞杂的工程。儿童必须学会对需要记忆的事物进行分类，例如，狗是动物、香蕉是水果等。图式（schema）能使我们的世界变得有序，更易记忆和分类。

> Schema means shape, or plan. A schema is a cognitive framework or concept that helps organize and interpret information. In Piaget's theory, a schema is not only the category of knowledge but also the process of acquiring that knowledge. He believed that people are constantly adapting to the environment as they take in new information and learn new things. Schemata allow us to take shortcuts in interpreting the vast amount of information. However, these mental frameworks also cause us to exclude pertinent information to focus instead only on things that confirm our pre-existing beliefs and ideas. Schemata can contribute to stereotypes and make it difficult to retain new information that does not conform to our established ideas about the world.

这里先介绍一下图式的概念。图式是人类用来为他们通过感觉器官接收的信息分配含义的辅助工具。图式描述的是一种思维或行为类型，用来组织资讯的类别，以及资讯之间的关系。它也可以被描述为先入为主思想的心理结构，表示世界某些观点的框架，或是用于组织和感知新资讯的系统。该模式使人们能够在任何情况下快速轻松地找到自己的思绪出路，并做出相对理性的行为。从技术上讲，心理学中的图式是一种心理知识结构，它以抽象的、概括的形式包含有关特定对象或概念的信息。该模式不应被理解为记忆中的实体，而是作为对如何在信息处理中使用所学知识的说明。图式的例子包括社交模式、刻板印象（stereotype）、社会角色、脚本（script）、世界观（world view）。在皮亚杰的认知发展论中，儿童根据他们所经历的互动来构建一系列的图式，用来帮助他们理解世界。

图式具有如下功能：

(1)图式会影响注意力和新知识的吸收。

(2)图式可以帮助理解世界和快速变化的环境。

(3)图式控制着人们的感知和信息处理，进而控制着他们的行为。图式是内隐记忆的内容，如果现实显示出与现行方案的差异，那么只有当它们非常显眼，"不容忽视"时才会被感知。

(4)图式帮助人们组织当前知识，并为将来的理解提供框架。

儿童必须学会图式。语言的习得是图式的必要条件，因为语言为图式提供了名称。有研究表明，2 岁的儿童已经能够区分儿童和成人，5 岁的儿童可以区分大小孩、小小孩、成人和老年人。他们会知道周边的人属于哪一类群体，他们喜欢什么、不喜欢什么，学习自己属于什么样的群体，遵守怎样的社会习俗和规范。这些能力都是在社会化过程中习得的。

5.4.3　道德社会化 Socialization of Morality

为了有效地进行社会互动，道德社会化和法律社会化是必须的。杜威（John Dewey，1859—1952）提出了道德发展的三个层次：①行为的前道德或者成规前期——由生物和社会刺激导致的行为动机；②行为的成规期，个体在团体中接受的规范并进行评判的反思；③由个体自己的思维和判断所引导，因此没经过反思不会接受团体的标准。

John Dewey was an American philosopher, psychologist, and educational reformer. He was one of the most prominent American scholars in the first half of the twentieth century.

皮亚杰经由实际访谈和观察（对游戏的规则）定义了儿童道德推理的阶段：

(1)前道德阶段（the stage of pre-morality）：对规则的权责没有感觉。

(2)他律道德阶段（the stage of heteronomous morality）：是非善恶只考虑后果，不考虑行为的动机即服从的规则。

(3)自律道德阶段（the stage of autonomous morality）：道德的判断，除考虑到的规范，也考虑情景因素。

1955 年，科尔伯格（Lawrence Kohlberg，1927—1987）经过长期跨文化的研究（cross-cultural research），再一次确认了道德的层次和阶段（stages of moral development）：

Lawrence Kohlberg was an American psychologist best known for his theory of stages of moral development. He served as a professor in the Psychology Department at the University of Chicago. Lawrence Kohlberg（1958）agreed with Piaget's（1932）theory of moral development in principle but wanted to develop his ideas further. He used Piaget's storytelling technique to tell people stories involving moral dilemmas. Kohlberg's theory proposes that there are three levels of moral development, with each level split into two stages. Kohlberg suggested that people move through these stages in a fixed order, and that moral understanding is linked to cognitive development. The three levels of moral reasoning include preconventional, conventional, and postconventional.

（1）道德成规前期（preconventional stage）：幼儿园到小学中年级。

阶段1：回避惩罚服从取向——儿童因缺乏是非观念，恐惧惩罚而服从就范。

阶段2：相对功利取向——对行为好坏的判断，只依行为结果而定，受罚的行为是坏的，因此为求报偿而遵守规范。

（2）道德循规期（conventional stage）：小学中年级以上，甚至到成人。

阶段3：寻求认同取向——个体顺从团体要求，符合成人意见，期求别人的赞许，表现出从众行为。

阶段4：顺从权威取向——个体服从团体规范，严守公共秩序，遵守法律权威，用法判断是非。

（3）道德自律期（postconventional stage）：青年后期人格成熟后。

阶段5：法制观念取向——有责任心和义务感，尊重法制，相信法律是为大家的公益，但却是由人订立的。

阶段6：价值观念取向——相信道德的普遍价值，价值判断全凭自己的良知，有所为有所不为。

儿童从父母、同辈、学校及媒体中不断学习符合社会需要的道德，并做出符合社会需要的道德行为，并进一步强化已有的道德认知结构。

5.4.4 成就动机 Achievement Motivation

Achievement motivation, also referred to as the need for achievement, is an important determinant of aspiration, effort, and persistence when an individual expects that his performance will be evaluated in relation to some standards of excellence. Such behavior is called achievement-oriented. The goal of achievement-oriented activity is to succeed, to perform well in relation to a standard of excellence or in comparison with others who are competitors.

工作是社会生活中很重要的部分，会影响到人们在经济或其他资源的分配。许多成人工作有着不同的成就动机，如薪水或者其他的奖励。毫无疑问，社会化的一部分就是工作定向。两岁的儿童能够意识到成人工作是为了赚钱。孩子们知道工作和钱的关系，钱可以用来购买食物、衣服和玩具。因此孩童很小的时候就知道工作的意义。父母、学校和媒体都会影响儿童的职业定向（vocational direction），并对儿童未来的职业定向起着潜移默化的影响。

不仅个体的职业导向受社会化影响，个体的成就动机（achievement motivation）也被社会化影响。成就动机指的是个体追求自认为有价值的工作，并使之达到完美状态的动机，这是一种以高标准要求自己、以力求取得活动成功为目标的动机。成就动机理论（achievement motivation theory），是美国心理学家大卫·麦克莱兰（David McClelland）和约翰·威廉·阿特金森（John William Atkinson）以默里（H. A. Murray）的成就需要理论为基础发展而来的理论。

一个社会或群体通常将成就大小看成评判一个人成功与否的标准，同时对取得个人成就的人给予各种赞赏和奖励。个人的成就动机决定着个人成就的大小，成就动机是一种重要的社会性动机，它对个体的工作和学习都有很大的推动作用。从个体的角度而言，成就动机是一个人在社会化过程中逐渐形成的适应社会生活的重要基础之一，是激励自我成就感和意志力的心理机制，是决定一个人事业成功与否的关键因素。心理学对成就动机的定义是人们在完成任务的过程中力求获得成功的内部动因，亦即个体乐意去做对自己重要和有价值的事情，并努力达到完美的一种内部推动力量。

精神分析学派和行为主义学派的心理学家也曾经对动机进行了研究，但是麦克莱兰认为：前人对动机的研究带有一定的局限性，关注的是人的基本需要，如饥饿、渴、安全的需要等。他更注重研究人的高层次需要（high-level needs）与社会性动机。他的研究主要受到了美国心理学家默里的需要理论及其研究方法的影响，使用主题统觉测验（thematic apperception test）进行测量研究。

麦克莱兰认为：人在不同程度上由以下三种需要来影响其行为：

（1）成就需要（need for achievement）：希望做得最好、争取成功的需要。

（2）权力需要（need for power）：不受他人控制、影响或控制他人的需要。

（3）亲和需要（need for affiliation）：建立友好亲密的人际关系的需要。

麦克莱兰研究还发现，具有强烈的成就需要的人渴望将事情做得更为完美，提高工作效率，获得更大的成功。个体的成就需要与他们所处的经济、文化、社会、政府的发展程度有关，社会风气也制约着人们的成就需要。

权力需要是指影响和控制别人的一种愿望或驱动力。不同人对权力的渴望程度有所不同。权力需要较高的人喜欢支配、影响他人，喜欢对别人发号施令，注重争取地位和影响力。

亲和需要就是寻求被他人喜爱和接纳的一种愿望。亲和需要者渴望友谊，喜欢合作而不是竞争的工作环境，希望彼此之间的沟通与理解，他们对环境中的人际关系更为敏感。有时，亲和需要也表现为对失去某些亲密关系的恐惧和对人际冲突的回避。亲和需要是保持社会交往和人际关系和谐的重要条件。

个人的成就动机与早期接受的独立性训练有关。独立性越强，成就动机越强。高成就动机父母会潜移默化地影响子女成就动机的形成，他们一方面及时对子女的成就给予奖励和赞赏；另一方面，他们也是儿童进行社会学习的榜样。麦克利兰指出成就动机是在一定的社会氛围（social atmosphere）下形成的，一个国家或群体的成就动机氛围会影响儿童成就动机的形成。

延伸阅读 Further Reading

思考 Thinking it Through：
社会化的重要性。

Introduction to Sociology：Understanding and Changing the Social World（Excerpt）

Why Socialization Matters

Socialization is critical both to individuals and to the societies in which they live. It illustrates how completely intertwined human beings and their social worlds are. First，it is through teaching culture to new members that a society perpetuates itself. If new generations of a society don't learn its way of life，it ceases to exist. Whatever is distinctive about a culture must be transmitted to those who join it in order for a society to survive. For U.S. culture to continue，for example，children in the United States must learn about cultural values related to democracy：they have to learn the norms of voting，as well as how to use material objects such as voting machines. Of course，some would argue that it's just as important in U.S. culture for the younger generation to learn the etiquette of eating in a restaurant or the rituals of tailgate parties at football games. In fact，there are many ideas and objects that people in the United States teach children about in hopes of keeping the society's way of life going through another generation.

Socialization is just as essential to us as individuals. Social interaction provides the means via which we gradually become able to see ourselves through the eyes of others，and how we learn who we are and how we fit into the world around us. In addition，to function successfully in society，we have to learn the basics of both material and nonmaterial culture，everything from how to dress ourselves to what's suitable attire for a specific occasion；from when we sleep to what we sleep on；and from what's considered appropriate to eat for dinner to how to use the stove to prepare it. Most importantly，we have to learn language—whether it's the dominant language or one common in a subculture，whether it's verbal or through signs—in order to communicate and to think.

Nature Versus Nurture

Some experts assert that who we are is a result of nurture—the relationships and caring that surround us. Others argue that who we are is based entirely in genetics. According to this belief，our temperaments，interests，and talents are set before birth. From this perspective，then，who we are depends on nature.

One way researchers attempt to measure the impact of nature is by studying twins. Some studies have followed identical twins who were raised separately. The pairs shared the same genetics but in some cases were socialized in different ways. Instances of this type of situation are rare，but studying the degree to which identical twins raised apart are the same and different can give researchers insight into the way our temperaments，preferences，and abilities are shaped by our genetic makeup versus our social environment.

For example，in 1968，twin girls born to a mentally ill mother were put up for adoption，separated from each other，and raised in different households. The adoptive parents，and certainly the babies，did not realize the girls were one of five pairs of twins who were made subjects of a scientific study (Flam 2007).

In 2003，the two women，then age thirty-five，were reunited. Elyse Schein and Paula Bernstein sat together in awe，feeling like they were looking into a mirror. Not only did they look alike but they also behaved alike，using the same hand gestures and facial expressions (Spratling 2007). Studies like these point to the genetic roots of our temperament and behavior.

Though genetics and hormones play an important role in human behavior，sociology's larger concern is the effect society has on human behavior，the "nurture" side of the nature versus nurture debate. What race were the twins? From what social class were their parents? What about gender? Religion? All these factors affected the lives of the twins as much as their genetic makeup and are critical to consider as we look at life through the sociological lens.

Extreme Isolation

We have just noted that socialization is how culture is learned，but socialization is also important for another important reason. To illustrate this importance，let's pretend we find a 6-year-old child who has had almost no human contact since birth. After the child was born，her mother changed her diapers and fed her a minimal diet but otherwise did not interact with her. The child was left alone all day and night for years and never went outside. We now find her at the age of 6. How will her behavior and actions differ from those of the average 6-year-old? Take a moment and write down all the differences you would find.

In no particular order，here is the list you probably wrote. First，the child would not be able to speak；at most，she could utter a few grunts and other sounds. Second，the child would be afraid of us and probably cower in a corner. Third，the child would not know how to play games and interact with us. If we gave her some food and utensils，she would eat with her hands and not know how to use the utensils. Fourth, the child would be unable to express a full range of emotions. For example, she might be able to cry but would not know how to laugh. Fifth, the child would be unfamiliar with, and probably afraid of, our culture's material objects, including cell phones and televisions. In these and many other respects, this child would differ dramatically from the average 6-year-old youngster in the United States. She would look human, but she would not act human. In fact, in many ways she would act more like a frightened animal than like a young human being, and she would be less able than a typical dog to follow orders and obey commands.

As this example indicates, socialization makes it possible for us to fully function as human beings. Without socialization, we could not have our society and culture. And without social interaction, we could not have socialization. Our example of a socially isolated child was hypothetical, but real-life examples of such children, often called feral children, have unfortunately occurred and provide poignant proof of the importance of social interaction for socialization and of socialization for our ability to function as humans.

One of the most famous feral children was Victor of Aveyron, who was found wandering in the woods in southern France in 1797. He then escaped custody but emerged from the woods in 1800. Victor was thought to be about age 12 and to have been abandoned some years earlier by his parents; he was unable to speak and acted much more like a wild animal than a human child. Victor first lived in an institution and then in a private home. He never learned to speak, and his cognitive and social development eventually was no better than a toddler's when he finally died at about age 40 (Lane, 1976).

(Reference: pressbooks.howardcc.edu/soci101/chapter/4-1-the-importance-of-socialization)

6 社 区
Community

The Definition of Community Development

Leaders in towns, cities, and villages all over the world know that their communities do not simply spring up overnight. The particular elements that make up a community need to be placed in the appropriate environment, under the appropriate circumstances, and they need to be cultivated into something that is both successful and cohesive as a whole. It takes time, effort, and a lot of patience to get results. Certainly, it isn't going to be an easy task for anyone to do.

Community development is a crucial aspect for any municipal area. Civic leaders dedicate resources and sections of their budgets toward community development because of the value it holds for their residents. It's a major part of urban planning, and the two frequently are tied together even when they are separated. As a result, it is incredibly important to have an understanding of what community development entails and what can be done to ensure its success.

This article will explore the basics of community development. Clearly defining community development and what its primary elements include allows for a better understanding of the more complex aspects discussed later on. Additional topics of this article include the value of community development, both domestically and internationally, and who in the community is involved in the process.

Community Development Defined

Many people mistake community development as another name for urban planning. It's often what people think of first when the concept is brought up. While the two are similar and can have a symbiotic relationship in a community, they are not the same. Community development is defined by the United Nations as a process where the conditions of social and economic progress are created through participation within the community and reliance on community initiatives. Different communities tend to use different means to achieve this, but it is generally a universal concept regardless.

Until recently, community development was imagined as a type of gentrification and renovation for poor, decrepit neighborhoods in desperate need of improvement. This has been the typical view of community development for many years and is still treated as such to some degree today. However, many communities use community development as a means of general improvement for the benefit of all. The goal(s) a community has will often focus on providing resources to residents of all socioeconomic levels in the neighborhood, and giving them the opportunities to use services they need when they need them.

It should be noted that when discussing community development, "community" isn't necessarily specific to a particular geographic area—although that will often be the case. The concept can be applied to communities of identity, interests, or culture and heritage. There's a central theme to each community, something that ties its members together in the first place. The actions taken for community development will often need to focus on that theme and the individual elements associated with it in order for a plan to be formulated and for things to be successful. In many instances, the involvement and participation of community members is necessary as they are each individual components that make up the whole. This also makes each community unique, so paying attention to the individual elements is very important.

Interested in learning more? Why not take an online Community Development course? How is community development done? In many cases, it's through the implementation of different policies and practices by leaders and residents within the community. This may be done with the assistance or involvement of local, state, and/or federal government, but it is not always a necessity. There are resources available throughout multiple levels of government for communities to obtain a healthy, safe, and equal environment for their residents, but they are not the only options community leaders have. Whatever methods and means a community uses for community development will be dependent on aspects such as the community's goals, location, size, internal resources (e.g. budget and funding), and existing condition.

International and Domestic Value

Much of the value community development has is contingent on what it can do for a community when properly implemented and maintained. The process is applied because a community and its members have a particular set of goals that they want to achieve, thus the value lies in the process' success under those particular circumstances. There are going to be some communities who see a different kind of value from community development due to the variety of factors involved, aside from what it is that they sought to achieve.

Community development does over some value on a more general level, applicable regardless of the circumstances. This includes:

Improved Quality of Life: One of the primary purposes of community development is to improve things for those in the community. The resources that are made available through the process are intended to improve the overall quality of life for the residents that use them. This can include anything from safety to health and well-being and then some. Again, this will be subject to the existing circumstances before the process is implemented and what is done during the process. This is certainly the largest measure of community development's value, and it is often equal to or greater than the cost of achieving it in most cases.

Unity: Community development prompts the residents and leadership of a community to come together to reach a collective goal. That collaboration generates a sense of unity throughout the community and brings home the idea that everyone has earned a place in it. Most people interpret that as meaning that they have value within their community, that they belong as an integral part of the whole. It can be both valuable and beneficial for the community to be united as it can help ensure the continued success of the process of community development, and everything that has been brought into the community through it.

Openness and Communication: When people are able to successfully work together as a united group, they tend to have strong communication abilities. Nothing can really get done without effective communication, so it's both an important part and byproduct of community development. Studies that have looked into community development have found that communication is essential for communities to achieve their goals. It was also found that openness is an equally essential value, as it affords communities with some degree of flexibility and the ability to grow in different ways. Communities that have gone through the process of community development will often find that the communication and openness amongst residents and leaders has improved over all and aids in their continued progress.

Sustainability: It does warrant some attention as part of the value of community development. The process of community development allows communities to be more autonomous and self-sustaining than they were before. The improvements made bring forth new resources and changes that empower the community to take action on its own. The promotion of self-sustainability is another key aspect of community development, and it certainly contributes to its value for those that apply it to their own communities.

For many communities, sustainability is something that repeatedly pays off and has a higher value in the long run when compared to the cost of its original implementation.

Stability: Community development itself can be a stabilizing force for communities to build upon and grow from. As mentioned before, many of the communities that have long used community development use it as a means of improving themselves on a large scale. Since it is often a long process, the stability it provides is crucial to its success. It very much lays the foundation that the community builds its improvements upon. Many of those communities lack that stability in the first place, so it is an incredibly valuable commodity that cannot necessarily be generated on its own.

Most of the above is applicable for both domestic and international communities. There is value that is applicable to international communities, whether that means communities throughout the world or domestic communities that are culturally diverse.

Education: Whenever there is any kind of diversity present in a community— domestic or international—there is usually interaction between the different cultures and interests. When that happens, there is the opportunity for residents to learn about those that are different than them in their community. Education is something that is available through community development and can be used to implement some of the improvements the process brings about. It also provides the chance for new ideas and concepts found in different cultures to be introduced into the community and to cultures where they are not currently present. Depending on the circumstances, this can help boost the other values of community development already discussed.

Global Cohesion: Communities are not merely small, individual groups that are isolated and independent from each other. In many cases, they intersect with other communities and are a part of larger ones. For example, a neighborhood is its own community, but it's also part of the community of a city or town, which is part of the community of the state, and so on. This is a byproduct of globalization, where the interactions and integration of different people, cultures, and nations intersect on multiple levels. In terms of community development's value, this can build upon the unity that a community has by generating a global cohesion within a particular community and those it intersects with. This can help with the community's internal collaboration amongst residents and with the communities that it works with.

Economic Growth: While economic growth is often a goal of a community going through the process of community development, it does give the process a lot of value on an international level. This is another byproduct of globalization, which often plays a role in economic growth in general. Internationally speaking, it fuels the community's global cohesion and developmental progress. Steady economic growth brings in new resources and maintains the connections with existing ones, fostering progress.

Who Is Involved in Community Development?

While it may be obvious that the community is involved in community development, the particular roles that different members play may not be. Involvement and participation are required to some degree, so it's important to identify the roles in play. Those who are involved are not necessarily going to be those directly impacted by community development, and may simply benefit when applied on a larger scale.

The Residents: The residents of a community are the ones who are going to be intimately involved and impacted by community development. They are the ones who actually take action and put the effort into making improvements to their community using their particular knowledge and skillset. Residents often do this through their employment in the community or through volunteer efforts, although it can also be done through their normal activities.

The Local Government: Most of the leadership in community development will be found through the local government. They are the ones who organize and plan things, identify goals, and possibly provide funding during the process. Members of the local government are going to be the ones that guide the rest of the community in their efforts and make sure things stay on track. They may also be the ones who first initiate the process of community development and recognize that it needs to occur in the first place. In a sense, it's a supervisor or coordinator—like role that's paired with the worker role of the residents and other community members.

The State and Federal Government: As mentioned before, the government on the state and federal levels may play a role in community development through things like assistance programs and other similar resources. This isn't going to be universal for every community that goes through community development, but its common enough for the potential to be there. The involvement of state and/or federal governments are often going to need to be invited into the process by the community itself, usually through application for the programs they offer. No invitation, no involvement. However, upper levels of government may get involved without an invitation if the improvements made through community development intersect with other communities, such as roadwork and new construction.

(Reference: www.universalclass.com/articles/business/the-definition-of-community-development.htm)

6.1　社区概述 Introduction to Community

社区(community)是社会学的主要研究对象,在进行具体社会研究的过程中,往往以社区为单位,对社会变迁进行分析。

社区概念的产生及发展已有上百年的历史,并且随着社会的发展,越来越广泛地被社会学研究所应用,成为社会学研究者经常使用的基本概念之一。

6.1.1　社区概念的起源 Origin of the Community Concept

"社区"一词源于拉丁语,原意是亲密的关系和共同的东西。大多数学者都认为"社区"这一概念最早是由德国社会学家 F. 滕尼斯(Ferdinand Tönnies,1855—1936)在 1887 年出版的《社区与社会》(*Community and Society*)一书中首先提出的,指与"社会"相对的,通过血缘(consanguinity)、邻里(neighborhood)和朋友关系建立起来的人群组合。后来也指:共享共同价值观或文化的人群,因为居住于同一区域互动影响而形成的社群(ecological association)。中文通常将"community"一词译为共同体、团体、集体、社区等,故中文版常将 *Community and Society* 译为《共同体与社会》或《社区与社会》。

Ferdinand Tönnies was a German sociologist, economist, and philosopher. He was a significant contributor to sociological theory and field studies, best known for distinguishing between community and society. He co-founded the German Society for Sociology together with Max Weber and Georg Simmel and many other founders. Tönnies, Max Weber, and Georg Simmel are considered the founding fathers of classical German sociology.

在汉语中,"community"是舶来品,早期和"社会"不作区分,也不收录在词典中。"community"一词在中文里最后被译为"社区",费孝通起到了非常重要的作用。20 世纪 30 年代,费孝通和同学在燕京大学学习社会学时,他和同学一起翻译老师英语授课内容,才组合"社"和"区"两字创造出"社区"一词对应英语单词"community",并用"社会"对应"society"以区别于社区,此后这一新造词遂在汉语中广为使用。

Fei Xiaotong or Fei Hsiao-tung was a Chinese anthropologist and sociologist. He was a pioneering researcher and professor of sociology and anthropology; he was also noted for his studies in the study of China's ethnic groups as well as a social activist. At missionary-founded Yenching University in Peiping, which had China's best sociology program, he was stimulated by the semester visit of Robert E. Park, the University of Chicago sociologist. For an M. A. in anthropology, Fei went to nearby Tsinghua University where he studied with Pan Guangdan. Fei's first fieldwork experience, in the rugged mountains of Guangxi province in the far south, ended tragically after Fei's leg was crushed by a tiger trap, and his young bride Wang Tonghui died seeking help. His last post before his death in 2005 was as Professor of Sociology at Peking University.

在具体指称某一人群的时候,有时会侧重其"共同文化"和"共同地域"两个基本属性的其中一点。如"徐家汇社区""五角场社区"等是侧重其共同地域属性;而"华人社区""客家社区"等则侧重其共同文化属性(cultural attribute)。无论所指侧重哪个要素,"社区"一词都是强调人群内部成员之间的文化维系力与内部归属感(sense of belonging)。

6.1.2 社区概念的发展历史 Development of the Community Concept

1. 国外学者对社区概念的界定 Definition of Community Given by Foreign Scholars

在滕尼斯首先提出社区概念之后,国外其他学者也对这一概念从不同的角度进行了界定,并已发展出百十余种,但从大体上来讲,具有代表性的概念主要有以下几个:

(1)滕尼斯在《社区与社会》一书中将"社区"与"社会"两个概念进行了区别。他认为社区是指由若干有亲族血缘关系的同质人口(homogeneous population)组成的社会联合团体,强调血缘的纽带作用;而社会则是由不同价值观念的异质人口所组成的社会联合团体,强调自主选择性。滕尼斯的社区概念实质是指向了传统乡村社会(traditional rural society)的代表——家族,而社会则指向了现代工业化(industrialization)和城市化(urbanization)的产物。他认为,随着现代工业社会(modern industrial society)的发展,社区会逐渐向社会发展,人与人之间是通过劳动分工与法理契约(legal contract)维系在一起的。此时,滕尼斯的有关社区的概念与现代社会中我们所理解的社区概念有很大的差异。

Though there is no direct English translation, the term gemeinschaft roughly is translated as community. According to Tönnies' theory, a community could be defined as a group of people that shared common bonds around traditions, beliefs, or objectives. Tönnies used the word "community" to describe people that actively worked together to maintain their bond and further their goals. An important element of community is that the relationships and bonds are based on direct personal interaction. A good example of community would be a church or other religious institution. In this case, those that attend the church on a regular basis have formed relationships with other attendees and have bonded around their shared beliefs, values, and traditions. Moreover, there tends to be a sense of support and collectivity in these types of environments that foster a feeling of togetherness and belonging.

（2）美国芝加哥大学（University of Chicago）社会学系教授帕克（Robert E.Park，1864—1944）是最早对社区下定义的社会学家之一，他从社区的基本特点上对社区下定义。他认为社区的基本特点可以概括为：①以区域组织起来的人口；②这些人口不同程度地扎根于他们所占有的土地上；③生活在社区中的每个人都处于一种相互依存的关系中。他强调了人口与土地、人与人之间相互依赖的关系。

（3）1955 年，美国社会学家希勒里（George A. Hillery）通过文献统计（document statistics），发现了 94 种社区定义。1981 年，燕京大学社会学系毕业生、美籍华裔社会学家杨庆堃（C. K. Yang，1911—1999）发现了 140 多种社区定义。在这些定义中，社区被界定为群体、社会系统、地理区域和生活方式等。希勒里提出："社区是指包含着那些具有一个或更多共同性要素以及在同一区域保持社会接触的人群"。（ Hillery，1955）

2. 国内学者对社区概念的界定 Definition of Community Given by Chinese Scholars

费孝通认为的社区主要是指以地区为范围，人们以地缘（geographical relationship）为基础而形成的互助合作（mutual cooperation）关系。地缘因素是社区得以形成的主要原因。

《中国大百科全书（社会学卷）》指出："社区是指以一定地理区域为基础的社会群体"。

3. 社区概念的最终界定 Final Definition of Community

以上仅仅是介绍了几种国内外有关社区的具有典型意义的概念，还有很多学者从不同的角度对社区进行了界定。综合历年来中外学者关于社区的概念界定情况，本书对社区进行如下界定：所谓社区就是指聚居在一定区域内，由一定数量居民组成的，具有内在互动关系与区域文化特征的生活共同体。

根据社区的定义可以看到，社区具有以下特征：一定的地理区域（geographic region），有一定数量的居民（residents），有居民间的社会互动（social interaction），形成独特的区域文化（regional culture），共同生活而形成的聚居群体。

6.1.3　社区理论的起源 The Origin of Community Theory

桑德斯（Irwin Taylor Sanders，1909—2005）在《社区论》（*The Community：An Introduction to a Social System*）一书中提出了三种社区研究的模式，即社会体系论、社会冲突论、社会场域论。如果说区位理论属于专门研究社区的理论，那么桑德斯的三种模式则属于运用社会学的一般理论来研究社区的典范。

社区理论研究是社区研究的重要组成部分，社区理论的研究起源于西欧，在美国得到极大发展。西方社会由于其工业化和城市化进程远早于中国，在社区研究方面有许多成果值得我们借鉴。在发展的 100 多年的时间里，社区理论研究经历过衰落和复兴，发展到现代社会，已成为一个成熟的理论研究体系。

1887 年，德国社会学家滕尼斯出版了《社区与社会》一书，标志着社区理论的诞生。书中，滕尼斯主要比较了社区与社会两种社会形态，认为社区是传统社会的社会关系的表现，建立于情感的基础上，是典型的传统家族社会的性质。而现代工业社会发展后，人与人之间的关系建立于理性基础上，法律与契约是维系社会关系的标准，人与人之间的情感被弱化。滕尼斯在区别了这两个概念的基础上，认为随着社会工业化与城市化的进一步加剧，人与人的组织类型由社区逐渐转向社会是社会发展的必然结果，并随之会引发一系列的问题，应对此进行持续性的研究。

> *Community and Society* was written by Ferdinand Tönnies in 1887 for a small coterie of scholars，and over the next fifty years continued to grow in importance and adherents. It was translated into English by Charles P. Loomis，who well described it as a volume which pointed back into the Middle Ages and ahead into the future by attempting to answer these questions："What are we? Where are we? Whence did we come? Where are we going?" If the questions seem portentous in the extreme，the answers Tönnies provides are modest and compelling.

社区理论被提出来后迅速传到美国，并得到极大的发展，形成了社区理论研究的几大研究派别，下面就社区理论的发展给予简单的介绍。

6.1.4　社区理论的发展 The Development of Community Theory

最早的社区理论研究之一，是在 20 世纪 20—30 年代享誉美国的芝加哥学派中展开的。该学派所提出的人文生态学的研究方法在很长一段时间内影响了美国的社区研究。

1. 人文生态学理论 Human Ecology

（1）古典人文生态学理论（classical human ecology）。人文生态学理论又称为人文区位理论，以美国城市社会学家帕克为首的芝加哥学派对芝加哥都市化过程进行研究的过程中，借用生物学中的区位学概念解释了这一现象，为社区研究提供了一个新的研究视角，并取得了极大的成果。帕克在人类生态学、族群关系、移民、同化、社会运动和社会解组等领域的工作为人称道,被认为是对美国社会学影响最深远的人物之一。

Human ecology refers to the study of the relationship between humans and their natural, social, and built environments. The term has been described as an attempt to apply the interrelations of human beings a type of analysis previously applied to the interrelations of plants and animals. Park himself explains human ecology as, "fundamentally an attempt to investigate the processes by which the biotic balance and social equilibrium are disturbed, the transition is made from one relatively stable order to other".

Park and Ernest W. Burgess were leading practitioners of human ecology. Much of the theory of what came to be called "classical human ecology" was stimulated by Park's writings and teaching at Chicago. Park argued that the basic process underlying social relationships was competition; however, because of human interdependence due to the division of labor, this competition always involves elements of unplanned cooperation. In this way, people come to form symbiotic relationships, both at the spatial and cultural levels. These ideas are developed in the collection of essays (many by Park himself) on *The City* (1925) and his monograph on *Human Communities* (1952).

　　20 世纪 20—30 年代,芝加哥学派在社区研究过程中创立了人类生态学理论,帕克成为这一学派的创始人。他借助生物学理论,研究都市环境的空间格局。帕克认为竞争是社区生活的主导,从而影响都市空间的结构。竞争存在于社区层面之上,而在竞争之上还存在着共生关系,这种共生关系也体现了帕克所提出的社会关系,因此,他认为社区是社会的基础。同时,由于对土地的竞争,形成了不同功能与需要的自然区域,它会影响整个社会的发展计划,自然区域也成为人文生态学理论的基本分析单位。

The Chicago School refers to a school of thought in sociology and criminology originating at the University of Chicago whose work was influential in the early 20th century. Conceived in 1892, the Chicago School first rose to international prominence as the epicenter of advanced sociological thought between 1915 and 1935. Their research into the urban environment of Chicago would also be influential in combining theory and ethnographic fieldwork.

　　此后,麦肯齐(R. D. Mckenzie)对这一理论进行了进一步的补充,提出了中心化、集中、隔离等生态过程的概念,并认为形成区位过程时最重要因素是人口的增加。伯吉斯(Ernest W. Burgess)则提出了都市同心圆假说。这些学者的研究都被称为古典人类生态学说。

　　(2)社会文化区位理论(social and cultural ecology)。社会文化区位理论是人文生态学理论的一个流派,主要代表人物是美国学者怀利(W. Wylie);社会文化区位理论主要强调文化因素。该流派在批判古典人文生态学理论忽略文化因素的基础上,强调文化在人类行为中的重要作用,认为人们的区位行为除受自然变量影响外,文化变量也是其重要因素;并且以文化和价值观为核心解释都市社区结构和发展。

（3）新正统区位理论。主要代表人物有霍利（Amos Henry Hawley）和邓肯（Otis Dudley Duncan，1921—2004）。为了对古典人文生态学（区位学）进行修正，一些学者在早期研究的基础上对区位学进行了复兴。1950 年，霍利出版了《人类生态学：一个关于社区结构的理论》一书，标志着新正统区位学的正式提出。

> Otis Dudley Duncan was an American sociologist whose study of the black population of Chicago（1957）demonstrated early in his career the validity of human ecology as an extension of the discipline of sociology. He was one of the most influential sociologists of the 20th century.

邓肯提出了"人类生态结构丛模式"（the ecological complex），指出了人口、组织、环境和技术四个变量，英文缩写为 POET。他认为区位学理论的基础就是这四个概念及其相互关系，社区的变化与发展体现在这一模式架构中。

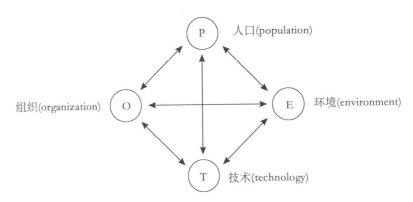

邓肯人类生态结构丛 POET 模型（Duncan 1961，1964）

由于区位理论偏重于空间因素的分析，同时也由于现实中社区变迁的复杂性，因此该理论并不能解释社区内发生的所有现象和问题。这就要求用新的研究视角和理论来研究社区。

2. 中镇综合研究理论 the Middletown Studies

在传统区位学理论发展的同时，美国社会学家罗伯特·林德和海伦·林德夫妇（Robert Lynd and Helen Lynd）和他们的研究团队开创了对中镇进行的综合研究。在美国，有许多城市名为中镇，但是他们取名为中镇的研究对象并非真的中镇，而是印第安纳州的一座美丽小城曼西市（Muncie），这是一座典型的美国小镇。最初，林德夫妇是为了研究中镇的宗教信仰和宗教活动的情况，后来他们发现，宗教生活与社区中的其他制度和机构有着密切的关系，所以开始研究宗教与社区中其他现象之间的关系。

The Middletown studies were sociological case studies of the white residents of the city of Muncie in Indiana initially conducted by husband-and-wife sociologists Robert Staughton Lynd and Helen Merrell Lynd. The Lynds' findings were detailed in *Middletown：A Study in Contemporary American Culture*，published in 1929，and *Middletown in Transition：A Study in Cultural Conflicts*，published in 1937. The word middletown was meant to suggest the average or typical American small city. There are many places in the US actually named Middletown，the Lynds were interested in an idealized conceptual American type，and concealed the identity of the city by referring to it by Middletown. The Lynds and a group of researchers conducted an in-depth field study of the white residents of a small American urban center to discover key cultural norms and social change.

1929 年,《中镇：现代美国文化研究》(*Middletown：A Study in Contemporary American Culture*)一书出版。书中描写了中镇居民的各种活动与宗教信仰情况,涉及谋生、成家立业及空闲时间使用等众多方面的情况,并解释了产生此种中镇现象的原因。几年后,林德夫妇又来到中镇做进一步的调查,并于 1937 年出版了《转型中的中镇》(*Middletown in Transition：A Study in Cultural Conflicts*)一书,分析了社会经济对社区的影响。

林德夫妇及其研究团队对中镇的综合研究方法促使社会学家们在研究社会现象的时候开始关注社区中众多因素的影响作用。与此同时,也引起了社会学家们对社区权力的关注与研究。

3. 社区权力理论 Community Power Theory

如前所述,西方社会学对社区权力结构的研究始于林德夫妇的《中镇》,大规模研究开始于 1953 年。1953 年,美国社会学家弗洛伊德·亨特(Floyd Hunter，1912—1992)出版了《社区权力结构》(*Community Power Structure*)一书,标志着社区权力研究的开始。亨特研究的内容侧重于社会中政治权力的分布和运用,研究目的是了解、评价社区中的政治生活质量。

Floyd Hunter was an American social worker and administrator, community worker, professor and author. He was an originator of the "power structure" in contemporary sociology. Hunter's influence on theoretical developments in sociology and other disciplines that utilize the concept of "power" was substantial. His methodology, which consisted of the "reputational" approach also had a profound influence on the debate over how scholars should conduct "power" studies.

作为一名社会工作者(social worker),以及后来成为一名社工行政人员,亨特在工作中发现了许多社区发展过程中的障碍,这促使他开始研究当地的权力分配(distribution of power)问题,并与当地的领导者沟通、消除社区发展中的障碍。亨特认为,社区中的民主形同虚设，社区中的官员对他们所在社区的重要决定没有多少影响力。

针对亨特所提出社区权力问题的研究，美国政治学家、当代政治学巨擘、民主理论大师、耶鲁大学政治学荣誉讲座教授、前美国政治学会主席罗伯特·阿伦·戴尔（Robert Alan Dahl，1915—2014）于 1961 年出版了《谁在进行统治》（*Who Governs? Democracy and Power in an American City*）一书，他没有采用亨特所使用的访谈法，而是通过不同的方法从已有的决策中找出对立的决策者及相应的支持者，弄清究竟是何人的决策占据绝对地位。研究发现，经民主选举产生的市长在社区决策中起着核心作用。

Robert Alan Dahl was an American political theorist and Sterling Professor of Political Science at Yale University who supports this view. In the late 1950s and early 1960s, he was involved in an academic disagreement with C. Wright Mills over the nature of politics in the United States. Mills held that America's governments are in the grasp of a unitary and demographically narrow power elite. Dahl responded that there are many different elites involved, who have to work both in contention and in compromise with one another. If this is not democracy in a populist sense, it is at least polyarchy (or pluralism). In perhaps his best-known work, *Who Governs?* (1961), he examines the power structures (both formal and informal) in the city of New Haven, Connecticut, as a case study. He is considered one of the greatest theorists of democracy in history.

在这两个研究之后，对社区权力的研究开始迅速发展起来，并出现了关于社区精英论与多元论的讨论问题。

总之，社区权力结构（community power structure）关注的主要问题是：社区内部的权力、权力的性质和来源、权力之间的关系、权力的强弱程度、行使权力的责任人等。它是社区政治结构的一个重要方面，直接影响着社区的发展。

4. 社区冲突理论 Theory of Community Conflict

社区冲突理论的主要代表人物是詹姆斯·塞缪尔·科尔曼（James Samuel Coleman，1926—1995）。长期以来，社会学家们对社会冲突的研究主要是着眼于整个社会；直到 1957 年，美国社会学者科尔曼发表《社区冲突》（*Community Conflict*）一书，社会学者才开始在社区范围内研究社会冲突。《社区冲突》一书标志着社区冲突研究的开始。

James Samuel Coleman was an American sociologist, theorist, and empirical researcher, based chiefly at the University of Chicago. He was elected president of the American Sociological Association in 1991. He studied the sociology of education and public policy, and was one of the earliest users of the term social capital. His *Foundations of Social Theory* (1990) influenced sociological theory. His *The Adolescent Society* (1961) and "Coleman Report" (*Equality of Educational Opportunity*, 1966) were two of the most cited books in educational sociology.

科尔曼在书中分析了社区冲突的三个根源：经济争端、政治争端和价值观的冲突。这三个根源导致了社区的种种冲突与矛盾，并在社区冲突问题的解决上起到非常重要的影响作用。科尔曼认为，社区冲突之间会彼此强化，因此有必要在冲突产生初期就制止此类恶性循环。此后的一些学者在科尔曼研究的基础上，对社区冲突理论进行了更加细致的研究工作，并在社会学界取得了极大的影响作用。

之后，美国学者桑德斯开始研究社区权力结构。桑德斯在《社区论》中提出，任何一个社区的冲突都包括以下三个要素：对立的关系、不同的权力分配以及社区居民的情绪反应。社区冲突会因对立关系类型的不同而有所不同。他还把社区变迁与社区冲突联系起来，提出要了解社区变迁，就必须了解社区冲突。

5. 社区行动理论 Community Action Theory

社区行动理论与其他理论相比，更重视研究社区中的具体行动，分析社会的具体行动过程，是一种微观意义上的社区研究理论。社区行动包括真正发生在社区内的具体行动，同时还包括与这一社区行动相关联的社区行为。因此，要对社区行动理论所观察到的具体社区行动进行仔细的区别与分析。这一学派的主要代表人物有美国学者哈罗德·考夫曼（Harold F. Kaufman）、劳伦斯·格林（Lawrence W. Green）与梅约。

综上，社区理论的发展历经西欧与美国之后，开始在世界范围内传播开来，并取得了长足发展，影响了现代社会中众多国家的社会发展力量与速度。

6.2 社区的基本要素与功能 Elements and Functions of Community

6.2.1 社区的基本要素 Basic Elements of Community

根据社区的概念，社区必须满足一定的条件才能得以形成，从而成为居民生活的共同体。从大体上来讲，社区必须具备以下七个基本要素：

（1）地域（territory）。每个社区都是在独特的地域空间中存在的，独特的社区地域空间为社区居民提供了生活与互动的场所。

(2)人口(population)。社区是由一定数量的人口聚居而成的,一定数量与质量的人口是社区存在的基本前提。社区当中的人口是指在该社区内长期生活,相互之间已形成相对稳定的生活方式,具有一定数量与质量的人口聚居体。

(3)物质保障(material guarantee)。社区中的人口要想不断地发展下去,并促进社区的不断进步,其前提是社区能够为社区中的居民提供基本的物质设施保障,保证社区居民正常地生产与生活。

(4)社会关系(social relations)。社会分工使得社区人口的互动与依赖成为可能。丰富的社会互动构成了社区文化的重要内容,社区的文化就是来源于实践过程中社区成员的互动,对其进行总结、归纳与分析就构成了社区文化。

(5)组织结构(organizational structure)。社区居民的交往与互动是有一定的规则和行为模式的。社区中的组织结构主要指社区内正式与非正式的组织结构,还包括为保证社区组织有效运行并发挥作用的社区中的正式规章制度(rules and regulations)、法律条款(articles of law),以及社区中的舆论(public opinion)等。社区通过组织的运行,充分地调动与利用社区与社会中的有效资源,以达到社区高度发展的目的。社区的组织有正式组织与非正式组织(formal & informal organization)之分,例如,家庭、邻里、娱乐群体、游戏群体等都属于非正式组织;而党政机关、居(村)委会、学校、医院等则属于正式组织。这两种组织形式在社区发展过程中都是必不可少的,都会起到相应的积极作用。

总之,无论是何种形式的组织形式,它们都是社区的重要组成部分,并且是促进社区发展的重要力量。

(6)文化心理(cultural psychology)。不同的社区在发展过程中会形成不同的文化心理特征。社区的文化心理特征不仅包括在社区中形成的文化价值观、行为规范、传统习俗、生活方式等,还包括受社区文化影响而形成的社区居民的心理意识、思想动态以及对社区产生的认同感与归属感。文化心理特征是每个社区所独有的,因此这是社区最本质的要素所在,是对不同社区进行区分的重要依据。

(7)经济要素(economic factors)。社区居民在长期生活与互动中形成的生产、交换、分配、消费等经济活动。

以上七个方面构成了社区的基本要素,各要素之间互相影响,共同构成了社区的整体特征,任何一个要素出现问题,社区都会相应地出现问题。

6.2.2 社区的基本功能 Basic Functions of Community

不同的社区会表现出不同的具体作用,但从社区整体来讲,社区具有以下最基本的功能:

(1)经济功能(economic function)。任何一个社区都要满足社区成员的基本生存需求,这就要求社区必然存在相应的生产、交换、分配与消费的经济功能。

(2)政治功能(political function)。社区的政治功能主要是指社区中的各级政治组织、政治团体与机构等在国家政治制度的引导下,保护社区居民的基本安全,实现社区居民的政治权力,发挥社区的政治管理功能。

(3)社会化功能(function of socialization)。社会成员社会化的媒介除了每个成员所在的家庭、工作或学习所在的单位或学校之外,还有一个重要的场所,就是其日常居住所在的社会小氛围,主要表现为居民所在的社区。

(4)社会保障功能(function of social security)。社区结合国家实行的各种保障与福利服务,根据不同社区的优势与特点,主要为社区中的弱势群体(vulnerable groups)提供种类繁多的社会保障与社会服务的功能。社区以互帮互助为原则,为社区中的老、弱、病、残、幼等弱势群体实行照顾与关怀,为这些弱势群体提供上门服务。

(5)社会整合功能(function of social integration)。社区既要使社区成员的需求得到满足,又要实现自身的有效管理,这主要是通过社区的社会整合功能实现的。社区生活丰富多彩,为居民提供了经济、政治、教育、娱乐、福利、宗教、社会参与等多方面活动的机会,提高了社区成员的素质,促进了社区成员的交往,挖掘了居民的潜能,强化了社区居民对社区的认同感(sense of identity)与归属感(sense of belonging),增强了社区居民的凝聚力(cohesion)。这些有利于社区自身的管理与发展,更有利于社会对社区的控制与整合,便于社会的稳定。

以上仅仅是对社区基本功能的一般讨论,随着社会的发展与进步,社区会不断产生更多新的功能,以不断完善社区的功能体系。

6.3　社区发展 Community Development

经联合国倡导,社区发展在第二次世界大战后立刻引起了世界各国的重视。近年来,社区发展(community development)受到世界各国的推广而得到迅速地发展。

> The United Nations referred to community development as "a process designed to create conditions of economic and social progress for the whole community with its active participation"(United Nations,1955). This definition captured an approach to working with people that can be used across all countries.

6.3.1　社区发展的含义 Meaning of Community Development

社区发展从15—16世纪的社区救助、17—18世纪的社区组织、再到19—20世纪的社区发展运动,已经历了上百年的历程。

欧洲工业革命(Industrial Revolution of Europe)之后,德国、法国、英国为了应对工业发展(industrial development)所带来的社会问题,充分利用社区的人力、物力、财力资源,在社区内展开了一系列社会工作，调动了社区居民的积极性、提升了居民参与社区事务的主动性，培养社区居民的自治精神（spirit of autonomy）和互助精神。第一次世界大战期间，美国政府为适应战时的需要，在全国普遍开展了战时服务（wartime service），社会工作由此得以迅速发展，并引起了社会学家的广泛关注和研究。

20世纪初，受欧美社区社会工作发展的影响，美国社会学家F.法林顿于1915年首先提出了社区发展的概念。1928年美国社会学家J.斯坦纳在其所著的《美国社区工作》一书中专门设置了"社会变迁和社区发展"一章，并对社区发展的内涵进行了论述。之后，又有几位美国社会学家对社区发展的定义、社区发展的基本方法和社区发展的理论作过较详细的论述，并为这一概念的发展和广泛应用奠定了基础。此后这一概念不断被完善，逐渐形成了完备的社区发展理论体系。

联合国于1955年发表的《通过社区发展促进社会进步》（"Social Progress Through Community Development"）专题报告中指出，社区发展（community development）的目的是赋能个体与群体，帮助他们获得改变社区的技能；动员和教育社区内居民积极参与社区建设，充分发挥创造性，与政府一起大力改变贫穷落后状况，以促进经济的增长和社会的全面进步。

> The United Nations defines community development as "a process where community members come together to take collective action and generate solutions to common problems." Community development seeks to empower individuals and groups of people with the skills they need to effect change within their communities. These skills are often created through the formation of social groups working for a common agenda. Community developers must understand both how to work with individuals and how to affect communities' positions within the context of larger social institutions.

近年来，我国社会学家开始对社区进行深入研究。于显洋（2006）认为，社区发展的含义包括广义与狭义两个层次。广义的社区发展乃泛指国家或者某个地区所有事物的发展与过程，包括社区的政治、经济、文化、教育、卫生、环境、服务、管理等各个方面。社区发展的范围包括城市、乡村和集镇居民所居住的地理范围等。狭义的社区发展是指基层社区建设与社会发展的事项与过程，以及具体问题的解决过程。

徐永祥（2021）则认为，所谓社区发展，概指居民、政府和有关的社会组织整合社区资源、发现和解决社区问题、改善社区环境、提高社区生活质量的过程，是塑造居民社区归属感（社区认同感）和共同体意识、加强社区参与、培育互助与自治精神的过程，是增强社区成员凝聚力、确立新型和谐人际关系的过程，也是推动社会全面进步的过程。

结合社区发展的历史，综合社区发展的概念，本书对"社区发展"的概念给予以下表述：所谓社区发展，就是指社区居民充分利用社区资源、发现和解决社区问题、加强社区建设、促进社区参与、培养社区领袖的社区互动过程，目的是赋能社区居民、提升合作能力、增强社区成员的归属感与凝聚力、提高社区整体的生活质量、改善社区环境、解决社区问题,最终实现社会公平与社会进步。

6.3.2 社区发展的意义 Purpose of Community Development

社区发展在世界各国都有着重要的战略意义。结合社区实际,积极推行社区发展,这在社会变迁中有着非常重要的意义,表现在以下四个方面:

(1)提高生活质量(enhance quality of living)。促进社区发展,不仅能改善社区的自然环境状态,同时还能及时解决社区中存在的社会问题,使社区成员之间和谐相处,形成良好的社会环境。

> The community development should focus on the well-being and quality of living. The initiative may focus on economic, physical, and/or social development. A multi-year initiative may focus on all these components. However, the community initiative is most successful when the community takes one step at a time.

(2)保障人权(secure human rights)。人民的幸福生活是最大的人权,而幸福生活的最大前提是人的生命和健康。社区发展中一个非常重要的问题就是利用资源的有效开发与使用最大限度地保障社区居民的生命权和健康权。社区中存在各种社会组织,政府也会为社区发展提供大量的便利条件,从社区居民的根本利益与需求出发,充分利用社区与社会中的资源,保障居民有清新的空气、干净的水源、安全的食品以及良好的医疗。

> The community initiative should focus on human rights principles. The community and practitioners must adopt the Universal Declaration of Human Rights in their work. The first three articles of the Universal Declaration of Human Rights states that "All human beings are born free and equal in dignity and rights"; "Everyone is entitled to all the rights and freedoms without distinction of any kind, such as race, color, sex, language, religion, political or other opinion, national or social origin, property, birth or other status", and "Everyone has the right to life, liberty, and security of person".

(3)提升社区领导力(promote community leadership and ownership)。社区发展过程中要求社区成员积极主动地参与到活动中来,公平地给予每位社区成员民主平等的社会环境,让社区成员发挥各自的最大能力、服务技能、自信心与社区发展愿景。与此同时,社区发展过程中还会对社区中有领导才能的成员进行积极的培养,锻炼他们逐渐成为社区领袖,从而能够组织各种社区活动,使社区在社区成员的领导下独立地发展。

> The most important principle is, through the community development process, to actively working with the community to increase leadership capacity, skills, confidence, and aspirations.

(4)提升社会公平(promote social justice)。社区的一个重要功能就是公平地为社区成员提供各种社会保障和社会服务。随着社会的发展和社会分工的加强,居民需求的满足不再仅仅来自于个人或家庭,还有很大一部分来自于社会,而最能直接并有效地提供这一服务的单位就是社区。社区是实现社会保障与社会福利的有效保证,社区发展的同时就是在促进社会的进步。

> As transformative community workers, our work must be guided by social justice principles, especially equity and inclusion. Community workers work with the community and critically examine the root causes of poverty, marginalization, and exclusions. Therefore, community practitioners work with excluded community members and equip them with knowledge, skills, and resources for their empowerment.

6.3.3　社区发展的原则 Principles of Community Development

1955 年,联合国在《通过社区发展促进社会进步》(Social Progress Through Community Development)的文件中,提出社区发展的 10 条基本原则:

(1)社区各种活动必须符合社区基本需要,并以居民的愿望为根据制订首要的工作方案。

(2)社区各个方面的活动可局部地改进社区,全面的社区发展则需建立多目标的行动计划和各方面的协调行动。

(3)推行社区发展之初,改变居民的态度与改善物质环境同等重要。

(4)社区发展要促使居民积极参与社区事务,提高地方行政的效能。

(5)选拔、鼓励和训练地方领导人才,是社区发展中的主要工作。

(6)社区发展工作特别要重视妇女和青年的参与,扩大参与基础,求得社区的长期发展。

(7)社区自助计划的有效发展,有赖于政府积极、广泛的协助。

(8)实施全国性的社区发展计划,须有完整的政策,建立专门行政机构,选拔与训练工作人员,运用地方和国家资源,并进行研究、实验和评估。

(9)在社区发展计划中应注意充分运用地方、全国和国际民间组织的资源。

(10)地方的社会经济进步,须与国家全面的进步相互配合。

以上社区发展与社区工作的原则都注重社区自身的建设与发展,利用社区内的资源与力量实现社区进步,同时,社区发展应该是有计划、有步骤的,与社会整体发展相适应,与社区居民的根本利益相适应。

6.3.4　中国的社区发展 Development of Chinese Communities

1. 中国社区发展的现状 Current Situation of Community Development in China

我国社区的真正发展是在 1978 年改革开放之后,市场经济进入了我们的生活领域,社区开始发生根本性的变化。农村实行了家庭联产承包责任制,城市则由原来的"单位制"走向"市场经济",集镇社区也随之迅速发展起来,大量的自由经营开始出现。在这样的变革背景中,中国的社区发展越来越成熟,并取得了一系列的明显成果。

中国的社区发展现状主要表现为以下几个方面:

(1)社区组织结构建设规范化。在改革开放后,我国借鉴了大量的西方社区理论,并结合我国实际,开始建立专业化的社区,典型的表现就是社区的组织结构规范化。1999 年,民政部正式启动了"全国城市社区建设实验区"工程,在北京、上海、广州、天津等地社区的带领下,越来越多符合我国社会发展状况的社区模式被各地接受和效仿,这更加促进了社区发展的规范化。

(2)社区建设深入发展。1991 年,民政部提出了"社区建设"这一概念。概念提出后,在我国社会成员的努力之下,社会各地的社区建设都得到了长足的发展。社区的自然环境保护受到人们的重视,人们开始自主地通过各种方式利用并保护社区资源。

(3)社区功能趋于完备。随着社会的进步与发展,社区不再像改革开放前一样,主要是对社区成员进行行政管理。改革开放后,市场经济出现,社区志愿者与各类民间服务组织大量涌现,同时也伴随着专业社区工作的出现,社区的功能开始多样化。

(4)社区发展呈现出专业化趋势。我国社区发展过程中,虽然还存在大量的行政人员对社区进行行政性的而非专业性的管理,但与改革开放前相比,从事社区工作与进行社区研究的专门人员越来越多。

(5)智慧社区(smart community)应运而生。智慧社区概念起源于美国,是顺应科技发展的产物,主要由基础设施层、功能应用层和决策管理层共同组成,包括智慧政务、智慧民生、智慧家庭和智慧物业四大模块,是社区管理的新模式。20 世纪 80 年代末,我国智慧社区开始发展,分为社区智能化、社区数字化、社区智慧化三阶段。当前我国智慧社区发展模式及建设存在着部分地区思想认识上有待加强、缺乏统一的规划、缺乏统一的智慧社区建设标准、建设资金不足、资源开发力度不够、技术人才短缺等问题;我国智慧社区未来发展的方向是网络覆盖化、系统集成化、设备智能化和设计生态化以及创新我国智慧社区发展的思路。

> A smart community is one that uses information technology, innovation and data to be more efficient, solve problems, and create new opportunities for people, businesses, and organizations. A smart community enables improved service delivery, economic development, and livability with a reduced environmental footprint.

也有学者认为,智慧社区发展中产生问题的根源是以国家的管理型设计、资本的经营型设计和专家的科学型设计为代表的"设计本位"理念。这种理念驱动下的智慧社区虽然在强化行政管理、降低可见成本、体现专业精神等方面取得了收效，却为社区发展留下了"反治理行为""设计脱离群众"等一系列弊病。智慧社区的未来发展需要感知并服务于生活中具有多样性和深入性的居民需求，尊重并充分汲取生活中各类行动主体的治理经验，以"生活本位"的视角重新审视智慧社区的规划和建设，以技术进步推动生活质量的提升。因此，提出了智慧社区未来发展的趋势应该是从设计本位到生活本位。

2022 年 5 月，我国九部门（民政部、中央政法委、网信办、发展改革委、工业和信息化部、公安部、财政部、住房城乡建设部、农业农村部）印发《关于深入推进智慧社区建设的意见》的通知。该通知首先对智慧社区下了定义：智慧社区是充分应用大数据、云计算、人工智能等信息技术手段，整合社区各类服务资源，打造基于信息化、智能化管理与服务的社区治理新形态。该通知指出了智慧社区建设的重要任务有以下六项：集约建设智慧社区平台，拓展智慧社区治理场景，构筑社区数字生活新图景，推进大数据在社区的应用，精简归并社区数据录入，加强智慧社区基础设施建设改造。

（6）社区基金会（community foundation）助力社区发展。社区基金会源于 1914 年美国克利夫兰社区基金会；此后，美国社区基金迅速发展。1921 年，加拿大成立了美国本土之外的第一个社区基金会。20 世纪 80 年代，社区基金会在英国兴起。随后，世界其他国家和地区相继出现社区基金会。从本质上来看，社区基金会是一个慈善组织，是一种资金源于社区又服务于社区的运营形态。其功能是筹集资金和使用资金；其优势是资金来源多样，价值中立，服务范围弹性化等；其价值在于能够解决社区问题，动员社会资源，提供项目资助，吸引不同资源主体。我国于 2008 年成立了首家社区基金会——深圳桃源居社区基金会。社区基金会的成立，有助于满足社区的独特需求，增强社区治理能力，但同时也对社区的专业服务能力等提出了新的挑战。

> Community foundations are instruments of civil society designed to pool donations into a coordinated investment and grant making facility dedicated primarily to the social improvement of a given place. The first community foundation was set up in Cleveland in 1914 by Frederick Goff. Others soon followed including the California Community Foundation and the Chicago Community Trust. The first Community Foundation in Canada, The Winnipeg Foundation, was established in Winnipeg in 1921. Since the 1980s, a number of private foundations in the United States have created initiatives to develop community foundations in various states.

2. 中国社区发展存在的主要问题
Major Problems in the Development of Chinese Communities

我国社会是典型的城乡二元结构（the urban-rural dual structure）模式，主要表现为城乡之间的户籍壁垒，在制度与管理上把城市和农村截然分开，形成城乡二元结构的分治格局。具体来说，城乡二元制在制度上把城镇居民和农村居民在身份上分为两个不同的社会群体,在公共资源配置和基本公共服务上向城镇和城镇居民倾斜,农村得到的公共资源和农民享有的基本公共服务明显滞后于城镇和城镇居民,农民不能平等参与现代化进程、共同分享现代化成果。城乡二元结构是制约城乡发展一体化的主要障碍,也是社区发展的主要阻力。

The urban-rural dual structure is a historical phenomenon common in developing countries. The urban-rural dual structure refers to the urban-rural dual economic and social structures. It originated from the planned economy system, hukou is the core problem. The government divides its residents into two groups, agricultural and non-agricultural hukou (household registration). On this basis, dozens of related institutional arrangements have been constructed. This system artificially separates the urban and rural areas. China's urban-rural dual structure has the unique characteristics of the system due to special reasons.

概括来说,中国社区存在的主要问题有以下几个方面:首先,我国这种典型的城乡二元结构把我国社区主要分成城市社区与农村社区两种类型。这两种类型的发展极其不均衡,物质、文化、资源分布不均衡导致城乡差距越来越大,使各地发展都处于不同的层次中。这不利于我国社区发展统一化,更不利于社会整体的发展。

其次,社区管理人员以行政领导而非社会服务人员自居。我国的社区组织中的社区管理者常常是以行政领导者的角色与社区居民发生互动,这样,工作者与居民之间的关系就容易出现管理与被管理的关系。

最后,社区工作者专业化程度不高,工作繁杂,负担较重。随着现代社区理论的发展,社区发展越来越要求社区工作者运用专业的方法加强社区建设。我国的社区理论虽已有所发展,但还没有普及到全国各地的社区,大多数的社会工作者仍然是在凭借个人经验从事社区服务工作,而实际上,这已远远不能满足社区居民的需求。

3. 中国社区未来发展趋势 Future Development Trend of Chinese Communities

结合我国社区目前发展的状况及存在的问题,我国社区未来发展的趋势将具有以下特点:①城乡社区一体化协调发展;②社区工作专业化程度高,社区工作者都发展成专业的社会工作者,以专业的社区发展理论去指导社区发展实践;③智慧社区的发展与社区基金会的运营将成为未来中国社区发展的亮点。

我国智慧社区尚处于起步阶段,存在覆盖范围不够大、技术设施不够先进、管理效率不高等问题。期待未来我国的智慧社区朝着实用、人性、便利、高效的方向发展。

社区基金会自20世纪80年代落户中国后,逐渐呈现出其助力社区发展的优势。但在这个过程中,也出现了一些问题:如水土不服、资金来源单一等。期待在未来发展中,社区基金会能接受市场的考验,尝试创办符合中国文化的社区基金会。

总之,我国社区具体情况复杂,条件多变,各地发展不均衡,未来社区的发展也是一个长时段的过程,它不仅仅涉及社区中具体要素的变化,还涉及到社区成员、社区工作者的变化,以及城乡二元体制的变革。社会不断进步、不断发生转型，这都会给社区建设者提出各种各样的难题。现实的社区建设会以未来社区发展为目标，逐渐形成合理的、符合中国国情的社区结构。

6.4 社区的研究方法 Community Research Methods

6.4.1 社区研究方法的概念及特点
The Concept and Characteristics of Community Research Methods

自 19 世纪末滕尼斯提出社区研究之后，欧美大量学者开始运用各种方法从事社区研究工作，社区研究成为社会学研究的重要内容。

在具体的社区研究方法上，欧美学者主要借鉴了社会学、人类学等相关学科的研究方法，对社区整体进行研究。综合来说，社区研究方法主要是指运用某种有效的资料收集方法对社区进行材料收集并加以整理和分析的过程。

社区研究方法的特点为：

(1)以社区整体为研究对象。

(2)客观地收集与分析社区资料。

(3)对社区进行全方位、多角度的分析与研究。

6.4.2 社区研究的基本方法 Basic Community Research Methods

社区的研究方法很多，不同的研究方法适用不同的研究目的和研究对象。这里只介绍几种比较常用的研究方法。

1. 问卷调查法 Questionnaire Survey

A questionnaire is a research instrument that consists of a set of questions or other types of prompts that aims to collect information from a respondent. A research questionnaire is typically a mix of close-ended questions and open-ended questions.

问卷调查法简称问卷法，它是研究者在一定理论指导下，根据研究目的设计调查问卷，依此对被调查者进行资料收集与资料分析。这种方法是进行社会调查常用的方法，它可以收集大量被调查者的客观资料，从而进行科学的统计分析，具有一定的客观性与科学性。根据社区研究的目的和调查对象的特点，可采用不同的方式完成问卷调查。

问卷调查法的优点是便于实施、调查结果较客观且容易量化、便于统计分析、适合大规模调查。其关键是问卷设计。设计问卷需要注意的问题有：问卷中所涉及的问题应该与调查目的相一致(uniformity)，合理而科学地提出问题，问题之间要有连贯性和逻辑性

(question sequence)。设计问卷必须要遵循以下原则：明确研究范围（identify the scope of your research）；力求简洁（keep it simple）；每次只问一个问题（ask only one question）；选项灵活（be flexible with your options）；了解问卷对象（to know your audience）。

问卷一般分为前言、主体与结语三个部分。前言主要表明研究的目的与意义、匿名保证以及调查者的身份或所属机构；主体主要指具体的问题、回答方式以及对回答的指导语；结语一般是表示感谢或征询被调查者对问卷的意见。

问卷调查分为结构式问卷调查（structured questionnaire）与非结构式问卷调查（unstructured questionnaire）。

问卷调查的形式有网上调查（online questionnaire）、电话调查（telephone questionnaire）、上门调查（in-house questionnaire）、邮件调查（mail questionnaire）。直接问答方式、送发式、邮寄式和报刊式等是比较传统的问卷发送方式。随着互联网技术的发展，目前，很多问卷调查都是在互联网上进行的，也有许多适合问卷调查的 App 应运而生，提高了问卷设计、回答、回收、统计的效率，极大地方便了问卷调查方法的使用。

2. 访谈法 Personal Interview Survey

A personal interview survey is a survey method that is utilized when a specific target population is involved. The purpose of conducting a personal interview survey is to explore the responses of the people to gather more and deeper information.

访谈法又称为访问法，它是通过调查者直接与被调查者面对面交谈（face-to-face interview）来获取资料的研究方法。访谈法强调沟通，但又和日常的交谈有不同之处，大多数的访谈都是有一定计划与目的的，因此，这种方法在社区调查中也是经常使用的方法。

访谈法可以让调查者有效地控制调查节奏，并能根据需要随时调整所要调查的内容，还可以直接与被调查者接触，通过被调查者的言行获得间接的观察资料。访谈法最大的优势是能够就调查者感兴趣的问题进行深度个人访谈（in-depth individual interview）。但这种方法要求调查者与被调查者相互信任，这样才能获得真实准确的资料。这种方法带有很强的主观能动性，容易受到受访者个人因素的影响，也较容易在对调查结果进行分析的过程中产生偏差。因此，只有受过专门训练的调查者才能驾驭这个方法。访谈法还有另一个缺点，那就是比较费时费力，工作成本较高。

访谈法主要分为结构式访谈（structured interview）与非结构式访谈（unstructured interview），个别访谈（individual interview）与集体访谈（group interview），直接访谈（direct interview）与间接访谈（indirect interview）。结构式访谈也称为标准化访谈（standardized interview），指调查者预先设计好访谈提纲，按照预定的程序和步骤进行访谈；非结构式访谈又称为非标准化访谈（non-standardized interview），指调查者并没有预先设计访谈提纲，而是就某一主题或问题与被调查者展开讨论，从中获得有效的资料；个别访谈指对单个的调查对象进行访谈；集体访谈则指就同一问题向多个调查者进行访谈，一般会采取会议的方式进行；直接访谈指调查者与被调查者以面对面的方式进行访谈；间接访谈则指调查者利用某种工具与被调查者进行访谈，二者不会采取面对面的方式，现代社会中常利用电话或网络实现间接访谈。现代互联网技术的发展，视频会议的便利，大大增加了间接访谈的频率。

3. 观察法 Observation

Observation is the active acquisition of information through the senses from a primary source. Human senses are limited and subject to errors in perception, scientific instruments were developed to aid human abilities of observation, such as weighing scales, clocks, telescopes, microscopes, thermometers, cameras, and tape recorders. The term also refers to any data collected during the scientific activity. Observations can be qualitative, that is, only the absence or presence of a property is noted, or quantitative if a numerical value is attached to the observed phenomenon by counting or measuring.

观察法是指调查者通过自己的感官对正在发生的事情进行观察与记录的一种调查方法。这种方法强调人的观察能力的充分发挥，它除了使用人自身的听觉和视觉等感官功能外，还会借助拍照、录像、录音等方式来增强人自身的感官功能，以获得更多的直接材料。在社区研究中，在对社区进行长期跟踪调查时往往使用这一研究方法。

观察法分为结构式观察（structured observation）与非结构式观察（unstructured observation）以及参与式观察（participant observation）与非参与式观察（nonparticipant observation）。结构式观察（structured observation）指有明确研究目的、研究步骤与研究对象的观察方法，它往往是研究者在观察之前已设计好相关的研究步骤，并依据确定的观察表格或观察卡片来进行观察；非结构式观察则没有明确的研究过程和步骤，而只是依照研究目的进行观察；参与式观察指研究者参与到被观察者的具体活动中，成为被观察群体的一员，通过与被观察者共同活动来获得资料；非参与式观察则是指研究者作为一个局外人在被观察者不知情的情况下进行的观察。

4. 文献法 Documentary Research

Documentary research is often conducted by social scientists to assess a set of documents for historical or social value, or to create a larger narrative through the study of multiple documents surrounding an event or individual. Documentary research is the use of outside documents to support the viewpoint or argument of an academic work. The analysis of the documents in documentary research would be either quantitative analysis or qualitative or both. The key issues surrounding types of documents and our ability to use them as reliable sources of evidence on the social world must be considered by all who use documents in their research. It is often related to Content Analysis research methodologies.

文献法就是指以研究目的为指导，阅读、收集、鉴别、整理、分析各种文献资料和其他可记录信息的方法。这种研究方法不仅仅是一个材料收集的过程,更是一个材料整理与分析的过程。它能够帮助研究者找到并分析出观察对象的早期历史发展情况,使观察者更全面地了解被观察者的情况。文献法获得的信息可以在文字中寻找,也可以在其他可记录信息的资料中寻找,例如录音带、录像带等。这是一种间接获得资料的方法,因此在使用时一定要保证文献资料的权威性和可信性。社区研究中,在了解社区基本信息时,这种方法是必不可少的。

根据内容的性质,文献可以分为定量的数据资料和定性的数据资料。定量的数据资料主要运用数字的变化来描述一种社会事实,对这类资料进行分析时,一般会借助专业的社会统计软件进行统计分析;而对于定性的数据资料,一般会采用内容分析的方法完成资料的整理与分析工作,它通过资料的性质描述来表现社会事实。不同文献可根据需要使用相应的方法,或者把两种方法结合起来使用。

5. 实验法 Experiment

An experiment is a procedure carried out under controlled conditions in order to discover an unknown effect or law, to test or establish a hypothesis, or to illustrate a known law, or determine the efficacy or likelihood of something previously untried.

Experiments provide insight into cause-and-effect by demonstrating what outcome occurs when a particular factor is manipulated. Experiments vary greatly in goal and scale but always rely on repeatable procedure and logical analysis of the results. There also exist natural experimental studies.

实验法是按照某种假设设计的、通过人为控制某些变量,对选定的一组研究对象的结果进行检测从而获得资料的一种方法。在心理学与社会心理学的研究中经常使用这一方法,对社区进行研究的过程中也可以采用这一方法,因为社区相对来说有特定的社会空间,研究者有能力在这有限的空间内对变量进行控制,从而观察到社区在变量改变后的表现结果。

实验法主要分为实验室实验法(laboratory experiments)与实地实验法(field experiments)。实验室实验法指在严格指定与控制的人为环境中进行的实验。它要求创造出来的实验环境尽可能地与现实接近,并且整个过程是能够严格控制的。这种方法标准化程度高,实验室可重复使用但仍与现实的真实环境存在差距,观察结果可能与现实不符。

实地实验法则是指在实际生活中进行的、控制部分变量的实验。这种实验的实验环境是真实的生活,因此很多变量因素是实验者所不能把握控制的。实地实验又可以分为严格控制的实地实验和较少控制的实地实验。前者中的被观察者知道他们在参与实验,有意识地会按照研究者的目的去行为;后者中的被观察者不知道自己在参与某项实验,观察者只能通过一些可控的变量对被观察者施加影响。

Field experiments are so named to distinguish them from laboratory experiments, which enforce scientific control by testing a hypothesis in the artificial and highly controlled setting of a laboratory. Field experiments have the advantage that outcomes are observed in a natural setting rather than in a contrived laboratory environment. It is often used in the social sciences, and especially in economic analyses of education and health interventions.

6. 人类生态学方法 Human Ecology

人类生态学强调空间与方位的研究方法，由芝加哥学派首创。它主要是通过分析人类行为与区位空间、生态结构之间的关系，来研究社区的时空活动特征。这里的区位空间与生态结构不仅仅是生物学意义上的自然与生态环境，还包括社区居民生活所在的经济、政治和社会文化环境。可见，人类生态学方法是将人类行为与环境要素结合起来进行分析的过程。

The Chicago School refers to a school of thought in sociology and criminology originating at the University of Chicago. Conceived in 1892, the Chicago School first rose to international prominence as the epicenter of advanced sociological thought between 1915 and 1935, when their work was the first major bodies of research to specialize in urban sociology. Following the Second World War, a "second Chicago School" arose, whose members combined symbolic interactionism with methods of field research (today known as ethnography).

利用人类生态学(human ecology)比较有名的学者主要是美国芝加哥大学社会学系教授伯吉斯，他于 1925 年提出了城市环境区位分析的同心圆模式，美国经济学家霍伊特(H. Hoyt)于 1939 年提出了城市环境区位分析的扇形模式，美国学者哈里斯(C. D. Harris)和乌尔曼(E. L. Ullman)于 20 世纪 40 年代提出了城市环境区位分析的多核心模式。

Ernest Watson Burgess was a Canadian-American urban sociologist at the University of Chicago. Burgess' groundbreaking research, in conjunction with his colleague, Robert E. Park, provided the foundation for The Chicago School. In *The City* (Park, Burgess, & McKenzie, 1925) they conceptualized the city into the concentric zones (concentric zone model), including the central business district, transitional (industrial, deteriorating housing), working-class residential (tenements), residential, and commuter/suburban zones.

7. 人类学方法 Anthropology Methods

人类学方法整合了人文及社会科学的研究方法；其对社区的研究强调对社区的生活形态、文化特质和社会内容进行考察。它把人类学对社会的观察研究方法应用到社区的观察研究之中，注重的是社区研究的文化比较，以期能够对不同社区的文化特征进行有效的分析。人类学方法的优势是能深入到人群中，通过与不同群体的对话，以及使用参与式观察

（participart observation）、文本分析（text analysis）等方法，获取第一手资料（firsthand material）。我国早期学者像吴文藻、费孝通等人都特别强调人类学的方法。

　　吴文藻在 1935 年前后，写了多篇文章介绍社区研究，如《现代社区实地研究的意义和功用》（载《北平晨报》1935 年 1 月 9 日）。在担任燕京大学社会学系主任时，派出多名学生到多地（如福州、江村、山西等）进行实地调查（fact-finding investigation），调查范围包括乡村领袖冲突问题、宗族组织问题、社会经济问题、礼俗和社会组织问题、侨民问题、社会组织问题等。

> Wu Wenzao was a Chinese sociologist，anthropologist，ethnologist. He was admitted into Tsinghua University at 1917. In 1923，his schoolmate Pan Guangdan persuaded him to go abroad to study at Dartmouth College after his graduation from Tsinghua. Wu Wenzao is one of the pioneers and the guide of Chinese ethnological anthropology. Since the early 1940s，he has vigorously advocated the academic thought of Chinese ethnological anthropology. Wu Wenzao's thought guided the development direction of Chinese ethnological anthropology.

　　费孝通是吴文藻的学生，他 1933 年毕业于燕京大学，获社会学学士学位，之后转去清华大学研究生院读人类学。费孝通的博士论文《江村经济》（Peasant Life in China），被誉为"人类学田野调查和理论工作发展中的一个里程碑"，成为国际人类学界的经典之作。他先后对中国黄河三角洲、长江三角洲、珠江三角洲等进行实地调查，提出既符合当地实际、又具有全局意义的重要发展思路与具体策略。

> Fei Xiaotong was a Chinese anthropologist and sociologist. He was a pioneering researcher and professor of sociology and anthropology. He and his colleagues established Chinese sociology and his works set up a foundation for the development of sociological and anthropological studies in China，they also introduced social and cultural phenomena of China to the international community.

　　吴文藻和费孝通通过社会调查，培养了大批人才，对社会学调查研究的发展贡献极大。他们主要运用田野考察的方法进入到我国农村社区甚至偏远地区（remote region）住户中进行比较观察与研究，取得了具有重要意义的成果。

8. 社会网络分析方法 Social Network Analysis

> Social network analysis is the process of investigating social structures through the use of networks and graph theory.

　　社会网络分析方法是一种社会学的研究方法，也称为结构分析法（structural analysis），是在社会网络理论的基础上建立起来的，主要用来分析社会网络的关系结构及其属性。社会网络理论认为,社会网络是由许多节点以及节点之间的关系构成的一个网络结构(network structure)。社会成员之间不断地交往与互动使得网络结构的形成成为可能。每一位社会成员(或组织)就是这张网中的节点,他们会与许多其他成员建立联系。社会成员之间的关系有亲密与稀疏之分,在社会网络中就相应地表现为强关系与弱关系。社会成员都会有自己的社会网络关系,他们会利用网络关系中的资源,促进个人的进步与发展。社区如同一个小社会,也会形成相互交错的人与人之间的关系,社会网络分析方法就可以分析社区成员的网络关系形成状况,从而可以进一步分析社区成员在社会网络结构中的具体位置以及所能获得的资源与资本。这也是获得社区资料的一种方法。

Social network theory is the study of how people, organizations or groups interact with others inside their network. Understanding the theory is easier when you examine the individual pieces starting with the largest element, which is networks, and working down to the smallest element, which is the actors.

延伸阅读 Further Reading

思考 Thinking it through:

问卷调查与实地调查的区别何在?

Need to Know the Distinction Between a Questionnaire vs Survey?

There is a significant difference between a questionnaire and a survey. A survey is defined as the evaluation of experiences or opinions of a group of people via questions as opposed to a questionnaire which is defined as a collection of written or printed questions with an answer choice made to conduct a survey.

Questionnaire

A questionnaire is a set of questions typically used for research purposes which can be both qualitative as well as quantitative in nature. A questionnaire may or may not be delivered in the form of a survey, but a survey always consists of questionnaire.

A questionnaire used in qualitative research asks open ended questions via email, telephone or face-to-face meetings. A questionnaire used in quantitative research asks more closed ended questions with restricted options to answer.

There are two types of questionnaires:

Questionnaires that evaluate variables that is separate, including questions regarding an individual's behavior, facts and preferences.

Questionnaires that measure factors incorporated into a scale like those about individual identities and different attributes, index and traits.

Survey

A survey is a sophisticated quantitative research method comprised of questionnaire with the intention of efficient gathering of data from a set of respondents. A survey mainly consists of closed ended questions with very few open ended questions for free form answers.

Modern online surveys are used for data oriented business, scientific and academic research studies. Questionnaire is an integral part of a survey. But there may not be the intention of a survey vs questionnaire.

The respondent can explain the answer in a descriptive style in case of open-ended questions or a respondent can be asked to choose a response or an answer from a pre-defined set of options in case of close-ended questions.

It's vital to remember that you decimate, distribute or use questionnaire but you don't conduct a questionnaire. The list of questions in a survey is called questionnaire. So the questionnaire is a tool to conduct a survey.

Flexibility, costs, coverage, willingness to take part, and the exactness of the reactions/responses can impact the method for directing surveys.

Surveys are the customary method for completing research in which the respondents are addressed with respect to awareness, demographics, motivations, behavior.

In the end, surveys and questionnaires have more in common than different, one being part of the other, with the only distinction being in how they are presented to a respondent.

Other Highlights About Questionnaire vs Survey

Questionnaires are set up in such a way in order to not aggravate the respondent. When a survey is a interview and not a questionnaire, it can be in-depth and open ended. A questionnaire requires not create precise or legitimate responses from the respondent. When the survey is in the form of an interview it is very much possible to get honest, true and detailed responses.

(Reference: www.questionpro.com/blog/questionnaire-vs-survey-difference/amp/)

7 社会工作
Social Work

Global Definition of Social Work
by International Federation of Social Workers

The following definition was approved by the IFSW General Meeting and the IASSW General Assembly in July 2014:

Global Definition of the Social Work Profession

"Social work is a practice-based profession and an academic discipline that promotes social change and development, social cohesion, and the empowerment and liberation of people. Principles of social justice, human rights, collective responsibility and respect for diversities are central to social work. Underpinned by theories of social work, social sciences, humanities and indigenous knowledges, social work engages people and structures to address life challenges and enhance wellbeing. The above definition may be amplified at national and/or regional levels."

Commentary notes for the Global Definition of Social Work

The commentary serves to unpack the core concepts used in the definition and is detailed in relation to the social work profession's core mandates, principles, knowledge and practice.

The social work profession's core mandates include promoting social change, social development, social cohesion, and the empowerment and liberation of people.

Social work is a practice profession and an academic discipline that recognizes that interconnected historical, socio-economic, cultural, spatial, political and personal factors serve as opportunities and/or barriers to human wellbeing and development. Structural barriers contribute to the perpetuation of inequalities, discrimination, exploitation and oppression. The development of critical consciousness through reflecting on structural sources of oppression and/or privilege, on the basis of criteria such as race, class, language, religion, gender, disability, culture and sexual orientation, and developing action strategies towards addressing structural and personal barriers are central to emancipatory practice where the goals are the empowerment and liberation of people. In solidarity with those who are disadvantaged, the profession strives to alleviate poverty, liberate the vulnerable and oppressed, and promote social inclusion and social cohesion.

The social change mandate is based on the premise that social work intervention takes place when the current situation, be this at the level of the person, family, small group, community or society, is deemed to be in need of change and development. It is driven by the need to challenge and change those structural conditions that contribute to marginalization, social exclusion and oppression. Social change initiatives recognize the place of human agency in advancing human rights and economic, environmental, and social justice. The profession is equally committed to the maintenance of social stability, insofar as such stability is not used to marginalize, exclude or oppress any particular group of persons.

Social development is conceptualized to mean strategies for intervention, desired end states and a policy framework, the latter in addition to the more popular residual and the institutional frameworks. It is based on holistic biopsychosocial, spiritual assessments and interventions that transcend the micro-macro divide, incorporating multiple system levels and inter-sectorial and inter-professional collaboration, aimed at sustainable development. It prioritizes socio-structural and economic development, and does not subscribe to conventional wisdom that economic growth is a prerequisite for social development.

The overarching principles of social work are respect for the inherent worth and dignity of human beings, doing no harm, respect for diversity and upholding human rights and social justice.

Advocating and upholding human rights and social justice is the motivation and justification for social work. The social work profession recognizes that human rights need to coexist alongside collective responsibility. The idea of collective responsibility highlights the reality that individual human rights can only be realized on a day-to-day basis if people take responsibility for each other and the environment, and the importance of creating reciprocal relationships within communities. Therefore, a major focus of social work is to advocate for the rights of people at all levels, and to facilitate outcomes where people take responsibility for each other's wellbeing, realize and respect the inter-dependence among people and between people and the environment.

Social work embraces first, second and third generation rights. First generation rights refer to civil and political rights such as free speech and conscience and freedom from torture and arbitrary detention; second generation to socio-economic and cultural rights that include the rights to reasonable levels of education, healthcare, and housing and minority language rights; and third generation rights focus on the natural world and the right to species biodiversity and inter-generational equity. These rights are mutually reinforcing and interdependent, and accommodate both individual and collective rights.

In some instances, "doing no harm" and "respect for diversity" may represent conflicting and competing values, for example where in the name of culture, the rights including the right to life, of groups such as women and homosexuals, are violated. The Global Standards for Social Work Education and Training deals with this complex issue by advocating that social workers are schooled in a basic human rights approach, with an explanatory note that reads as:

Such an approach might facilitate constructive confrontation and change where certain cultural beliefs, values and traditions violate peoples' basic human rights. As culture is socially constructed and dynamic, it is subject to deconstruction and change. Such constructive confrontation, deconstruction and change may be facilitated through a tuning into, and an understanding of particular cultural values, beliefs and traditions and via critical and reflective dialogue with members of the cultural group vis-à-vis broader human rights issues.

Social work is both interdisciplinary and transdisciplinary, and draws on a wide array of scientific theories and research. "Science" is understood in this context in its most basic meaning as "knowledge". Social work draws on its own constantly developing theoretical foundation and research, as well as theories from other human sciences, including but not limited to community development, social pedagogy, administration, anthropology, ecology, economics, education, management, nursing, psychiatry, psychology, public health, and sociology. The uniqueness of social work research and theories is that they are applied and emancipatory. Much of social work research and theory is co-constructed with service users in an interactive, dialogic process and therefore informed by specific practice environments.

This proposed definition acknowledges that social work is informed not only by specific practice environments and Western theories, but also by indigenous knowledges. Part of the legacy of colonialism is that Western theories and knowledges have been exclusively valorized, and indigenous knowledges have been devalued, discounted, and hegemonized by Western theories and knowledge. The proposed definition attempts to halt and reverse that process by acknowledging that Indigenous peoples in each region, country or area carry their own values, ways of knowing, ways of transmitting their knowledges, and have made invaluable contributions to science. Social work seeks to redress historic Western scientific colonialism and hegemony by listening to and learning from Indigenous peoples around the world. In this way social work knowledges will be co-created and informed by Indigenous peoples, and more appropriately practiced not only in local environments but also internationally. Drawing on the work of the United Nations, the IFSW defines indigenous peoples as follows:

They live within (or maintain attachments to) geographically distinct ancestral territories.

They tend to maintain distinct social, economic and political institutions within their territories.

They typically aspire to remain distinct culturally, geographically and institutionally, rather than assimilate fully into national society.

They self-identify as indigenous or tribal.

Social work's legitimacy and mandate lie in its intervention at the points where people interact with their environment. The environment includes the various social systems that people are embedded in and the natural, geographic environment, which has a profound influence on the lives of people. The participatory methodology advocated in social work is reflected in "Engages people and structures to address life challenges and enhance wellbeing." As far as possible social work supports working with rather than for people. Consistent with the social development paradigm, social workers utilize a range of skills, techniques, strategies, principles and activities at various system levels, directed at system maintenance and/or system change efforts. Social work practice spans a range of activities including various forms of therapy and counseling, group work, and community work; policy formulation and analysis; and advocacy and political interventions. From an emancipatory perspective, that this definition supports social work strategies are aimed at increasing people's hope, self-esteem and creative potential to confront and challenge oppressive power dynamics and structural sources of injustices, thus incorporating into a coherent whole the micro-macro, personal-political dimension of intervention. The holistic focus of social work is universal, but the priorities of social work practice will vary from one country to the next, and from time to time depending on historical, cultural, political and socio-economic conditions.

It is the responsibility of social workers across the world to defend, enrich and realize the values and principles reflected in this definition. A social work definition can only be meaningful when social workers actively commit to its values and vision.

ADDITIONAL MOTIONS THAT WERE PASSED AT THE IFSW GENERAL MEETING RELATING TO THE GLOBAL DEFINITION OF SOCIAL WORK

"No part of this definition shall be construed in a way to interfere with any other parts of this definition"

"Amplifications on national and/or regional levels shall not interfere with the meaning of the elements of the definition and with the spirit of the whole definition"

"As the definition of social work is the key element for establishing the identity of an occupational group, a future revision of this definition has to be initiated only after precise evaluation of the implementation process and the need for change. Adding further comments is to be first choice before altering the definition."

UPDATED INFORMATION ON IFSW AND COVID-19

In many countries social workers are supporting communities that are affected or fearful of the Covid-19 Virus. Social work has an essential frontline role in the fight against the spread of the virus through supporting communities protect themselves and others through physical distancing and social solidarity.

Key functions of social work at this time include:

——ensuring that the most vulnerable are included in planning and response.

——organizing communities to ensure that essentials such as food and clean water are available.

——advocating within social services and in policy environments that services adapt, remain open and pro-active in supporting communities and vulnerable populations.

——Facilitating physical distancing and social solidarity.

——As a profession, advocating for the advancement and strengthening of health and social services as an essential protection against the virus, inequality and the consequent social and economic challenges.

（Reference：www.ifsw.org/what-is-social-work/global-definition-of-social-work/）

7.1　社会工作概述 Introduction to Social Work

社会工作(social work)是现代社会结构中的一个重要组成部分,是为了解决社会问题、从社会实践中产生并逐渐走向专业化的一个学科。作为一门新兴学科和一种新的解决社会问题的职业,社会工作目前已逐步为我国政府、学术界和社会各界所接纳。

7.1.1　什么是社会工作 What Is Social Work

Social work is an academic discipline and practice-based profession concerned with meeting the basic needs of individuals, families, groups, communities, and society as a whole to enhance their individual and collective well-being. Social work practice draws from academic areas, such as psychology, sociology, health, political science, community development, law, and economics to engage with systems and policies, conduct assessments, develop interventions, and enhance social functioning and responsibility.

不同国家在不同时期由于政治、经济、社会和文化背景的差异,对社会工作的理解也各有不同。早期有些国家是把社会工作当作一种个人的慈善事业,后来则把社会工作理解为是政府、非政府组织或其他组织与个人进行的有组织的活动,再后来有些国家从专业服务的角度定义社会工作,认为社会工作是由政府、非政府组织或其他组织与个人所推动的,以协助任何个人发挥其最大潜能从而获得最美满、最有效生活为目的的专业服务活动。

我国根据自己的国情,一般把社会工作做如下界定:社会工作是社会建设的重要组成部分;它坚持助人自助的宗旨,遵循专业伦理规范,是在社会服务与管理等领域,综合运用专业知识、技能和方法,帮助有需要的个人、家庭、群体、组织和社区,整合社会资源,协调社会关系,预防和解决社会问题,恢复和发展社会功能,促进社会和谐的职业活动。

上述定义至少包含了如下几个内涵:①社会工作是一种助人活动。②社会工作是一种专业。③社会工作是一种专门的职业。④社会工作是一种制度。

7.1.2　社会工作的起源 The Origin of Social Work

社会工作是伴随工业化引发的一系列社会问题而产生的,解决这些社会问题的理念和做法为社会工作的产生与发展奠定了实践基础。

1. 英国的《济贫法》The Poor Laws

The Poor Laws were a system of poor relief in England and Wales that developed out of the codification of late-medieval and Tudor-era laws in 1587—1598.

The system continued until the modern welfare state emerged after the Second World War. According to New World Encyclopedia, British Poor Laws were a body of laws designed during the Elizabethan era to provide relief for the poor population living throughout the United Kingdom. Such laws began in sixteenth century England and prevailed until after World War II and the establishment of the welfare state.

Poor Laws provided relief in various forms, including care for the elderly, sick, and infant poor, and the establishment of supportive work programs for all able-bodied poor.

《济贫法》是英国历史上一系列规定，其历史可追溯到中世纪晚期有关乞丐与流浪者的法规。从传统上来说，英国的贫困救济一般都是依赖教会，但随着大量贫困人口涌入城市，教会财力不足以支撑社会救济。在这个背景下，英国王室出台了一系列济贫法案，其中 1601 年颁布的《伊丽莎白济贫法》(Elizabethan Poor Law)最具有代表性。

《伊丽莎白济贫法》的基本原则是：帮助没有工作能力的人得到救济或赡养；给那些有劳动能力的人一份工作，让他们能够以此谋生。此后，英国政府在《伊丽莎白济贫法》的基础上，颁布了一系列相关的法律；例如 1662 年，斯图亚特王朝通过的《住所法》。此后，这一制度在英国各郡广泛采用，成为缓和阶级矛盾的重要措施。工业革命后，英国家庭手工业的没落造成了大量无业流民，贫困化加剧。这使得政府用于穷人救济的财政支出数额增加，旧的济贫法无法适应新形势的需要。于是，议会于 1834 年通过《济贫法（修正案）》(The Poor Law Amendment Act of 1834)，这是 1601 年以后最重要的济贫法，史称新济贫法。20 世纪以来，济贫法的重要性逐渐降低。待到 1946 年的《国民保险法》和 1948 年的《国民救助法》通过后，卫生部主管的社会保险已完全代替济贫，济贫法失去作用。

《济贫法》是社会福利史上的大事，正是因为《济贫法》的颁布，使得慈善不再是教会专属的社会活动，从侧面推动了社会工作的形成。

2. 德国的汉堡制与爱尔伯福制 Hamburger and Elberfeld System in Germany

德国也是工业化较早的国家，在 18 世纪后叶与英国的处境相似。汉堡制和爱尔伯福制是当时德国解决贫困问题的两个亮点。

(1)汉堡制(Hamburger Model)是历史上德国曾实施的一种对济贫事务进行管理的制度，因起源于德国的汉堡市而得名。工业革命后，18 世纪的德国汉堡市人口骤增、贫富差距加大，城市穷人和乞丐人数渐增，他们列队街市并沿门乞讨，成为当地一个最严重的社会问题。

为了解决这个问题，汉堡市参照了英国济贫法案，由布什教授草拟救助方案，于 1788 年建立了以社区为单位管理济贫事务的制度，将全市划分为 60 个区，每区设 1 名监督员，并设一中央办事机构，综理全市的济贫业务。史称"汉堡制"(王思斌，2014)。

汉堡制的宗旨(mission)是设法帮助穷人自力更生(self-reliance)。具体措施包括为失业者介绍工作、为贫困者提供救济、将贫苦儿童送往工艺学校学习技能及接受识字教育、把患病者送往医院诊治、规定对上门乞讨者不准施舍等，并联络各社会救济机关协同工作。汉堡制共实行了 13 年，收效很大，汉堡市的社会状况为之改观。后因济贫事务增多且日趋复杂，这一制度已无法适应变迁了的社会，1892 年代之而起的新汉堡制对它做了重大修改。汉堡制彰显了社会工作助人自助(help people to help themselves)的价值观。

(2)爱尔伯福制(Elberfeld System)是一种对社会救济事务进行管理的制度，因起源于德国爱尔伯福市(Elberfeld)而闻名。该市效仿汉堡制对于社会救济事务的初次尝试是在 1850 年，开始正式实施是在 1852 年，在实际操作中赈济员由本地区志愿者义务担任，对受助者状况进行深入细致调查，为现代社会个案工作方法的产生奠定了基础，在济贫事务管理方面为后来的社会工作者积累了宝贵的经验。

> The Elberfeld system was a system for aiding the poor in 19th-century Germany.
>
> The first attempts to create a reformed poor relief system in Elberfeld began in 1800. The 1802 system was further extended in 1841. Key to the system was that the almoners and overseers served voluntarily. They came mostly from the middle class. Women were also accepted as almoners. The Elberfeld system influenced the reorganization of relief systems in most of the German cities. Attempts to introduce the system in non-German cities were unsuccessful.

德国汉堡制与爱尔伯福制的精神和做法为许多国家所仿效,影响很大,是社会工作史上的里程碑之一。

3. 慈善组织会社 Charity Organization Society

> Charity Organization Society was a private charity that existed in the late 19th and early 20th centuries. The society was mainly concerned with distinction between the deserving poor and undeserving poor. The society believed that giving out charity without investigating the problems behind poverty created a class of citizens that would always be dependent on alms giving. Instead of offering direct relief, the societies addressed the cycle of poverty. Neighborhood charity visitors taught the values of hard work and thrift to individuals and families. The COS set up centralized records and administrative services and emphasized objective investigations and professional training. There was a strong scientific emphasis as the charity visitors organized their activities and learned principles of practice and techniques of intervention from one another. The result led to the origin of social casework. The COS movement was introduced into the United States by two men from Buffalo, New York who were deeply concerned about the expanding destitution caused by the Long Depression of the 1870s. One was an Episcopal rector, Rev. Stephen. H. Gurteen. He traveled to England and spent the summer of 1877 learning about the London Charity Organization Society.

慈善组织会社(Charity Organization Society,COS or Associated Charities)是一家慈善组织,1869 年成立于英国,是志愿服务组织的先驱。其前身是 1869 年在英国伦敦成立的世界上第一个慈善组织"组织慈善救济及抑制行乞协会",旨在协调组织志愿者救济贫困人民。

慈善组织会社帮助的对象包括穷人、病患、孤儿甚至是罪犯。他们的理念是个体要为自己的贫穷负责,要培养解决贫困的能力;反对政府增加财力支出及消耗大量的社会公共资源去救助贫困;他们将穷人进行区分,以"授人以渔而非授人以鱼"为济贫原则,帮助有能力的受助者尽己所能去维持基本生活。

之后,慈善组织会社的影响逐渐扩展到英国其他城市,后影响至美国。1877 年,一位曾经参访过慈善组织会社的美国牧师斯蒂芬·汉弗莱斯·格廷（Rev. Stephen Humphreys Gurteen）受此会社影响，在美国纽约布法罗成立了美国第一个慈善组织会社。

该组织坚持助人自助的朴素理念，在实施救助过程中，不是简单地提供物资援助，而是通过联络、协调资源的方式进行救助。不仅如此，他们还帮助贫困者管理钱财，培育他们量入为出的生活习惯，并不时就开销问题提供建议。慈善组织会社的助困实践，为社会工作的个案工作方法开创了先河。

4. 睦邻运动 Settlement Movement

The settlement movement was a reformist social movement that began in the 1880s and peaked around the 1920s in the United Kingdom, the United States and Australia. Its goal was to bring the rich and the poor of society together in both physical proximity and social interconnection. Its main object was the establishment of settlement houses in poor urban areas, in which volunteer middle-class settlement workers would live, hoping to share knowledge and culture with, and alleviate the poverty of their low-income neighbors. The settlement houses provided services such as daycare, English classes, and health care to improve the lives of the poor in these areas. The movement gave rise to many social policy initiatives and innovative ways of working to improve the conditions of the most excluded members of society. In general, the settlement movement, and settlement houses in particular, have been a foundation for social work practice in this country.

睦邻运动是志愿者组织发起的社区居民自助互助运动。该运动发生在 19 世纪 80 年代的英国，其背景是广泛存在的贫困问题、失业问题和犯罪问题，这些问题成为社会发展的巨大威胁。

英国最早开始和完成工业革命，其经济发展水平远超其他国家。但英国城市的贫困问题一直未得到解决，由此导致的社会矛盾日益尖锐。睦邻运动就是在这样的时代背景下，首先在英国拉开了帷幕。

推动睦邻运动的，除了一些实证社会科学家以外，主要是教会界人士。他们主张让受过高等教育的人和穷人共同生活，使穷人获得接受教育和享受文化生活的机会；同时，知识分子深入穷人区可促进他们对贫困问题的深切了解，有助于贫困问题的解决。

社区睦邻运动的发起人是东伦敦教区的牧师巴内特（C. Samuel Augustus Barnett）。他早年就读于牛津大学，毕业后到东伦敦教区任职。这一教区是伦敦最贫困的教区之一，于是巴内特动员人们为改造社区出力。他首先向当时就读于牛津大学和剑桥大学的贵族子弟们发出了倡议，号召他们前往东伦敦教区为穷人服务，并邀请他们与穷人一起住在教区内，了解穷人的生活状况，并研究解决脱离贫困的方法。

牛津大学经济学讲师汤恩比（Toynbee）也投身社区服务穷人。1883 年汤恩比因病去世后，为纪念他伟大的献身精神，巴内特于 1884 年在伦敦东区建立了大学社区睦邻服务中心，命名"汤恩比服务所"（Toynbee Hall Settlement House）。

继"汤恩比服务所"之后，许多助困服务机构相继在英国成立，这些机构都设立在穷人区；社区睦邻运动轰轰烈烈地开展起来。许多社会学家也加入到睦邻运动的行列中。这使得睦邻运动成为一场社区改造运动。睦邻运动的一大成果是提高了国家对社区贫困的认识，许多睦邻工作者后来也成为推动国家社会福利政策的重要人物。社区睦邻运动的独特方法，它所提倡的人道主义服务精神和所取得的成就，无疑给当时面临种种社会问题而束手无策的政府指出了一条可行之路，因而在短期内迅速传遍欧洲大部分国家，美国受这一运动的影响最大，开展得最为广泛。澳大利亚、东南亚及日本等国也竞相效仿。

第二次世界大战后，社区睦邻运动的影响逐渐减弱，社会保障制度逐渐成熟，政府开始十预社会问题的解决，社会工作从自发的慈善事业阶段走向政府参与组织管理阶段。社区睦邻运动也被更加完善和系统的社区工作替代。

5. 沪东公社 Yangtze-poo Social Center

我国 1917 年沪江大学（University of Shanghai）社会学系在上海杨树浦工人区创建的"沪东公社"，是中国第一家社区服务机构，开启了近代中国的社区服务先河。

上海是中国近代对外开放商埠最早的地区之一，也是近代中国工业的发源地。早期，在上海的杨树浦地区，工厂林立，人口密集，工人的居住条件和生活条件较差，社会矛盾突出。1917 年，杨树浦地区诞生了中国第一家社区服务机构——沪东公社，开启了近代中国的社会服务事业先河。沪东公社由布朗大学毕业生葛学溥（Daniel H. Kulp Ⅱ，1888—1980）创办。葛学溥于 1932—1933 年出版了《华南乡村生活：家族主义社会学研究》（*Country Life in South China：the Sociology of Familism*）。书中记录了他在中国南方进行的社会调查。

Brown-in-China was an effort on the part of Brown to support a school of Social Science at Shanghai College in China. It was initiated by Daniel H. Kulp in 1921 after he had spent six years at the College. His plan was approved by the president, alumni representatives and the Cammarian Club. Brown assisted in the support of Kulp as a teacher in Shanghai. In 1921-1922 Professor James Q. Dealey spent a semester teaching at Shanghai College, and in 1923-1924 Professor Harold S. Bucklin spent a year there, while Kulp spent the year at Brown, teaching and studying. A pamphlet prepared by Bucklin, "A Social Survey of Sung-ka-Hong," was printed in both English and Chinese. The Department of Sociology of Shanghai College started the Yangtzepoo Social Center with Kulp as director in the factory district of Shanghai. The self-supporting center had a budget of $20,000 and a staff of three Americans and thirteen Chinese workers. Herbert D. Lamson joined the Brown-in-China effort in social work and teaching in Shanghai in 1926, but returned in the spring of 1927 because of unsettled conditions in China.

1914 年，浸会大学（1915 年改名为沪江大学）创办了中国最早的社会学系。然而，所谓的社会学系，其实只设有一门社会学课程，由美国布朗大学毕业生，年轻的葛学溥讲授（阎明,2010)。在教授"社会调查"课程的过程中,葛学溥指导学生在杨树浦地区的东部搜集有关住房、人口、工业、教育等方面的资料,并制成图表,这是在中国大学实施较早的社会调查。葛学溥于同年在沪江大学校内组织了"沪江社会服务团",附设八个小组,开展面向贫民的社会服务工作,这八个组包括乡村组、学生福利组、平民教育组、卫生组、娱乐组等。1917年,葛学溥将社会服务范围进一步扩大,在校外设立了一个社区服务中心"杨树浦社区中心"即"沪东公社"。沪东公社提供服务的主要内容是教育,从给工人开设补习班起步发展到开设夜校,学生规模逐渐扩大。除教育外,沪东公社还开办了民众图书馆、民众代笔处、民众食堂和民众茶园、民众同乐会、施诊所等。

1937年"八一三"事变,上海成为抗日前线,战争造成几十万难民流离失所。1938年1月15日,沪东公社接收了复兴收容所,前后总共收容约900位难民。不仅如此,公社还将难民按性别和年龄分组进行识字教育,同时组织难民开展生产活动,1939年5月结束难民所事务。

为了使成年难民获得一技之长,沪东公社还开设了职业培训班。最值得一提的是其高级机械和驾驶班。至1941年12月8日太平洋战争爆发,汽车培训班总共办了8届,共毕业学生260余人,其中大部分转入内地服务运输事业。1952年,全国高等院校进行院系调整,沪江大学撤销,所属各院系并入华东师范大学、复旦大学、上海财经经济学院。

沪东公社首开中国社会工作教育之先河,与燕京大学的北平协和医院社会服务部南北呼应,构成了中国近现代最初的社会工作形态。尽管在创建之初带有浓厚的宗教色彩,但它开展的大众教育、社会改良和慈善救济活动,却无不体现出社会工作的思想。如对弱势群体的关照,建立中国第一家社区服务机构;关注时代问题,不断扩展服务对象与服务领域;实务、专业教育和学术研究"三位一体"共同推进。沪东公社所秉承的价值理念和开展的服务实践,在一定程度上反映了社会工作思想在近代中国的萌芽与发展过程,值得当代学者仔细研究和学习,以汲取历史经验发展当代中国社会工作(李卓等,2017)。

7.1.3 社会工作的发展 Development of Social Work

1. 从志愿性工作到行业性工作的转变
The Transformation from Voluntary Work to Industrial Work

随着工业化的发展,越来越多的农业人口和传统手工业者失去了安身立命之本,贫困与犯罪成为主要的社会问题,只靠志愿服务很难满足社会需求,需要全职受薪工作者来服务社会,他们不仅要理解贫民的处境、更要具有专门的知识,第一个全职社会工作岗位出现在美国环境委员会。1887年,纽约州的布法罗开始使用受过专业训练的人员与案主建立联系。随着行业性社会工作的展开和行业协会的成立,作为行业的社会工作与志愿群体区分开来。

2. 从行业性到专业性的转变 The Transformation from Industry to Specialty

社会问题的加剧使得人们对社会工作的要求越来越高。仅仅依靠志愿者的爱心和善心去解决社会问题,在数量和水准上都远远不够。19世纪20年代,社会工作受到社会学发展的影响，以社会学为基础，以新的视角看待助人活动。

1910年美国哥伦比亚大学和芝加哥大学开设了社会工作相关课程，1912年波士顿大学社会工作学院开设了医疗社会工作课程。这些课程为社会工作从行业性向专业性的转变提供了理论准备和知识储备。

1917年玛丽·里士满（Mary Richmond，1861—1928）出版了《社会诊断》（Social Diagnosis），创立了个案工作的社会诊断模式，界定了社工在个案工作中的职责；标志着社会工作的诞生。理士满被誉为专业社会工作的创始人。

3. 社会工作专业标准的提出

The Development of Professional Standards for Social Work

1915年，美国教育学家亚伯拉罕·弗莱克斯纳（Abraham Flexner，1886—1959）提出了社会工作专业的六条标准：即社会工作的职业活动需建立于智力与个人责任、社会工作的职业训练要以知识而非日常活动为基础、社会工作的实用取向需高于理论取向、社会工作技能是可以被传授的、社会工作职业具有内部组织性、社会工作职业须被利他动机推动。

> Abraham Flexner（1866—1959）was an American educator who concentrated on the medical and scientific fields. He developed his own school focused on preparing students for college and was known for his criticisms of American education：1）professional activity is based on intellectual action along with personal responsibility；2）the practice of a profession is based on knowledge, not routine activities；3）there is practical application rather than just theorizing；4）there are techniques that can be taught 5）a profession is organized internally；6）a profession is motivated by altruism, with members working in some sense for the good of society.

欧内斯特·格林伍德（Ernest Greenwood，1910—2004）于20世纪50年代提出了社会工作专业的五项特质：理论体系系统化、权威性、认可性、伦理性和文化特质。

> Ernest Greenwood was one of the most distinguished faculty members at the UC Berkeley School of Social Welfare.

查尔斯·加文（Charles D. Gavin）于20世纪90年代提出社会工作专业的七条标准：理论体系、知识基础、大学训练、产生收入、对实务活动的专业管理、内在道德或伦理、可观察的结果。

4. 社会工作在中国的发展 The Development of Social Work in China

社会工作是现代社会结构不可或缺的组成部分，是补偿社会变迁损失、修正市场失败、追求社会公平和改善人类福祉的社会机制，其基本功能是通过解决社会问题满足人类需要。

社会工作在中国的发展经历了如下阶段：1949年之前，在大学的社会工作课程与实地调研。1949 年—20 世纪 80 年代中期,靠行政框架解决社会问题的行政性非专业化的社会工作模式。20 世纪 80 年代中期之后,社会工作课程作为应用社会学在一些大学恢复起来。1986 年,国家决定在北京大学等学校设立社会工作与管理专业,之后各大高校纷纷设立社会工作专业。2004 年,《社会工作者国家职业标准》出台。2006 年,《社会工作者职业水平评价暂行规定》和《助理社会工作师、社会工作师职业水平考试实施办法》颁发,社会工作者开始有了独立的职业水平等级和资质证书。《社会工作者职业道德指引》也于 2012 年底正式向社会发布,这被视为社会工作者的行为准则。2006 年,社会工作专业人才培养规划正式纳入国家顶层设计。当年 10 月,中共中央在《关于构建社会主义和谐社会若干重大问题的决定》,首次提出要"建设宏大的社会工作人才队伍"。2010 年 4 月,《国家中长期人才发展规划纲要(2010—2020 年)》正式印发,纲要明确了要加快中国经济社会发展,必须重视和培养六类重点人才,社会工作人才位列其中。2011 年 11 月,中央 18 个部委联合印发《关于加强社会工作专业人才队伍建设的意见》,2012 年 3 月,中央 19 个部门和组织和群团组织联合发布《社会工作专业人才队伍建设中长期规划(2011—2020 年)》,对社会工作专业人才的教育、培训、评价、使用、激励等提出了具体要求。2015 年,中国社会工作学会成立,会员由来自社会工作专业教育研究、社会工作行政管理、社会工作实务及关心、支持社会工作事业发展的组织和个人组成。

改革开放以来中国社会进入结构转型期,整个社会发生了翻天覆地的变化。在人们享受改革开放成果的同时,也不得不面对社会问题丛生、越轨行为屡见不鲜的现实,这为社会工作的发展提供了千载难逢的机遇;同时也对社会工作者提出了巨大挑战。随着经济发展与社会转型,中国人民的生活方式也发生了重大变化,消费文化和娱乐文化发生了很大改变。社会工作如何解决社会问题、满足群体基本需要? 这些都是摆在社会工作者面前的紧迫问题。

学者们对社会工作在中国的发展历程进行了梳理,既提炼出优势也指出了不足:如服务领域"冷热不均",受益群体覆盖不均衡、不充分;服务地区"梯度差异"显著,中西部贫困地区服务缺口大;本土实务经验不足,欠缺与传统工作方法的对话与糅合;行业发展尚欠规范,专业督导与项目评估亟待加强(魏爽,2020)。

7.2 社会工作的价值观 Values of Social Work

社会工作是"满载价值"的专业,可以说是在所有助人专业中,最具价值取向的专业。

7.2.1 社会工作的价值与伦理思想的演进
The Value of Social Work and the Evolution of Ethical Thought

在整个社会工作的发展历史中,它的基本使命是追求社会正义、采取集体主义思想,主张社会中的个人对他人负有责任。社会工作的价值基础内涵了社会工作对社会正义、社会公平的持久承诺,但这并不意味着社会工作的价值取向就只有一种。随着社会工作发展环境的改变,社会工作的价值观也在不断地转变。迄今为止,已有六种不同的价值取向发展出来,其存在的时间长短也各有不同:家长式取向(the paternalistic orientation)、社会正义取向(the social justice orientation)、宗教取向(the religious orientation)、临床取向(the clinical orientation)、专业自我保卫取向(the self-defensive orientation)、中立取向(the neutral orientation)。虽然这六种取向在概念上是不同的,但是它们并不一定互相排斥。换句话说,它们可能同时存在于实务工作者的价值观中,并同时存在于社会工作历史发展的不同阶段。

(1)家长式取向。此观点主要是存在于19世纪末至20世纪初,当友善访问与慈善组织会社开始兴起之时,人们普遍认为饥饿、贫穷、失业等问题的根源在于个人的道德缺陷,因此,要真正解决这些问题,必须提高个人的道德品质。社会工作专业的使命也在于提升案主的正直品格,帮助他们运用自己的内在能力去过有意义的生活,而不是依赖政府或民间的财政帮助。

> According to Stanford Encyclopedia of Philosophy, paternalism is the interference of a state or an individual with another person, against their will, and defended or motivated by a claim that the person interfered with will be better off or protected from harm. It is action that limits a person's or group's liberty or autonomy in order to promote their own good.

(2)社会正义取向。根据此观点,贫穷、失业、犯罪以及一些精神疾病,往往与个人的人格、道德上的缺陷无关,而是源于社会结构的问题。因此,要解决这些问题,必须经过基本的社会改革。例如:对妇女与弱势团体的补偿政策、机会平等、财富再分配、人道的社会福利给付服务等。"睦邻组织运动""新政""与贫穷作战""大社会"等的政策都可反映出此观点。

> Social justice refers to the fair distribution of wealth, opportunities, and privileges within a society. It refers to the view that everyone deserves equal economic, political and social rights and opportunities. Social workers aim to open the doors of access and opportunity for everyone, particularly those in greatest need.

(3)宗教取向。宗教取向包含了家长式与社会正义取向的特质。此观点主张专业的中心任务是将自己的宗教信仰转变成有意义的社会服务。

(4)临床取向。近年来在个案工作中伦理两难的议题已逐渐受到重视,这也反映出临床取向对于社会工作价值的观点。此现象尤其自20世纪70年代末期开始已成为当代专业伦理潮流的一部分。此派讨论的议题包括案主保密的责任、知后同意、父权主义、利益的冲突、揭发机构或专业内部的不当行为、守法与遵守机构的规章等。部分因为社会工作一直关切案主价值与工作者价值观的关系,故此派取向强调价值冲突与伦理两难的议题。

（5）专业自我保卫取向。此派是现阶段社会工作伦理与价值中重要的一部分。与临床取向相比，临床取向着重于案主利益（包括个人、家庭、小团体、社区及社会）的社会工作伦理，而此派关切对实务工作者的保护。其基本关切议题是有关于对于各种类型的过失或不当治疗的辩述以及最主要的是有关专业人员应负责任的议题与逐渐升高的法律诉讼风险等。

（6）中立取向。此派的特征是强调价值中立，将实务工作视为纯技术性的。例如在 20 世纪 20 年代"精神医学"洪流时期的实务工作者，他们避免运用有关于价值或伦理的概念，而运用心理动力的专用术语来厘清人类行为的奥秘。另外，诸如心理治疗技术、方案评估、成本效益分析等也可归类于此种取向。然而，这个取向并非是价值中立的，只是其价值基础隐而不显罢了。

> The concept of value-neutrality was proposed by Max Weber. It refers to the duty and responsibility of the social researcher to overcome his personal biases while conducting any research. It aims to separate fact and emotion and stigmatize people less. It is not only important in sociology but outlines the basic ethics of many disciplines.

7.2.2　社会工作的理念 The Idea of Social Work

一般社会工作的理念可以说与积极性的"人道主义"（humanitarianism）紧密关联。人道主义哲学有三个基本假设：第一是对人的尊重；第二是相信每个人都是独特的；第三是坚信人有自我改变、成长和不断进步的能力。

> According to Cambridge Dictionary, humanitarianism is a belief in improving people's lives and reducing suffering. Humanitarianism is based on a view that all human beings deserve respect and dignity and should be treated as such. Therefore, humanitarians work towards advancing the well-being of humanity as a whole.

若将此价值信念运用于社会工作实务当中，便会形成如下一些实践准则：①接纳他人，即积极地了解别人独特之处，并设身处地地考虑别人的需要；②非评判的态度，即不以自己的意见去评判别人，但也不是道德观念上的模棱两可，而是尽力去理解别人做事的背后的理由和原因；③个别化，即不能千篇一律地去看别人的遭遇和问题，也不能凡事只有一种解决的办法；④保密原则；⑤案主自决原则，即鼓励案主承担责任。上述信念和原则都是经过长期实践总结出来的，因而是所有社会工作实务领域都应当遵循的基本理念（fundamental philosophy）。

积极的"人道主义"哲理及其实践原则，其核心在于尊重人，深信人性具有高度的可塑性和丰富的潜能。因此，社会工作的基本目标或本质不是为案主提供福利服务或直接替代案主解决问题，而是助人自助，即协助社会功能失调的案主，通过发挥其潜能，改善其生活与增进其幸福。为案主提供福利服务或直接替代案主解决问题,只能一时缓解案主的问题,而不能从根本上解决问题;而且这种解决问题的方式会使案主产生依赖心理,并损害其自尊与自助的能力。当然,帮助案主解决一些实际问题,有时也是取得案主信任的必要手段和步骤。

7.2.3 社会工作的使命和核心价值 The Mission and Core Values of Social Work

The NASW (National Association of Social Workers) Code of Ethics is a guide for the day-to-day conduct of a social worker. The NASW Delegate Assembly set up the first version in 1960. It has been revised several times but much of it remains as originally written. The moral framework is based on these social work core values:

Service, Integrity, Social justice, Competence. The importance of human relationships, Dignity and worth of the client. The code of ethics clearly defines laws, regulations and policies for people in the field to follow, and to hold them accountable if the rules are broken.

The code serves six purposes:

Provides core values upon which the social work occupation is based.

Creates distinct ethical standards that should direct social work practices and represent the core values.

Guides social workers in their professional considerations and obligations when ethical uncertainties occur.

Provides ethical standards to which the social work profession can be held liable.

Establishes the profession's mission, values and ethical principles and standards for new social workers.

Makes standards by which the social work profession can assess if a social worker has engaged in unethical practices. Social workers who pledge to abide by this code must comply with its provisions and disciplinary rulings.

The NASW promotes these ethical objectives for social workers to consider and practice. That said, social work research, policies and agency regulations should be used at all times.

美国社会工作者协会成立于 1919 年,并于 1958 年发展出了社会工作最初的价值体系。1960 年,美国社会工作者协会通过了第一个社会工作人员伦理守则。1960—2008 年,该守则共历经五次修改。

社会工作专业的使命立基于一组核心价值。这些伴随社会工作走过专业历史的核心价值是社会工作独特的目标与远景的基础。其核心价值主要涉及服务社会主义、个人尊严与价值、人际关系的重要性、廉正和能力。核心价值和由此衍生出的原则必须配合不同的人类社会环境及其复杂性而定。

7.2.4　社会工作价值的本质 The Nature of Social Work Values

虽然我们都认为社会工作包含了价值观、知识体系以及专业技巧,同时也认定价值是非常重要的,但是大部分的研究都集中于知识与技巧层面,少有研究是探讨实务中价值观的运用问题。理论界或课程设计者也未深入地关切这个主题。过去社会工作者坚守社会工作价值,但是并没有加以实际运用与发展。我们似乎只是凭直觉固守社会工作价值,表明自己是人道主义的象征,但我们尚未严肃地将社会工作价值视为此专业的重要支柱。

社会工作价值是该专业中最重要的一部分。在社会工作中,价值观在以下几个方面扮演了关键的角色:社会工作使命的本质;社会工作者与案主的关系、与同事的关系、与社会的关系;社会工作者服务方法的运用;实务工作中伦理两难的解决。

社会工作价值是社会性的。社会工作价值并非仅仅是一些信念和口号,而是包含了社会工作对弱势族群的深切关注,以及对社会公平与社会正义的持久承诺。

社会工作价值是信念但更是行动。对社会工作价值的熟悉当然是重要的,毕竟,实务工作者对于社会工作价值的信念与支持能够给予其一种激励,使其维持有意义的专业生涯。

7.3　社会工作的知识体系 The Body of Knowledge in Social Work

社会工作专业必须发展其知识基础。社会工作的知识基础包括:①社会工作者关于自我、专业和干预的知识;②社会工作者关于案主的知识;③社会工作者关于案主问题或改变领域的知识;④社会工作者关于社会和文化环境的知识。

美国社会工作者协会把社会工作的典型知识定为:①人类行为和整体环境的知识;②心理学的知识;③人类沟通方式的知识;④群体过程和群体与个体相互影响的知识;⑤文化遗产,包括宗教信仰、精神价值、法律和其他社会制度对个人、群体和社区的意义及影响的知识;⑥社区发展与变迁的知识;⑦社会服务和社会资源的知识;⑧自我概念和专业自觉的知识。

社会工作的知识体系通常由四类知识所组成:①通识知识,包括社会科学与人文科学的知识,如社会学、政治学、经济学、法学、史学、哲学、人类学等。②人类行为的知识,包括人的情绪、认知、行为、发展等知识。人的行为不是个体的行为,包括人与人的互动,以及人与社会的互动。③实施理论。这是社会工作实务发展出来的理论,包含社会工作助人行动的本质、助人的过程、干预的策略等。④特殊人口群的知识。针对不同的服务领域与对象,如儿童、少年、身心障碍者、老人、女性、成人、原住民、流动人口、穷人、犯罪者、娼妓、艾滋病人、吸毒者等的了解,包括这些人的特性,以及部门的特性。

上述这些知识主要来自以下独立学科或研究领域:①社会学。社会学为社会工作提供了广泛的知识基础。②心理学。心理学对于社会工作的影响可以归结为对于心理层面的重视。③人类学。

7.4 社会工作的专业方法 Professional Approaches to Social Work

社会工作者对于社会工作是一种专业性服务要有充分认识。今天我们遭遇的问题,不是仅靠爱心、热心及慈悲就能解决的,而是必须接受社会工作专业教育和训练,具备社会工作专业技能后才能解决的。

迄今为止的社会工作历史,直接社会工作方法,尤其是社会个案工作占有长期的发展优势。这种历史传统让社会工作从业者普遍相信,直接工作方法尤其是个案工作方法是实务的真正源泉,直接服务方面的训练与经验是从事间接服务工作(包括社会工作行政)的必要条件和可靠基础。

7.4.1 个案工作方法 Social Case Work

Social case work is a primary method of professional social work. It is concerned with the adjustment & development of individuals towards more satisfying relations in different situations. It follows a systematic approach to studying & diagnosing the client's problem. It aims to find individual solutions to clients' problems. The focus of social case work is on an individual. Social case work is also an art of helping individuals to work out better social relationship and adjustment, it is a way of helping individual to use their own resources both material and psychological for the treatment and prevention of personal and social problems.

个案工作方法是社会工作实务三大主要方法之一,也是最早发展的社会工作方法。所谓个案工作方法就是由专业社会工作者运用有关人与社会的专业知识和技巧,为个人和家庭提供解决物质和情感方面的问题的支持和服务,目的在于帮助个人和家庭减轻压力、解决问题,达到个人和社会的良好福利状态。

1. 个案工作的性质和目的 Nature and Purpose of Social Casework

个案工作是一个助人自助的过程。个案工作不是直接替代案主解决问题,直接替代案主解决问题往往只能达到一时的缓解而不能从根本上消除问题产生的根源。而且,这种解决问题的方式可能会使案主产生依赖心理,并损害其自助的能力。

个案工作的目的可以从社会和个人两个层面去理解。在社会层面,积极的目的是在社会公平和正义的前提下,保障每一个社会个体的尊严和权利。消极的目的,则在于减轻或遏止因个人或家庭功能失调而引起的社会问题,维持社会的安定和发展。

在个人层面,个案工作的目的是帮助每一位受助者了解和接纳本身的长处和短处,促进他们解决问题的能力和决心,使其有效地适应社会环境和满足自己的期望,从而进一步发挥潜能,建立信心,过上有意义和有满足感的生活。

2. 个案工作专业关系 Casework Professional Relations

个案工作是以心灵影响心灵的工作。根据个案工作学者的研究,一个有意义有效果的个案工作关系,应包括下列特质:①助人关系应是双方的关系,需要社会工作者与受助者两方面的投入和配合;②助人关系只有单一的目标,就是帮助受助者解决问题,提高解决问题的能力,进而充分发挥其潜能;③助人关系除了基于专业的理论和知识外,也包括人与人之间的情感的交流;④助人关系不一定总是愉快和轻松的;⑤助人关系是包容和不批判的;⑥助人关系必须为受助者提供真正的选择。

3. 个案工作过程 Social Casework Process

个案工作过程是一个有计划、有方向、有步骤的解决问题的过程。个案工作的过程一般分为六个步骤:

(1)接案阶段(intake phase)。当一个人或个别家庭遇到困难或问题时,凭自己的能力不能解决,便需要外力来做出帮助。受助者有些是自己主动求助,有些是由别人或其他机构转介而来。当个人或家庭向机构求助时,个案工作员通常会立刻会见求助者,一方面了解其需求、需要和具体问题,另一方面则向受助者介绍机构服务的范围和权责以及个案工作的方式、方法和内容,包括对受助者的要求。接案阶段也是社会工作者与受助者建立初步关系的过程。

Intake is an administrative procedure to take in the person with problem, admit or enroll the person as a client of the agency. After this phase the case worker is able to asses the needs and problems of applicant person and how and where his needs can be best met.

(2)研究阶段(study phase)。接案完成后,受助者的个案便正式开展。资料搜集阶段主要的工作就是探讨问题和搜集主、客观资料,主要途径包括与案主面对面会谈、与案主重要关系人的面谈以及查阅文献等。

Study is a methodical examination of the client and his or her circumstances in relation to the client's condition. According to Mary Richmond, in social studies, the caseworker must secure all facts through logical and inferential reasoning in order to uncover the client's personality and the circumstance for effective action (treatment).

(3)分析与诊断阶段(assessment/diagnosis phase)。一般来说,诊断的目的和内容包括:第一,分析和评估案主面对问题的实际情况、问题的成因和症结以及问题对案主和身边有关人士的影响;第二,分析和评估案主的心理状况、思想与行为、人际关系和身处的境况;第三,评估案主本身的限制、长处和潜质;第四,评估环境因素的阻力和助力。

(4)制订服务计划阶段(treatment plan phase)。服务计划的制订,以个案分析和诊断为依据。计划首先须订出明确的目标,通常分为远期和近期目标。服务目标确定后,便可以开始设计服务或治疗的方法和步骤。

The Treatment Plan Phase is the main part of social case work with different steps and techniques. The case worker should plan about the treatment in different way thoroughly. The treatment plan is different in different case works according to the change of the client, problem, situation etc. But every social case work is done through the same methods. The focus in treatment should be given to the immediate problems. Total social casework process includes three stages or three phases they are the beginning, middle and ending. While treatment or intervention process different techniques are used for the identification and eradication of their problems.

（5）个案介入阶段（intervention phase）。这是个案工作过程中最主要的环节，前面讨论的各个步骤，都是为这一阶段所做的准备工作。个案介入的方式多种多样，可以是支持和鼓励、资讯和意见的提供、观念的澄清，也可以是行为的改变、环境的改善，乃至直接的干预等。

Intervention is to relieve the client's suffering and to restore, maintain, or improve an individual's social functioning who is in need of assistance. Its purpose is to is to improve the client's comfort, satisfaction, and self-awareness. This may necessitate improving the ego's adaptive capacities and the functioning of the person-situation system.

（6）结案与评估阶段（termination/evaluation phase）。这是个案工作过程中最后的阶段。社会工作者需要做三方面的工作：第一，帮助案主接纳结案的事实，处理离别情绪；第二，帮助案主回顾整个个案的过程；第三，对整个个案作整体评估。

Termination refers to the completion of the procedure. Termination occurs when the procedure is finished or when the worker lacks faith in the client's ability to deal with current and emerging issues. In social casework practice, evaluation gives critical input to both the caseworker and the client on whether the intervention program is succeeding as intended.

需要指出的是，以上所描述的个案工作过程和步骤，只是概念上的划分，实际的工作过程其实十分复杂，并不必然按照上述顺序进行，需要灵活运用。

7.4.2 小组工作方法 Social Group Work

Social group in the ordinary sense means that any collection of more than one individual, but sociologically it is a collection of individuals interacting with each other under a recognized structure. A social group is always motivated by some common goals and interests, characterized by some rules and regulations. Social group work is a method of social work that helps persons to enhance their social functioning through purposeful group experiences and to cope more effectively than when done individually with their personal, group or community problems.

小组工作方法是通过有意图性的小组经验来提高个人的社会运作功能，使他能更好地处理个人、群体及社区的问题。小组社会工作方法强调小组过程及小组动力去影响服务对象的态度和行为。小组成员解决问题的能力和潜力是通过成员间的分享、相互分担和相互支持而发挥出来。

1. 小组工作的性质和目标 Nature and Objective of Social Group Work

小组工作是通过专业的小组工作人员创设需要的社会团体，并运用专业知识与技术指导团体活动，以实现发展性、治疗性和社会行动目标。所谓治疗性目标，就是矫正不恰当的人格、行为和态度，提供解决特定问题的信息和途径，恢复与发展个人的社会功能；所谓发展性目标，是指提供社交和娱乐的机会，促进个人的社会化和全面发展；所谓社会行动目标，就是通过团体实现特定的社会目标。

2. 小组工作的原则 Principles of Social Group Work

（1）按计划形成小组原则（the principle of planned group formation）。

（2）小组目标明确化的原则（the principle of specific objectives）。小组都有其本身的目标，小组目标一般在设立小组前就已确定，但也经常会随小组的发展而改变。

（3）引导小组互动的原则（the principle of guided group interaction）。促使小组以及小组成员变化的主要动力来自于成员间的交互反应或互动。

（4）小组民主自决的原则（the principle of democratic group self determination）。在小组工作中，小组有最大的权利来决定小组活动，小组工作者应尊重小组的决定。

（5）运用社会资源的原则（the principle of resource utilization）。小组工作者应运用其对机构的了解以及对社区资源的丰富知识，协助小组有效地利用外部资源。

（6）评估的原则（the principle of evaluation）。在小组工作中，对过程、方案与结果进行持续的评估是非常重要的。

3. 小组工作的过程 Procedure of Social Group Work

（1）小组形成期（the forming stage）。在这个时期，小组成员开始产生角色意识，他们发现了自己的角色以及自己与他人的关系，弄清了小组目标和参与小组的方向，并开始对领导者或其他成员产生依赖感。

（2）风暴期（the storming stage）。这是团体的分化和再组时期。小组可能因冲突而分化，小组工作者应冷静面对，采取适当的干预策略。

（3）成就期（the performing stage）。小组经过分化、冲突而趋于整合。小组的目标变得明晰起来，并逐步得到实现。

（4）结案（the adjourning stage）。结案分成结案前的准备与结案后的追踪。在小组结案前，小组工作者应适时提醒小组成员做好分离的准备，并进行回顾与评估工作。

7.4.3　社区工作方法 Social Community Work

社区工作是社会工作的方法之一，是以社区为对象的社会工作介入方法。它通过组织社区内居民参与集体行动，去厘定社区需要，合力解决社区问题，改善生活环境及素质；在参与过程中，让居民建立对社区的归属感，培养自助、互助及自决的精神；加强市民的社会参与及影响决策的能力和意识，发挥居民的潜能，培养社区领袖才能，以达致更公平、公义、民主及和谐的社会。

1. 社区工作的性质与目标 The Nature and Objectives of Community Work

社区工作主要的核心是通过发动社区居民的参与，来改变社区层面的现状。其中社区资源的整合、社区居民在参与中自主能力的提升，对于社区归属感的培养，都是社区工作的重要元素。

Community organization or Community Based Organization refers to organization aimed at making desired improvements to a community's social health, well-being, and overall functioning. Community organization occurs in geographically, psychosocially, culturally, spiritually, and digitally bounded communities. Community organization includes community work, community projects, community development, community empowerment, community building, and community mobilization. It is a commonly used model for organizing community within community projects, neighborhoods, organizations, voluntary associations, localities, and social networks, which may operate as ways to mobilize around geography, shared space, shared experience, interest, need, and/or concern.

社区工作的目标可以分为两个层面：任务目标和过程目标。所谓任务目标，就是通过居民参与集体行动，影响政府的决策及社区资源的运用，改善社区设施及服务，解决社区问题。所谓过程目标，就是着重人的发展，通过共同工作，发展居民间的相互关心和合作态度，培养居民解决社区问题的信心和能力。

2. 社区工作的价值观与实践原则

Values and Practical Principles of Community Organization

（1）社区工作的价值观。社区工作价值观是社区工作实践的灵魂和方向，是发生争论时的判别标准，也是社区工作者投身社区工作的主要动力。

社区工作的价值观主要体现为：

具体目标原则（the principle of specific objectives）。

人的尊严原则（the principle of human dignity）。

社会正义原则（the principle of social justice）。

文化取向原则（the principle of cultural orientation）

民主原则（the principle of democracy）。

群众参与原则（the principle of people's participation）。

互助互动原则（the principle of inter-group approach）。

社会责任原则（the principle of social responsibility）。

（2）社区工作的实践原则（the Practical Principles of Community Work）。

社区工作的实践原则是根据社区工作的价值观制订出来的，是社区工作者在推行工作时所需要遵守的工作准则。社区工作的实践原则具体包括注重以人为中心的发展目标；根据社区的实际情况计划工作步伐；尊重社区自决；强调居民的自助参与；广泛及包容性的社区参与；民主及理性的社区行动方式。

3. 社区工作过程 The Process of Community Work

（1）建立专业关系。社区工作者建立专业关系一般从拜访社区重要人士与社区发展机构入手。

（2）搜集与社区生活有关的资料。社区工作者要了解的情况主要是三个方面，即社区生活、社区需求与社区资源。

（3）制定社区发展计划。社区发展计划根据对象与范围的大小，又可分为通盘规划与具体方案两种。

（4）采取社区行动。社区行动是事实社区计划的过程，包括会议、协调、财政、宣传等方面。

（5）成效评估。社区工作的评估应注意评估方法的科学性、评估主体的多元性以及评估内容的全面性。

以上简要分析了社会工作三大直接服务方法，也是社会工作中三种最重要的方法。实际上，社会工作专业方法还有很多，如社会工作行政、社会工作督导、社会工作咨询、社会工作研究等，限于篇幅，这里就不详细介绍了。

延伸阅读 Further Reading

思考 Thinking it through：

如何理解社会工作的价值观？

Six Core Social Work Values and Ethics

Every day，social workers stand up for human rights and justice and give voice to unheard and marginalized populations. They contribute to bettering individuals' lives，and by doing so，they improve society as a whole. Social workers are employed by nonprofits，the government，and private practices.

There were 713,200 social workers nationwide as of 2019，according to the U.S. Bureau of Labor Statistics，and that number is expected to increase by 13 percent between 2019 and 2029. Each of those social workers，regardless of the setting in which they choose to provide services，must adhere to the professional code of ethics established in 1996 by the National Association of Social Workers（NASW）Delegate Assembly and revised in 2017.

The NASW Code of Ethics "is intended to serve as a guide to the everyday professional conduct of social workers"，according to the NASW website. It outlines six ethical principles that "set forth ideals to which all social workers should aspire." This article will explore the six social work core values，which comprise：

Service

Social justice

Dignity and worth of the person

Importance of human relationships

Integrity

Competence

Professionals working as social workers understand the importance of these values. Individuals who are interested in pursuing a career in social work can earn an advanced degree，such as Tulane University's Online Master of Social Work，to prepare for the role，including learning more about social work values.

Six Ethical Principles of Social Work

Social workers devote themselves to serving their communities. They advocate for human rights through the following six social work core values：

1. Service

Empowering individuals，families，and communities is a primary goal of all social workers. Service is the value from which all other social work values stem. Social workers regularly elevate the needs of their communities above their own personal interests and use their skills and knowledge (from education and experience) to enhance the wellbeing of others. In addition，social workers often volunteer their time or expertise above and beyond their professional commitments.

For example，during the COVID-19 pandemic，many social workers coordinated mutual aid，community meals，and PPE drives.

2. Social Justice

Social workers advocate on behalf of the oppressed，the marginalized，and anyone who needs their voice amplified. They often focus on issues such as poverty，homelessness，discrimination，harassment，and other forms of injustice. Social workers provide information，help，and other resources to people seeking equality，and they educate people who may not directly experience discrimination about the struggles of others who may not have the same level of privileges in our society.

Social workers' efforts to address injustices includes examining their own biases and encouraging others to do the same. They work to create more equitable support systems and identify structural conditions that contribute to disparities in the health and well-being of individuals and communities.

3. Dignity and Worth of the Person

Social workers are mindful of individual differences in thinking and behavior，as well as cultural and ethnic diversity. Only by treating each person with dignity and respect can social workers promote their clients' capacity and opportunity to address their own needs and improve their personal situations. Social workers must be cognizant of their duties to both individual clients and to society as a whole，and seek solutions for their clients that also support society's broader interests.

Social workers seek to eliminate factors that threaten the dignity and worth of individuals，but they do so with a decentered approach that respects differences and honors self-determination. Rather than imposing their own values，social workers leverage the values of their clients and the communities they serve.

4. Importance of Human Relationships

Social workers connect people who need assistance with organizations and individuals who can provide the appropriate help. Social workers recognize that facilitating human relationships can be a useful vehicle for creating change，and they excel at engaging potential partners who can create, maintain, and enhance the well-being of families, neighborhoods, and whole communities.

Challenging social conditions, such as those created by the COVID-19 pandemic, highlight the essential role of human relationships in supporting health and healing. Social workers not only build and maintain strong relationships with individuals and communities, they also help their clients identify relationships that are helpful to them and let go of relationships that are not.

5. Integrity

To facilitate these relationships and empower others to improve their lives, social workers must act in a way that engenders trust. Each social worker must be continually aware of the profession's mission, values, and ethical principles and standards, and set a good example of these components for their clients. By behaving honestly and demonstrating personal integrity, social workers can promote the organizations with which they are affiliated while also creating the most value for the populations they serve.

One relevant trend in social work is the profession's use of and interest in social media. A study published by *Social Sciences & Humanities Open in* 2020 reports that the social work profession seeks to "regard data privacy protection as a human and civil rights issue" and "support inclusion of social media information in social work."

6. Competence

Professional social workers often hold undergraduate or graduate degrees in social work, but a fair amount of their knowledge comes from gaining on-the-job experience. As part of the social work values outlined in the NASW Code of Ethics, each social worker must practice within their scope of competence and avoid misrepresenting skills or experience to potential clients.

Social workers must constantly strive to expand their knowledge base and competence in order to make meaningful contributions to the profession and those they serve. Social work is a lifelong learning commitment, and continuing education can take the form of any activity that expands a social worker' knowledge and skill set: conducting personal study and research, attending webinars and conferences, or pursuing additional licenses or degrees.

Pursue a Career in Social Work

Ethics and values in social work encompass far more than compliance with regulations and requirements. The core beliefs that guide social workers ensure that while they work on behalf of their clients, they also work with clients, constantly learning as they empower others.

Whether you're new to the field of social work or a practicing professional looking to expand your knowledge and career options，Tulane University's Online Master of Social Work program can teach you the skills you need to enhance human well-being and provide basic human needs for all individuals and communities. Visit the Online Master of Social Work program to learn more about a curriculum that serves clients within their environments and builds upon individual and community strengths.

（Reference：www.socialwork.tulane.edu）

8　当代社会问题
Contemporary Social Problems

Understanding Social Problems（Excerpt）

As we move well into the second decade of the twenty-first century，the United States and the rest of the world face many social problems：poverty and hunger，racism and sexism，drug use and violence，and climate change，to name just a few. Why do these problems exist? What are their effects? What can be done about them?

This first chapter begins our journey into the world of social problems by examining how sociology understands social problems and gathers research about them.

Define "Social Problem"

A social problem is any condition or behavior that has negative consequences for large numbers of people and that is generally recognized as a condition or behavior that needs to be addressed. This definition has both an objective component and a subjective component. The objective component involves empirical evidence of the negative consequences of a social condition or behavior，while the subjective component involves the perception that the condition or behavior is indeed a problem that needs to be addressed.

The Natural History of a Social Problem

We have just discussed some of the difficulties in defining a social problem and the fact that various parties often try to influence public perceptions of social problems. These issues aside，most social problems go through a natural history consisting of several stages of their development.

Stage 1：Emergence and Claims Making

A social problem emerges when a social entity（such as a social change group，the news media，or influential politicians）begins to call attention to a condition or behavior that it perceives to be undesirable and in need of remedy. As part of this process，it tries to influence public perceptions of the problem，the reasons for it，and possible solutions to it.

Stage 2: Legitimacy

Once a social group succeeds in turning a condition or behavior into a social problem, it usually tries to persuade the government (local, state, and/or federal) to take some action—spending and policymaking—to address the problem. As part of this effort, it tries to convince the government that its claims about the problem are legitimate—that they make sense and are supported by empirical (research-based) evidence. To the extent that the group succeeds in convincing the government of the legitimacy of its claims, government action is that much more likely to occur.

Stage 3: Renewed Claims Making

Even if government action does occur, social change groups often conclude that the action is too limited in goals or scope to be able to successfully address the social problem. If they reach this conclusion, they often decide to press their demands anew. They do so by reasserting their claims and by criticizing the official response they have received from the government or other established interests, such as big businesses. This stage may involve a fair amount of tension between the social change groups and these targets of their claims.

Stage 4: Development of Alternative Strategies

Despite the renewed claims making, social change groups often conclude that the government and established interests are not responding adequately to their claims. Although the groups may continue to press their claims, they nonetheless realize that these claims may fail to win an adequate response from established interests. This realization leads them to develop their own strategies for addressing the social problem.

Theoretical Perspectives

Three theoretical perspectives guide sociological thinking on social problems: functionalist theory, conflict theory, and symbolic interactionist theory. These perspectives look at the same social problems, but they do so in different ways. Their views taken together offer a fuller understanding of social problems than any of the views can offer alone.

Functionalism

Functionalism, also known as the functionalist theory or perspective, arose out of two great revolutions of the eighteenth and nineteenth centuries. The first was the French Revolution of 1789, whose intense violence and bloody terror shook Europe to its core. The aristocracy throughout Europe feared that revolution would spread to their own lands, and intellectuals feared that social order was crumbling.

Today's functionalist perspective arises out of Durkheim's work and that of other conservative intellectuals of the nineteenth century. It uses the human body as a model for understanding society.

Functionalism views social problems as arising from society's natural evolution. When a social problem does occur, it might threaten a society's stability, but it does not mean that fundamental flaws in the society exist. Accordingly, gradual social reform should be all that is needed to address the social problem.

Functionalism even suggests that social problems must be functional in some ways for society, because otherwise these problems would not continue. This is certainly a controversial suggestion, but it is true that many social problems do serve important functions for our society. For example, crime is a major social problem, but it is also good for the economy because it creates hundreds of thousands of jobs in law enforcement, courts and corrections, home security, and other sectors of the economy whose major role is to deal with crime. If crime disappeared, many people would be out of work! Similarly, poverty is also a major social problem, but one function that poverty serves is that poor people do jobs that otherwise might not get done because other people would not want to do them. Like crime, poverty also provides employment for people across the nation, such as those who work in social service agencies that help poor people.

Conflict Theory

In many ways, conflict theory is the opposite of functionalism but ironically also grew out of the Industrial Revolution, thanks largely to Karl Marx (1818—1883) and his collaborator, Friedrich Engels (1820—1895).

According to Marx and Engels, every society is divided into two classes based on the ownership of the means of production (tools, factories, and the like). In a capitalist society, the bourgeoisie, or ruling class, owns the means of production, while the proletariat, or working class, does not own the means of production and instead is oppressed and exploited by the bourgeoisie. This difference creates an automatic conflict of interests between the two groups. Simply put, the bourgeoisie is interested in maintaining its position at the top of society, while the proletariat's interest lies in rising up from the bottom and overthrowing the bourgeoisie to create an egalitarian society.

In a capitalist society, Marx and Engels wrote, revolution is inevitable because of structural contradictions arising from the very nature of capitalism. Because profit is the main goal of capitalism, the bourgeoisie's interest lies in maximizing profit. To do so, capitalists try to keep wages as low as possible and to spend as little money as possible on working conditions. This central fact of capitalism, said Marx and Engels, eventually prompts the rise of class consciousness, or an awareness of the reasons for their oppression, among workers. Their class consciousness in turn leads them to revolt against the bourgeoisie to eliminate the oppression and exploitation they suffer.

Marx and Engels' view of conflict arising from unequal positions held by members of society lies at the heart of today's conflict theory. This theory emphasizes that different groups in society have different interests stemming from their different social positions. These different interests in turn lead to different views on important social issues. Some versions of the theory root conflict in divisions based on race and ethnicity, gender, and other such differences, while other versions follow Marx and Engels in seeing conflict arising out of different positions in the economic structure. In general, however, conflict theory emphasizes that the various parts of society contribute to ongoing inequality, whereas functionalist theory, as we have seen, stresses that they contribute to the ongoing stability of society. Thus, while functionalist theory emphasizes the benefits of the various parts of society for ongoing social stability, conflict theory favors social change to reduce inequality.

Symbolic Interactionism

Symbolic interactionism focuses on the interaction of individuals and on how they interpret their interaction. Its roots lie in the work of early 1900s American sociologists, social psychologists, and philosophers who were interested in human consciousness and action. Herbert Blumer, a sociologist at the University of Chicago, built on their writings to develop symbolic interactionism, a term he coined. Drawing on Blumer's work, symbolic interactionists feel that people do not merely learn the roles that society has set out for them; instead, they construct these roles as they interact. As they interact, they negotiate their definitions of the situations in which they find themselves and socially construct the reality of these situations. In doing so, they rely heavily on symbols such as words and gestures to reach a shared understanding of their interaction.

Symbolic interactionism views social problems as arising from the interaction of individuals. This interaction matters in two important respects. First, socially problematic behaviors such as crime and drug use are often learned from our interaction with people who engage in these behaviors; we adopt their attitudes that justify committing these behaviors, and we learn any special techniques that might be needed to commit these behaviors. Second, we also learn our perceptions of a social problem from our interaction with other people, whose perceptions and beliefs influence our own perceptions and beliefs.

Because symbolic interactionism emphasizes the perception of social problems，it is closely aligned with the social constructionist view discussed earlier. Both perspectives emphasize the subjective nature of social problems. By doing so，they remind us that perceptions often matter at least as much as objective reality in determining whether a given condition or behavior rises to the level of a social problem and in the types of possible solutions that various parties might favor for a particular social problem.

Applying the Three Perspectives

To help you further understand the different views of these three theoretical perspectives，let's see what they would probably say about armed robbery，a very serious form of crime，while recognizing that the three perspectives together provide a more comprehensive understanding of armed robbery than any one perspective provides by itself.

A functionalist approach might suggest that armed robbery actually serves positive functions for society，such as the job-creating function mentioned earlier for crime in general. It would still think that efforts should be made to reduce armed robbery，but it would also assume that far-reaching changes in our society would be neither wise nor necessary as part of the effort to reduce crime.

Conflict theory would take a very different approach to understanding armed robbery. It might note that most street criminals are poor and thus emphasize that armed robbery is the result of the despair and frustration of living in poverty and facing a lack of jobs and other opportunities for economic and social success. The roots of street crime，from the perspective of conflict theory，thus lie in society at least as much as they lie in the individuals committing such crime. To reduce armed robbery and other street crime，conflict theory would advocate far-reaching changes in the economic structure of society.

For its part，symbolic interactionism would focus on how armed robbers make such decisions as when and where to rob someone and on how their interactions with other criminals reinforce their own criminal tendencies. It would also investigate how victims of armed robbery behave when confronted by a robber. To reduce armed robbery，it would advocate programs that reduce the opportunities for interaction among potential criminal offenders，for example，after-school programs that keep at-risk youths busy in "conventional" activities so that they have less time to spend with youths who might help them get into trouble.

（Reference：saylordotorg.github.io/text_social-problems-continuity-and-change/s04-understanding-social-problems.html）

8.1 生态问题 Ecological Problem

社会问题(social problems)是社会学的研究领域之一。随着社会发展,各类社会问题层出不穷,社会学家们也因此越来越重视对社会问题的分析。社会问题是对社会生活正常秩序的极大挑战。本章将着重讨论生态问题、社会保障问题、贫困问题、家庭问题和恐怖主义。

21 世纪人类面临着诸多挑战,其中生态环境问题就是一个主要挑战。由于生态环境问题对人类生存和发展构成了广泛和严重的威胁,因而引起了国际社会广泛的关注。当前国际上关于生态安全或者环境安全的讨论也越来越多。

8.1.1 对生态系统的界定 Defining Ecosystem

生态系统(ecosystem)是由生物群落及其生存环境共同组成的动态平衡系统(homeostat)。生物群落(biocenosis)由存在于自然界一定范围或区域内并互相依存的一定种类的动物、植物、微生物组成。生物群落内不同生物种群的生存环境包括非生物环境(abiotic environment)和生物环境(biotic environment)。非生物环境又称无机环境(inorganic environment),如各种化学物质、气候因素等;生物环境又称有机环境(organic environment),如不同种群的生物。生物群落同其生存环境之间以及生物群落内不同种群生物之间不断进行着物质交换(exchange of substance)和能量流动(energy flow),并处于互相作用和互相影响的动态平衡(dynamic equilibrium)之中。这样构成的动态平衡系统就是生态系统。它是生态学(ecology)研究的基本单位,也是环境生物学研究的核心问题。

生态系统一词,最早于 1935 年由英国的生物学家亚瑟·坦斯利(Arthur Tansley,1871—1955)提出。

Arthur Tansley was an English botanist and a pioneer in the science of ecology. He is best known for coining the term ecosystem. Educated at Highgate School, University College London and Trinity College, Cambridge, Tansley taught at these universities and at Oxford, where he served as Professor of Botany until his retirement in 1937. Tansley was a pioneer of the science of ecology in Britain and introduced the concept of the ecosystem into biology. Tansley was a founding member of the first professional society of ecologists, the Central Committee for the Survey and Study of British Vegetation, which later organized the British Ecological Society, and served as its first president and founding editor of *the Journal of Ecology*.

1871 年,亚瑟·坦斯利出生在英国,他在儿时就表现出对植物学的浓厚兴趣,后来顺利进入剑桥大学攻读植物学和动物学。在其职业生涯早期,坦斯利曾前往埃及、马来西亚、斯里兰卡等多个国家研究植物。1935 年,坦斯利在《生态学杂志》发表论文,正式提出"生态系统"理念。在论文里,坦斯利创造了"生态系统"一词,指的是在一定的空间内,生物成分和非生物成分通过物质循环和能量流动互相作用、互相依存而构成的一个生态学功能单位;这个单位是由物理因子与生物所构成的整个环境。亚瑟·坦斯利认为,若想了解一种植物,必须同时了解植物周围的土壤、气候以及动植物生存状态。坦斯利认为地球生态环境是一个微妙平衡的系统;他意识到:虽然大自然形成一个生态系统需要若干年,但是食物链中除去任意一种物种,都会立刻打破自然循环的层级结构,并且将摧毁整个生态系统。从 1907 年任剑桥大学植物学讲师到创办期刊《新植物学家》并担当主编,再到成为英国生态学会主席和《生态学杂志》主编,坦斯利走到哪里,都在传播生态环境的观念。

But the fundmental conception is, as it seems to me, the whole *system* (in the sense of physics), including not only the organism-complex, but also the while complex of physical factors forming what we call the environment, with which they form one physical system. ... These *ecosystems*, as we may call them, are of the most various kinds and sizes. They form one category of the multitudinous physical systems of the universe, which range from the universe as a whole down to the atom. (Tansley, 1935:299)

生态系统在一定的时间和空间范围内,生物群落与非生物环境通过能量流动和物质循环所形成的一个相互影响、相互作用并具有自调节功能的自然整体。根据研究目的和对象,划定生态系统的范围。最大的是生物圈(biosphere),包括地球上的一切生物及其生存条件;小的如一片森林、一块草地、一个池塘都可以看作是一个生态系统。

8.1.2 人类活动与生态系统 Human Activities and Ecosystem

一个生态系统内,各种生物之间以及和环境之间存在一种平衡关系(equilibrium relationship),任何外来的物种或物质侵入这个生态系统,都会破坏这种平衡,平衡被破坏后,可能会逐渐达到另一种平衡关系。但如果生态系统的平衡被严重地破坏,可能会造成永久的失衡。

人类活动是造成生态系统失衡的最主要因素。自工业革命以来,人类对生态系统进行了前所未有的破坏,人类活动深刻影响了生态系统的运转。

人类在生产生活的过程中,不可避免地会向生态系统排放有毒有害物质,这些物质会在生态系统中循环,并通过富集作用积累在食物链(food chain)顶端的生物上(最顶端的生物往往是人)。毒素(toxin)在食物链的集中,使人类深受其害,因为人类既吃植物、又吃动物,且处于食物链的最顶端,会同时吸收植物和动物所积蓄的毒素。

农业活动（agricultural activity）就是人类破坏自然生态系统，创造自己的人为生态系统的范例，人类开垦荒地，人类种植自己需要的庄稼，人类为了保护庄稼除草和使用杀虫剂滴滴涕（dichloro-diphenyl-trichloroethane，DDT）等，都使得人为生态系统产生了对人类活动的依赖性；如果农田被抛荒，很快就会重新产生新的生态系统，要么杂草遍地，要么可能沙漠化（desertification），但不会自动恢复到原有的生态系统。DDT会在土壤中存留很长时间，因此即使土地多年不再使用这类化学品，长出的庄稼中还是会含有有毒物质。不仅如此，DDT以后还会残留在生物的器官里，通过食物链向上传递。

DDT（dichloro-diphenyl-trichloroethane）was developed as the first of the modern synthetic insecticides in the 1940s. It was initially used with great effect to combat malaria, typhus, and the other insect-borne human diseases among both military and civilian populations. It also was effective for insect control in crop and livestock production, institutions, homes, and gardens. DDT's quick success as a pesticide and broad use in the United States and other countries led to the development of resistance by many insect pest species.

人类活动造成物种的长距离迁移，也可能会对生态系统造成人类没有预料到的破坏，老鼠和苍蝇随着人类散布到全世界，人类随意带到澳大利亚的兔子，给澳大利亚的生态系统造成毁灭性的灾难。人类活动造成的环境污染也会从物质和能量方面破坏生态系统的平衡，会造成永久性的破坏。目前，外来物种（alien species）如水葫芦已经开始对中国的生态系统造成威胁，类似的案例不胜枚举。人类目前已经认识到生态系统平衡被破坏的后果，正在力图帮助恢复其平衡，但这需要付出资金和能量，恢复比破坏要困难得多。

工业革命之后，工厂林立；工厂烟囱排出大量的二氧化硫和二氧化氮，可以随酸雨（chemical rain）降落到几千公里之外。酸雨是全球三大环境危害之一，20世纪70年代以后，我国出现大范围酸雨，中国酸雨区是世界三大酸雨区之一，东亚酸雨区的一部分。中国的酸雨主要因大量燃烧含硫量高的煤而形成，多为硫酸雨，少数为硝酸雨，此外，各种机动车排放的尾气也是形成酸雨的重要原因。我国一些地区已经成为酸雨多发区，酸雨污染的范围和程度已经引起人们的密切关注。

除了以上问题，人类面临的生态问题还有资源枯竭（resource exhaustion）、雨林破坏（rainforest destruction）和全球变暖（global warming）等问题。这些问题，给人类社会的未来发展带来巨大挑战。

8.1.3　生态系统保护 Ecosystem Protection

最早倡导人与自然和谐共处的是新英格兰作家，亨利·戴维·梭罗（Henry David Thoreau，1817—1862）在其出版的著作《瓦尔登湖》（*Walden*）中，对当时正在美国兴起的资本主义经济（capitalist economy）和旧日田园牧歌式生活的远去表示痛心。

1962 年,美国海洋生物学家(marine biologist)蕾切尔·卡森(Rachel Carson,1907—1964)在其生态学著作《寂静的春天》(*Silent Spring*)中提出了农药 DDT 造成的生态公害与环境保护问题,唤起了公众对环保事业的关注。

1970 年 4 月 22 日,哈佛大学学生丹尼斯·海斯(Denis Hayes)发起并组织保护环境活动,得到了环保组织的热情响应,全美各地约两千万人参加了这场游行集会,促使美国政府采取了一系列治理环境污染的措施。后来,这项活动得到了联合国的首肯。之后,每年的 4 月 22 日便被定为"世界地球日"(World Earth Day)。

1972 年,联合国人类环境会议在瑞典斯德哥尔摩召开,并于同年 6 月 16 日签订了《人类环境宣言》(Declaration on the Human Environment),这是保护环境的一个划时代的历史文献(historical document),是世界上第一个维护和改善环境的纲领性文件(programmatic document),宣言中,各签署国达成了七条基本共识;此外,会议还通过了将每年的 6 月 5 日作为"世界环境日"的建议。

1982 年 5 月,为了纪念联合国人类环境会议(United Nations Conference on the Human Environment)召开 10 周年,促使世界环境的好转,国际社会成员国在规划署总部内罗毕召开了人类环境特别会议,并通过了《内罗毕宣言》(Nairobi Declaration)。《内罗毕宣言》指出了进行环境管理和评价的必要性和环境、发展、人口与资源之间紧密而复杂的相互关系。宣言指出:"只有采取一种综合的并在区域内做到统一的办法,才能使环境无害化和社会经济持续发展(sustainable economic development)。"

1987 年,世界环境与发展委员会(WCED)在给联合国的报告《我们共同的未来》(Our Common Future)中提出了"可持续发展(sustainable development)"的设想。

Sustainable development is a principle to meet human development goals while also sustain the ability of natural systems to provide the natural resources and ecosystem services on which the economy and society depend. The desired state is a society where living conditions and resources are used to continue to meet human needs without undermining the integrity and stability of the natural system. Sustainable development was defined in 1987 as "development that meets the needs of the present generation without compromising the ability of future generations to meet their own needs". As the concept of sustainable development developed,it has shifted its focus more towards the economic development, social development and environmental protection for future generations.

1992 年 6 月 3—14 日,联合国环境与发展大会在巴西里约热内卢举行。会议通过了《里约环境与发展宣言》(Rio Declaration)又称《地球宪章》(Earth Charter),这是一个有关环境与发展方面国家和国际行动的指导性文件。这次会议还通过了为各国领导人提供下一世纪在环境问题上战略行动的文件《联合国可持续发展二十一世纪议程》《关于森林问题的原则声明》《气候变化框架公约》与《生物多样性公约》(Convention on Biological Diversity)。非政府环保组织通过了《消费和生活方式公约》,认为商品生产的日益增多,引起自然资源的迅速枯竭,造成生态体系的破坏、物种的灭绝、水质污染、大气污染、垃圾堆积。因此,新的经济模式应当是大力发展满足居民基本需求的生产,禁止为少数人服务的奢侈品(articles of luxury)的生产,降低世界消费水平,减少不必要的浪费。

Crafted by visionaries over twenty years ago, the Earth Charter is a document with sixteen principles, organized under four pillars, that seek to turn conscience into action. It seeks to inspire in all people a new sense of global interdependence and shared responsibility for the well-being of the whole human family, the greater community of life, and future generations. It is a vision of hope and a call to action.

8.1.4 从三种视角看生态问题 Three Perspectives on Ecosystem

功能论者(functionalist)认为:无论生态问题多么严重,改善生态的需求多么迫切,仍然要从改变其他制度入手来改变社会的消费价值观。举例来说,在改变消费价值观之前,首先要改变企业的组织架构、营销手段和广告策略等。

冲突论者(conflict theorist)强调,那些提倡依靠自觉自发行为来改变个人价值观从而解决生态问题的想法都太过于天真了。他们认为,只要污染是有利可图的,只要利益驱动仍然是经济运行的基础,就很难彻底消灭污染问题。

相互作用论者 (interactionist)不相信经济发展或科技进步,他们看重的是人们的处境。他们认为,任何脱离处境、脱离文化的决策,都注定要失败。

8.2 社会保障问题 Social Security Problem

社会保障(social security)是一个十分古老的问题。自古以来,总有一部分社会成员会因各种原因陷入生活困境,需要政府、社会或他人的援助才能解决生存问题。各国政府为了维持社会稳定,缓和阶层矛盾与阶级对抗,在很早以前就制定并执行过如救灾、济贫和扶弱等政策措施。不过,由于社会保障(social security)要受到各国政治、经济、社会、历史文化乃至伦理道德等因素的影响,各国具体国情的差异又使其在实践过程中出现很大的差异,对社会保障的认识和理论界定也就很自然地存在差异。

Social Security established by legislation to maintain individual or family income or to provide income when some or all sources of income are disrupted or terminated or when exceptionally heavy expenditures have to be incurred. Thus, social security may provide cash benefits to persons faced with sickness and disability, unemployment, crop failure, loss of the marital partner, maternity, responsibility for the care of young children, or retirement from work. Social security benefits may be provided in cash or kind for medical need, rehabilitation, domestic help during illness at home, legal aid, or funeral expenses. Social security may be provided by court order, by employers (sometimes using insurance companies), by central or local government departments, or by semipublic or autonomous agencies.

8.2.1　社会保障制度的起源与发展
Origin and Development of Social Security System

社会保障制度(social security system)是社会发展和社会进步的产物,也是现代国家文明的重要标志之一。20世纪人类社会的重大发展之一就是社会保障制度的普及。现在世界上大多数国家和地区都建立了不同形式的社会保障制度。

In many societies charity has been the traditional way in which provision was made for the poor. Charitable giving has been encouraged by many different religions, and in many parts of the world religious agencies have long collected charitable donations and distributed help to those in need.

The imposition of obligations on communities to pay taxes in order to provide for the poor can be traced back for hundreds of years in a number of different societies. For example, part of the function of the Christian tithe was to provide for the poor. Town poor laws were passed in Germany from 1520 onward, and a law passed in 1530 clearly placed on towns and communities the obligation of sustaining the poor. In 1794 the Prussian states assumed the responsibility of providing food and lodgings for those citizens who were unable to support and fend for themselves. From the 16th century it became recognized in England that there were people who could not find work, and legislation was passed to provide work for the poor and houses of correction for rogues and idlers. From 1598 a clear obligation was placed on parishes to levy local taxes and appoint overseers of the poor in order to give relief to those who could not work and to provide work for those who could. This formed was the essence of the Elizabethan Poor Laws, an early provision of social assistance.

The Elizabethan Poor Laws were poorly enforced in the 17th century but widely used and liberalized by the end of the 18th century. A new Poor Law enacted in 1834，and reflecting a harsh moral view of poverty，required the poor persons to be admitted to the workhouse so as to receive relief only in kind，with occasional exceptions，but this again was by no means uniformly enforced，though it added greatly to the unpopularity of the Poor Laws. Some U.S. states copied the Elizabethan Poor Laws but exempted recent immigrants. The English Poor Laws were also introduced in Jamaica in 1682 for destitute European immigrants and much later in Mauritius （1902） and Trinidad （1931）. In Latin America the Spanish colonists，instead of establishing a public relief agency，gave grants to charities to provide "hospitals" for the poor and the Portuguese promoted lay brotherhoods.

社会保障制度的起源可以追溯到 100 多年前的德国。1883 年，德国的俾斯麦政府为缓和阶级矛盾，迫于压力，率先颁布"疾病保险法"；1884 年又制定了"伤害保险法"，1889 年颁布"老年残疾保险法"。

英国社会保障制度的首次立法是 1908 年制定的"养老金法"，1911 年又通过了"全国健康与失业保险法案"。1941 年 6 月，英国政府设立"社会保险及有关事业部会联系委员会"，牛津大学的威廉·亨利·贝弗里奇（William Henry Beveridge）提出了《社会保险及有关服务》。1945 年英国工党执政后，通过一系列重要立法，施行社会保险、工伤保险、家庭补助、全民医疗保险等法案。1948 年，工党首相宣称英国已经建成福利国家（welfare state）。此后，社会保障措施不时有所增改，保障范围不断扩大。20 世纪 80 年代以后，英国形成了一个十分庞大的保障体系，真正成为福利国家。

1935 年美国通过《社会保障法》（Social Security Act），开始全面实施社会保障制度，以摆脱经济大萧条的困境。从 20 世纪 50 年代起，美国政府对《社会保障法》多次修正，逐步扩大了社会保障范围。

发展中国家（developing country）在取得民族独立之后，在独立发展本国经济的同时，也根据各国的具体情况逐步发展了社会保障事业。特别值得一提的是，新加坡实行的中央公积金制度（central provident fund，CPF）别具一格，取得了显著成效，为世界各国所瞩目。

我国的社会保障制度是在 20 世纪 50 年代高度集中的计划经济体制下（highly centralized planned economy）建立起来的。保障的核心是以城镇劳动者为主，实行就业—工资—福利三位一体的保障模式，城镇劳动者的生、老、病、伤、残等均由单位包揽；在农村，则主要以家庭保障（family security）为主。20 世纪 80 年代中期开始实行城镇职工退休费用社会统筹（social pooling），改革企业养老保险制度至今，我国的社会保险制度改革已经逐步开展和深入。我国是在 1986 年制订和实施国民经济与社会发展第七个五年计划的文件中，第一次采用"社会保障"一词。十几年改革的重点是突出养老保险（endowment insurance）的改革和重建，并重点建立和完善失业保险制度（unemployment insurance）、医疗保险

（medical insurance）和生育保险制度（maternity insurance）等。

1998 年以来社会保障逐渐成为一项基本的社会制度。2008 年 4 月，合并原劳动与社会保障部和人事部，组建新的人力资源和社会保障部，明确其职责为统筹拟订人力资源管理和社会保障政策，健全公共就业服务体系，完善劳动收入分配制度，组织实施劳动监察。2015 年末，全国城镇职工基本养老保险（basic endowment insurance）参保人数为 3.54 亿人，城乡居民基本养老保险参保人数为 5.05 亿人，两者合计达到 8.59 亿人，比 2008 年的 2.2 亿人增长 2.9 倍，总体覆盖率达到 80% 以上。城镇职工和居民基本医疗保险参保人数为 6.66 亿人，新型农村合作医疗参合人数为 7.36 亿人（2014 年），三项合计已超过 14 亿人，我国已基本实现全民医疗保障。城镇职工工伤保险参保人数为 2.14 亿人，失业保险参保人数 1.73 亿人，生育保险参保人数达到 1.78 亿人。截至 2020 年底，全国经基本医疗保险参保人数达 13.6 亿人，参保覆盖面稳定在 95% 以上。

8.2.2　从三种视角看社会保障问题
Three Perspectives on Social Security System

功能主义者认为，社会保障问题源于社会变迁。拿备受关注的医疗保险来说，医疗技术的进步使得医疗行业的重点转向专家和大型医院。尽管病人的经济开销增加，但以医院为基础的医疗体系有效地为医院、医生和制药公司提供了收入。冲突论者把医疗保健机制视为一个垄断行业，一个有利可图的行业。符号互动论者则强调医患之间的互动，指出一个人健康与否，取决于他人的界定以及由此导致的自我认知。

8.3　贫困问题 Poverty Problem

贫困问题是当今世界面临的最严峻的挑战之一。联合国秘书长古特雷斯（Guterres）说："贫困是对我们这个时代的道德控诉"。联合国发布的有关数据显示，全世界在脱贫方面取得了积极进展，但是各国在减少贫困人口、提高卫生条件等方面仍然任重道远。

> Poverty is one of the very worst problems that the world faces today. The poorest in the world are often hungry, have much less access to education, regularly have no light at night, and suffer from much poorer health. To make progress against poverty is therefore one of the most urgent global goals.

8.3.1　认识贫困 Understanding Poverty

欧共体（European Community）在 1989 年《向贫困开战的共同体特别行动计划的中期报告》中给贫困下了一个定义："贫困应该被理解为个人、家庭和人的群体的资源（物质的、文化的和社会的）如此有限，以致他们被排除在他们所在的成员国的可以接受的最低限度的生活方式之外。"世界银行在以"贫困问题"为主题的《1990 年世界发展报告》中，将贫困界定为"缺少达到最低生活水准的能力"。

1998 年诺贝尔经济学奖获得者阿玛蒂亚·森（Amartya Sen）认为，贫困的真正含义是贫困人口创造收入能力和机会的贫困；贫困意味着贫困人口缺少获取和享有正常生活的能力。

> Amartya Sen, Indian economist who was awarded the 1998 Nobel Prize in Economic Sciences for his contributions to welfare economics and social choice theory and for his interest in the problems of society's poorest members. Sen was best known for his work on the causes of famine, which led to the development of practical solutions for preventing or limiting the effects of real or perceived shortages of food.

2019 年诺贝尔经济学奖得主阿比吉特·班纳吉（Abhijit V. Banerjee）与埃斯特·迪弗洛（Esther Duflo）夫妇在他们的著作《贫穷的本质：我们为什么摆脱不了贫穷》（*Poor Economics*：*A Radical Rethinking of the Way to Fight Global Poverty*）中提到了几个发人深省的问题：为什么穷人吃不饱饭还要买电视？为什么他们的孩子即使上了学也不爱学习？为什么他们放着免费的健康生活不去享受，却要自己花钱买药？为什么他们能创业却难以守业？为什么大多数人认为小额信贷、穷人银行没什么效用？他们指出：多年来的扶贫政策大都以失败而告终，原因就在于人们对贫穷的理解不够深刻。两位作者通过多年实验，揭示了穷人对于蚊帐、教育、经济等问题的看法，为当地政府消除贫困提供了许多有价值的建议。同时也启发我们，社会学研究不仅需要仰望星空者，更需要那些愿意通过实地调查揭示事实真相的脚踏实地者。

> The winners of the Nobel Prize in Economics upend the most common assumptions about how economics works in this gripping and disruptive portrait of how poor people actually live. Why do the poor borrow to save? Why do they miss out on free life-saving immunizations, but pay for unnecessary drugs? In *Poor Economics*, Abhijit V. Banerjee and Esther Duflo, two award-winning MIT professors, answer these questions based on years of field research from around the world. Called "marvelous, rewarding" by the *Wall Street Journal*, the book offers a radical rethinking of the economics of poverty and an intimate view of life on 99 cents a day. *Poor Economics* shows that creating a world without poverty begins with understanding the daily decisions facing the poor.

我们可以从宏观和微观两个层面来审视贫困。宏观层面是从整体角度来看待贫困。从这个角度来理解，那么，所有低收入国家（low-income country）都是贫困的国家，而所有高收入国家（high-income country）则不是贫困国家。这种贫困问题也称不发达状态，它是发展经济学研究的主题。微观贫困是从个人和家庭角度看待贫困。从这种角度来理解，所有国家都有贫困问题。这种意义上的贫困是个永恒的问题，除非收入和财富分配是绝对的平均。

经济发展只是为缓解贫困提供了可能性,但它无法为消除贫困提供保障,甚至有可能随着经济发展,贫困问题反而越来越严重,很多历史经验都已经证明了这一点。

目前,世界各地的发展出现了严重的不平衡态势。其中,亚洲在脱贫方面取得了巨大进展,而非洲大陆面临的贫穷、饥饿、疾病等问题依然严峻。全世界 46 个最不发达国家大部分在非洲。[①]自 1990 年以来,全球极端贫困人口的数量减少了 1.32 亿,但非洲撒哈拉以南地区的极端贫困人口却由 2.27 亿增加到 3.13 亿。

可见,贫困其实是一个既简单又复杂的现象。我们只能在一个更大的社会背景中来理解贫困。除了关注贫困者之外,我们还需要关注贫困文化。社会学的研究有助于我们理解物质贫困并不是大部分社会问题的主要原因。

8.3.2　消除贫困 Eradication of Poverty

可持续发展的第一个目标是"在全世界消除一切形式的贫困"。贫困是一种无声的危机,严重阻碍了贫穷国家的社会经济发展,也是当前地区冲突(regional conflicts)、恐怖主义(terrorism)蔓延和环境恶化等问题的重要根源。多年来,国际社会为消除贫困作了积极努力。

1992 年 12 月 22 日,第 47 届联合国大会根据联合国第二委员会(经济和财政)的建议,确定自 1993 年起把每年的 10 月 17 日定为"国际消除贫困日"(International Day for the Eradication of Poverty),用以唤起世界各国对因制裁、各种歧视与财富集中化引致的全球贫富悬殊(polarization of the rich and the poor)族群、国家与社会阶层的注意、检讨与援助。2000 年 9 月,联合国千年首脑会议一致通过了"千年发展目标"(Millennium Development Goals),承诺到 2015 年之前将世界极端贫困人口和饥饿人口减半。值得一提的是,2014 年中华人民共和国国务院将 10 月 17 日设立为我国首个扶贫日(Poverty Alleviation Day)。

The observance of the International Day for the Eradication of Poverty can be traced back to 17 October 1987. On that day, over a hundred thousand people gathered at the Trocadéro in Paris, where the Universal Declaration of Human Rights was signed in 1948, to honor the victims of extreme poverty, violence and hunger. They proclaimed that poverty is a violation of human rights and affirmed the need to come together to ensure that these rights are respected. Since then, people of all backgrounds, beliefs and social origins have gathered every year on October 17th to renew their commitment and show their solidarity with the poor.

除了联合国之外,世界银行(World Bank)也为消除贫困(eradication of poverty)做出了积极贡献。世界银行制定的全球极端贫困线(poverty line),最初于 1990 年设定的生活费"1 天 1 美元"的极端贫困线标准,反映了当时低收入国家的普遍情况。2008 年,根据世界

---

① 当今世界的最不发达国家有哪些?［EB/OL］.(2023 - 03 - 08)［2023 - 03 - 25］. https://www.163.com/dy/article/HVARF2O20553PQOU.html.

上 15 个最贫穷国家的最新平均贫困线，世界银行对极端贫困线进行了更新。2013 年世界银行股东国批准的共享繁荣目标，为我们提供了一个认识收入和机会不平等的窗口：虽然帮助极贫人口脱贫取得了显著进步，但很多人依然很贫困，这是因为他们缺少机会。关注底层 40% 的人口，有助于确保他们从国家经济发展中充分受益。

2014 年 4 月 10 日，世界银行在名为《共同富裕：结束极端贫困力》（*Prosperity for All：Ending Extreme Poverty*）的报告中指出：要想救助底层 40% 的人口，重要的是要了解他们的特点，但这些特点因国家而异。例如，在卢旺达，极贫人口占总人口的 63%；在哥伦比亚，极贫人口占总人口的 8%。在孟加拉国，底层 40% 的人口中有三分之二住在农村，而巴西底层 40% 的人口中有 23% 住在农村。在卢旺达，底层 40% 的人口中有 11% 拥有中学学历，而在土耳其有 55% 接受过中学教育。在就业方面，菲律宾底层 40% 的人口中有 63% 从事农业，而在约旦底层 40% 的人口中只有 11% 从事农业。

> The new World Bank paper, "Prosperity for All：Ending Extreme Poverty", begins by looking at progress to date in reducing global poverty and discusses some of the challenges of reaching the interim target of reducing global poverty to 9 percent by 2020, which was set by the WBG President at the 2014 Annual Meetings. It also reports on the goal of promoting shared prosperity, with a particular focus on describing various characteristics of the bottom 40 percent. A more detailed report with policy recommendations in the areas of ending extreme poverty and boosting shared prosperity is due for release at the Annual Meetings later this year.

要想解决贫困问题，就需要了解大部分贫困人口生活在哪里，同时还要把力量集中在贫困最普遍的地方。这需要世界 12 亿贫困人口生活的国家做出共同努力。就贫困人口数量而言，排在前五位的国家是印度（占世界贫困人口的 33%）、尼日利亚（7%）、孟加拉国（6%）和刚果民主共和国（5%）等，这五个国家加在一起在世界贫困人口中占了近 7.60 亿。再加上五个国家——印度尼西亚、巴基斯坦、坦桑尼亚、埃塞俄比亚和肯尼亚——将涵盖近 80% 的极贫人口。因此，报告认为，将重点放在这些国家，对于终结极端贫困至关重要。

为了达到消除贫困的目的，世界银行集团需要根据每个国家的城市化水平、能源需求程度、基本服务水平、每个公民的能力以及政府的能力定制援助方案。要想取得成功，需要大规模地实施具有变革性的解决方案，可以通过新兴城市改善环境卫生的项目、提高农业用水及其他用水效率的项目、扩大低收入人群的健康覆盖的项目以及在青年失业率高的地方推广以工代赈计划。

8.3.3　从三种视角看贫困 Three Perspectives on Poverty

功能主义者从两个方面来解读贫困。一是贫困的范围和性质是社会变迁的结果。科技的进步、劳动机会的减少以及歧视等因素使得一部分人口发现自己被困在其中，在这个后工业社会（post-industrial society）中显得脆弱而毫无准备。二是贫困并不代表社会制度的崩溃,而是社会系统中一个必不可少的部分。贫困可以推动人们去工作;但是,话说回来,虽然所有工作都对社会运转发挥着作用,但是报酬的等级化制造了社会的等级层次。如果贫困过于普遍,就会给社会带来沉重负担。积极方面是,贫困者形成了一个廉价劳动力群体(cheap labor force),从事那些没有人愿意干的脏活。

冲突论者认为,资本主义是贫困的根源。他们反对以社会化不充分或者价值观不正确来指责那些贫困人口。

相互作用论者关注人们认识和界定那些影响他们生活事件的方式。这种认识和界定,也会加强贫困的存在。如果他们所居住的街区是有着高失业率、严重犯罪、大量吸毒者和酗酒者,那么就没有什么值得学习的榜样。同时,贫困者也会受到标签分类的影响,社区、家庭、学校只给了他们低期望;消极的自我形象使他们被动地接受现状。因此,在相互作用论者看来,贫困既是一个经济陷阱,也是一个心理陷阱。

8.4　家庭问题 Family Problem

家庭(family)是个体在人生经历中接触最早、生活在其中时间最长的社会生活群体。家庭是社会的一个因子,是我们观察和了解社会的窗口。了解家庭问题,有助于我们更好地认识社会问题。

> Family is a group of persons united by the ties of marriage, blood, or adoption, constituting a single household and interacting with each other in their respective social positions, usually those of spouses, parents, children, and siblings. The family group should be distinguished from a household, which may include boarders and roomers sharing a common residence. It should also be differentiated from a kindred (which also concerns blood lines), because a kindred may be divided into several households. Frequently the family is not differentiated from the marriage pair, but the essence of the family group is the parent-child relationship, which may be absent from many marriage pairs.

8.4.1　认识家庭问题 Understanding Family Problem

家庭是指在婚姻关系、血缘关系或收养关系基础上产生的,具有情感纽带的社会单元,以共同的住处、经济合作和繁衍后代为特征。

从历史发展来看,家庭总是受到社会中反家庭因素的破坏,但是许多家庭问题却被置于个人化的领域,这是不恰当的。下面,我们从家庭暴力(domestic violence)、离婚(divorce)和家庭教育(family education)三个方面来分析家庭问题。

第一,关于家庭暴力。家庭暴力在整个世界范围内都是一个十分严峻的问题。针对妇女的暴力行为,尤其是亲密伴侣暴力和性暴力,是一个持续存在的重大公共卫生问题,也是违反妇女人权的问题。①

Domestic violence can be defined as a pattern of behavior in any relationship that is used to gain or maintain power and control over an intimate partner. Abuse is physical, sexual, emotional, economic or psychological actions or threats of actions that influence another person. This includes any behaviors that frighten, intimidate, terrorize, manipulate, hurt, humiliate, blame, injure, or wound someone. Domestic violence can happen to anyone of any race, age, sexual orientation, economic class, immigration status, religion, or gender. It can happen to couples that are married, living together, or who are dating. Domestic violence affects people of all socioeconomic backgrounds and education levels.

联合国的调查表明,2017 年,全世界有 87 000 名妇女被故意杀害,其中一半以上是被家庭成员中的亲密伴侣所杀害。令人震惊的是,暴力侵害妇女行为与癌症一样,已成为导致生育年龄的妇女死亡和丧失能力的重大原因,同时也是比交通事故和疟疾双重因素加起来还大的造成妇女罹患疾病的原因。

Any household member may potentially perpetrate or become a victim of domestic abuse regardless of age, race, gender, sexual orientation, faith or other social group. Therefore, potential victims include an intimate partner, a child or other relative. In response to this threat of escalating domestic abuse, the Secretary-General has called for the creation of safe ways for household members to seek support without alerting their abusers, including emergency warning systems in pharmacies and grocery stores. Working from home during an extended period may heighten stress and anxiety. Although being with immediate family members and loved ones could alleviate feelings of isolation, confinement may aggravate pre-existing inter-familial tensions where long-term abusive patterns are now exacerbated. Confinement may also create new tensions, resulting in domestic abuse.

其他研究也表明,有四分之一至二分之一遭受其伴侣侵犯人身的妇女蒙受身体伤害。即使暴力发生在数年以前,受虐妇女比非受虐妇女报告健康不良以及身体和精神问题的可能性也要高一倍。这包括自杀念头和企图、精神痛苦以及疼痛、眩晕等身体症状。② 此项研究是与伦敦卫生和热带医学学院、适宜卫生技术规划以及参加国的国家研究机构和妇女组织合作开展的。

---

① 消除针对妇女的暴力行为刻不容缓——联合国纪念"制止暴力侵害妇女行为国际日"[EB/OL]. (2020 - 12 - 01) [2023 - 03 - 25]. https://news.un.org/zh/story/2020/12/1072692.

② 21 世纪经济报道. 联合国:全球 1/3 女性受到暴力侵害,十年未有改善,疫情促暴力"隐形大流行"[EB/OL]. (2021 - 03 - 10)[2023 - 03 - 25]. https://new.qq.com/rain/a/20210310A08WZW00.

专家们意识到,婚姻中的暴力行为是一个严重的社会问题,但是确认和帮助被殴打妇女却很难,因为妇女们通常不愿意公开自己的遭遇。与此相关的是,目睹暴力行为的孩子会在心理上受到永久伤害,他们可能会相信:暴力是一种解决问题的可行方式。男孩长大后,可能会成为施虐者,而女孩则会同他人建立被虐待关系。除了妇女之外,儿童和 80 岁以上的老人也很容易遭受家庭暴力。

第二,离婚问题。离婚是指夫妻双方通过协议或诉讼的方式解除双方之间的婚姻关系,终止夫妻间权利和义务的一种行为。在办理离婚手续的过程中,男女双方通常都要面对许多复杂的问题,尤其是子女抚养权或监护权以及财产分配、子女抚养费等问题。不仅如此,离婚还会对成年人和儿童造成伤害。研究表明,与那些在完整家庭长大的孩子相比,父母离异的孩子读到高中毕业的可能性较小,更有可能从事低收入工作,更可能依赖社会福利来生活,而且更有可能早婚。不过,离婚对儿童最大的影响是,许多儿童因为父母离异而不得不降低生活水平,这是因为未获得监护权的父亲没有履行抚养的责任。甚至在父亲们有支付能力的情况下,也经常发生拒绝支付抚养费的事情。而那些再婚了的父亲更倾向于从过去婚姻留下的孩子身上解脱出来。

第三,家庭教育问题。家庭是社会的细胞,家庭教育是家庭的重要事务,父母是孩子的第一任老师。从历史上看,家庭教育曾经是人类教育最主要的形态,东西方皆然。现代学校教育的兴起出现在近 200 年左右的时期。自 20 世纪 60 年代以来人们开始对学校教育的等级性、排斥性和控制性进行批评,家庭教育的重要性日益突出,一度萎缩的家庭教育功能开始复苏,家庭教育的合法性在一些国家开始得到认可。在有些国家,数以百万计的儿童开始在家里接受正规教育。自 20 世纪 90 年代以来,由于各种原因,在我们国家也出现了越来越多的"私塾"或"在家上学"的现象。更加普遍的是,世界各国都非常重视家庭的学校教育参与,并将其作为成功教育的一个重要条件。我国的教育工作者也提出"家校共育"的理念,教育界普遍认识到,教育改革要想取得成功,没有广大家长的认同和积极参与是不可能的。

家庭教育面临的挑战很多,这里着重讲一条普遍被社会忽视的家庭教育问题:父亲的缺失。父亲对儿童心理发展的影响正日益受到研究者的重视。父亲缺失的研究使得研究者对父亲缺失家庭儿童和完整家庭儿童的人格特点进行对比,进而推理父亲的作用。它已成为当前对父亲作用研究的重要的研究范式。父亲缺失对儿童性别角色发展的作用、对儿童道德和犯罪行为的影响、对儿童人际交往能力、个体化发展等的影响,都不能小视。

8.4.2　解决家庭问题 Solving Family Problem

第一,对家庭暴力问题的应对。1960 年 11 月 25 日,三位多米尼加女性——米拉瓦尔三姐妹(Mirabal sisters)被杀害。为了纪念这一事件,1981 年 7 月,第一届拉丁美洲女权主义大会宣布把 11 月 25 日作为反暴力日。1993 年 11 月 25 日,联合国发表了《消除针对妇女的暴力宣言》。1999 年 11 月 3 日,联合国大会通过由多米尼加共和国提出、60 多个国家支持的倡议,将每年 11 月 25 日定为"国际消除家庭暴力日"。

2015 年 12 月 27 日,中华人民共和国第十二届全国人民代表大会常务委员会第十八次会议通过、2016 年 3 月 1 日起施行的《中华人民共和国反家庭暴力法》(Anti-Domestic Violence),将家庭暴力界定为家庭成员之间以殴打、捆绑、残害、限制人身自由以及经常性谩骂、恐吓等方式实施的身体、精神等侵害行为。按照表现形式划分,可分为身体暴力、情感暴力、性暴力和经济控制;按照受害者类型划分,可分为亲密伴侣暴力、儿童暴力、老年人暴力等 。2020 年 12 月 14 日,最高人民法院、全国妇联和中国女法官协会首次联合发布了人身安全保护令十大典型案例,向社会传递出多方联合治理的鲜明信号。

Matters to Research and Understand

• If you live outside your home country and are planning to leave your partner/ex-partner, get a divorce or separation, and/or establish child custody, start by consulting an attorney who understands the complexities of international divorce or separation and child custody proceedings as well as the immigration consequences of divorce or separation.

• If you can't afford an attorney, contact a free legal service organization or visit your local family court. They may be able to determine whether you are eligible for a free legal consultation or a pro-bono attorney. In the event that you are not eligible for a pro-bono attorney, you can still file on your own for a divorce or separation (pro se), protect your child custody rights, and obtain financial support for yourself and your children. A legal service organization or a court may provide you with all the necessary documentation and guide you through the process. Please refer to sections below on divorce and international child custody.

• Find a safe accommodation if you decide to leave. Your personal safety and the safety of your loved ones should always remain your priority, even if it means that you have to leave your home. If possible, prepare your departure in advance.

• If possible, don't leave without documentation and evidence of the abuse. If you feel threatened, call the police.

联合国对减少家庭暴力的建议:

(1)增加对在线服务和公民社会组织的投资。

(2)确保司法系统继续起诉施暴者。

(3)在药房和杂货店建立紧急警报系统。

(4)宣布庇护所为基本服务。

(5)为妇女提供安全的寻求支持的方式,而不会惊动施虐者。

(6)避免释放因任何形式的暴力侵害妇女行为而被判的囚犯。

(7)扩大公众意识运动,尤其是针对男性和男孩的运动。

第二,对离婚问题的应对。关于离婚问题,全世界一个普遍的做法是离婚冷静期的设立。下面谈谈我国的具体做法。

十三届全国人大三次会议表决通过了《中华人民共和国民法典》(Civil Code of the People's Republic of China)。这部法律自 2021 年 1 月 1 日起施行。民法典婚姻家庭编中关于"离婚冷静期"(cooling-off period)的规定有新的解读。《民法典》第一千零七十七条规定:"自婚姻登记机关收到离婚登记申请之日起三十日内,任何一方不愿意离婚的,可以向婚姻登记机关撤回离婚登记申请。前款规定期限届满后三十日内,双方应当亲自到婚姻登记机关申请发给离婚证;未申请的,视为撤回离婚登记申请。"意味着,如果通过协议离婚的方式,须先冷静的等待第一个三十日届满,最短三十一天可离婚,最长需要六十天。设立"离婚冷静期"是因为相比其他国家"我国目前的离婚程序过于简单,在实践中,存在很多的草率离婚、冲动离婚的现象。"因此,设立"离婚冷静期",就像是给离婚增加了一个"门槛"。

民政部 2022 年 3 月发布的统计季报数据显示,2021 年全年有 213.9 万对夫妻完成离婚登记。这一登记量比 2020 年(373.3 万对)下降了约 43%。当然,也有学者提出,离婚率下降也可能受到其他因素的影响。

第三,对家庭教育问题,尤其是对父亲缺席问题的应对。

卡西·卡斯滕斯(Cassie Carstens)在其著作《世界需要父亲》(*The World Needs a Father*)中提出,父亲是儿女们的生命教练,是道德伦理的榜样,父亲缺席给儿女带来的创伤影响深远,这伤痛制造了"人间地狱"。作者呼吁全世界的父亲们勇敢地正视现实,回归家庭;卡西·卡斯滕斯期待帮助世界各地的父亲们把父亲的责任带入到他们的家庭、文化和国家中。父亲们该怎样履行这一神圣的职责呢? 首先,他们要明白孩子在每个生命阶段的需要。之后,卡西·卡斯滕斯从"建立道德权威""赋予身份""提供安全感"和"肯定潜力"等四部分,帮助父亲们明白父亲的角色意味着什么。

If the family unit is a fundamental building block of society, the nucleus of that unit is the father, and when he causes damage, the ripples affect everyone. Drawing from decades of first-hand experience and a wealth of academic research, *The World Needs a Father* delves into the depths of the catastrophe that is fatherlessness, laying it open from an academic and personal perspective, and presenting a thorough, practical solution. *The World Needs a Father* was written with the intention of capturing the core of The World Needs A Father Master Trainer course in a format that is easy to access and digest, but it is also an invaluable resource for anyone who wants to be a better husband, father or mentor. It will challenge you, convict you, and encourage you to be the best father you can be within your context.

8.4.3　从三种视角看家庭问题 Three Perspectives on Family Problem

功能主义者把家庭看作在社会制度中发挥着基本功能的一个机制。家庭具有作为一个生产单位的经济功能、消费功能、教育功能、保护功能、娱乐功能等。冲突论者则将我们的视线引向家庭中的权力关系。那些离家从事工作的妇女比家庭主妇获得更多权力。对另一些妇女而言，离婚意味着摆脱了不平等的关系。相互作用论者注重对家庭角色的期待。

延伸阅读 Further Reading

思考 Thinking it through：

父亲的缺失，会给家庭带来哪些影响？

Father-Absent Homes：Implications for Criminal Justice and Mental Health Professionals

Abstract

The number of single-parent households in the United States has reached high levels in recent decades. As the extant literature suggests that children raised in single-parent households experience more physical and psychological problems compared to those raised in two-parent households, the implications of homes in which fathers are absent may be important to explore for criminal justice and mental health professionals. The present article aims to examine the extant literature base on father-absent homes, seeking to provide a fair and balanced account of this phenomenon. Specifically, we highlight ten adverse outcomes associated with homes missing a father. Findings suggest that a negative developmental trajectory may result for children lacking a father in the home, albeit further research in this area is warranted.

Please note：This article is part one of a two-part series that focuses on the topic of parental absence. Part two of this series will examine the impact of mother-absent homes and its implications for criminal justice and mental health professionals.

Introduction

The number of children who grow up without a father in the home in the United States has reached concerning levels. There exists a considerable research base that suggests that children raised in households lacking a father experience psychosocial problems with greater frequency than children with a father in the home (Allen and Daly, 2007). These problems have been found to extend into adolescence and adulthood and include an increased risk of substance use, depression, suicide, poor school performance, and contact with the criminal justice system (Allen and Daly, 2007). Lack of paternal involvement has also been associated with a higher likelihood of being bullied and experiencing abuse (Allen and Daly, 2007). Educating uninvolved fathers and helping them play a more active role in their child's life could benefit both families and communities. To bring this into focus, the present article aims to highlight ten adverse outcomes that may result from the absence of a father in a child's life: ① perceived abandonment, ② attachment issues, ③ child abuse, ④ childhood obesity, ⑤ criminal justice involvement, ⑥ gang involvement, ⑦ mental health issues, ⑧ poor school performance, ⑨ poverty and homelessness, and ⑩ substance use.

Adverse Outcome 1: Perceived Abandonment

Children who grow up without their fathers may come to resent paternal-figures due to perceived abandonment. These feelings may burgeon from a lack of trust and result in a heightened sense of anger. As a child grows into adolescence and young adulthood, these problems may contribute to contact with the criminal justice system, use of illicit substances, as well as a variety of mental health problems. These consequences may result in interpersonal dilemmas including the inability to develop strong social bonds. For example, anger stemming from abandonment can make it difficult for juveniles to establish friendships and relationships (Poehlmann, 2005).

Adverse Outcome 2: Attachment Issues

Attachment refers to the deep emotional bond that develops between a caregiver and a child (Bowlby, 1988). Children who come from a father-absent home are more likely to experience attachment-related problems than those from a two-parent household (King, 1994; Furstenberg & Cherlin, 1991; Seltzer, 1991). This may result in serious emotional issues throughout the lifespan. The inability to form a strong caregiver bond is associated with hypervigilance to anger and a misappropriation of hostile intent to neutral stimuli, both of which may result in conduct problems in the child. Such misconduct may have the unintended consequence of creating difficulties in the development of friendships and healthy romantic relationships (Hirschi, 1969; Jensen, 1972; Johnson, 1987). The active involvement of a father with his children can promote empathy and self-control for the child throughout life.

Adverse Outcome 3: Child Abuse

Many previous publications have linked the absence of a father in the home to higher risk conditions for mothers and their children. Children that grow up in such households are much more likely to be the victim of physical (including sexual) abuse and neglect compared with those who grow up in a two-parent household (Smith, Selwyn, Hanson, and Nobel, 1980). Children who grow up in a single parent home are twice as likely to be the subject of physical and/or emotional abuse (*America's Children*, 1997). In addition, the absence of a father results in an increased psychological burden on the child, as he or she must make sense of why his or her father is not present. This burden extends beyond the child to alternative caregivers such as the child's mother. Indeed, the needs of a child are hard to meet, even when a mother is very loving, committed, and caring. When children are surrounded by multiple caring adults (e.g., mothers, extended family members, community members), they are more likely to thrive and feel supported. If the mother is the only caregiver of the child, mounting stress over the considerable responsibilities of parenthood may increase the risk of her harming her children or herself.

Adverse Outcome 4: Childhood Obesity

Children with higher body mass indices (BMI) are more likely to come from father-absent homes (Finn, Johannsen, and Specker, 2002; Strauss and Knight, 1999). Another study found that a father's parenting style was a better predictor of whether a child would become obese (Wake, Nicholson, Hardy, and Smith, 2007). Fathers who were present and used more authoritarian parenting styles had children who were more physically fit than fathers who were absent and, if sporadically involved, used more of a permissive approach. Mothers' parenting styles had little to no effect on obesity and fitness levels.

Adverse Outcome 5: Criminal Justice Involvement

Family structure and the lack of paternal involvement are predictive of juvenile delinquency. The more opportunities a child has to interact with his or her biological father, the less likely he or she is to commit a crime or have contact with the juvenile justice system (Coley and Medeiros, 2007). In a study of female inmates, more than half came from a father-absent home (Snell, Tracy, and Morton, 1991). Youths who never had a father living with them have the highest incarceration rates (Hill and O'Neill, 1993), while youths in father-only households display no difference in the rate of incarceration from that of children coming from two-parent households (Harper and McLanahan, 2004). In addition, children who come from father-absent homes are at a greater risk for using illicit substances at a younger age (Bronte-Tinkew, et al., 2004). The absence of a father in a child's life may also increase the odds of his or her associating with delinquent peers (Steinberg, 1987).

Adverse Outcome 6: Gang Involvement

A high percentage of gang members come from father-absent homes (Davidson, 1990), possibly resulting from a need for a sense of belonging. Gaining that sense of belonging is an important element for all individuals. Through gangs, youth find a sense of community and acceptance. In addition, the gang leader may fill the role of father, often leading members to model their behaviors after that individual (Leving, 2009). Having a father in the child's life greatly reduces the likelihood of a child joining a gang (Leving, 2012).

Adverse Outcome 7: Mental Health Issues

Coming from a fatherless home can contribute to a child having more emotional problems, such as anxiety and depression. Fatherless children may start thinking that they are worth less than other children who have fathers and wonder why their father abandoned them. This may also lead to an increased risk of suicide and/or self-injurious behaviors. Children who do not grow up with a father are also more likely to be aggressive and exhibit other externalizing problems (Osborne and McLanahan, 2007). Children from a father-absent home are also more likely to become depressed, have suicidal thoughts, anxiety, social withdrawals, and school absences if they see or hear their parents fighting (Flouri, 2007). The mental health aspects associated with divorce on children will be discussed in a future article.

Adverse Outcome 8: Poor School Performance

Evidence suggests that not having a father at home may have a negative impact on a child's overall academic performance. Research has shown that children who come from a father-absent home are more likely to drop out of school when compared to children who live in a two-parent household (Whitehead and Holland, 2003; Popenoe, 1996; Blankenhorn, 1995; McLanahan and Sandefur, 1994; Sampson, 1987). Children from father-absent homes are also less likely to pursue higher education (Keith and Finlay, 1988). It is important to note that African American boys who identify their father as their role model demonstrate significantly higher grade point averages and are less likely to be truant from school (Bryant, 2003).

Adverse Outcome 9: Poverty and Homelessness

According to the U.S. Census Bureau (2011), children from absent-father homes are four times more likely to be living in poverty. Often children with an absent father also have less networking connections to aid them in the working world (Coleman, 1988). Furthermore, studies have shown that the cause of the father's absence matters little in relation to poverty and divorce (U.S. Bureau of the Census, 1998; McLanahan and Casper, 1995). Poverty also presents a obstacle for children pursuing well-paid jobs, which can result in increased stress and frustration (Cloward and Ohlin, 1960; Merton, 1957). Children from father-absent homes may also be more likely to shoplift and become chronic shoplifters (Manning and Lamb, 2003).

Adverse Outcome 10: Substance Use

Children who grow up in a home where a father is not present are at a greater risk for abusing alcohol and other drugs (Hoffmann, 2002). In one study, researchers examined the impact of father-absence on African American boys (Mandara & Murray, 2006). According to their findings, the boys who came from a home without a father were more likely to use drugs than boys who came from a home where a father was present. Involvement of a father can，hence，be a protective factor against child and adolescent substance use.

Conclusion

Given the large research base suggesting that children who grow up in homes without a father present adverse outcomes at rates significantly above those with fathers present，attention to this phenomenon is perhaps warranted by clinicians，researchers，and policymakers. It is important to point out that not all children who are raised in a father-absent home will experience adverse outcomes. This said，available evidence cannot be ignored. Rather，further investigation into single-parent homes and potential differences for children's developmental trajectories if they are raised solely by their fathers compared to their mothers could make a major contribution to the field.

（Reference：www.mnpsych.org/index.php%3Foption%3Dcom_dailyplanetblog%26view%3Dentry%26category%3Dindustry%2520news%26id%3D54）

参考文献 References

[1] 阿塔利.帕斯卡尔——改变世界的天才[M].鲁方根,赵伟,译.上海:上海人民出版社,2014.

[2] 波普诺.社会学[M].李强,等译.北京:中国人民大学出版社,1999.

[3] 陈彬.我国社会保障事业的发展历程及未来趋势[J].财经界,2017(12):3-5.

[4] 陈镕.离婚冷静期实施一年后,去年中国离婚登记人数大降43%[N/OL].第一财经,(2022-03-20)[2022-11-15]. https://www.yicai.com/news/101354574.html.

[5] 费雷尔,赫特,费雷尔.人力资源管理:第10版,双语教学版[M].北京:人民邮电出版社,2018.

[6] 费孝通.费孝通文集(第五卷)[M].北京:群言出版社,1998.

[7] 费孝通.我看到的中国农村工业化和城市化道路[J].浙江社会科学,1998(04):4-7.

[8] 顾东辉.社会工作概论[M].上海:复旦大学出版社,2008.

[9] 何雪松.社会工作理论[M].上海:上海人民出版社,2007.

[10] 黄红,沈黎.社会工作参与新型冠状病毒感染肺炎防控工作实务指引(第一版)[EB/OL].(2020-2-2)[2022-10-30]. https://caswe.pku.edu.cn/info/1065/1159.htm.

[11] 吉登斯,萨顿.社会学[M].赵旭东,等译.北京:北京大学出版社,2015.

[12] 康德.判断力批判(下卷)[M].北京:商务印书馆,1964:95.

[13] 克鲁克洪.文化与个人[M].高佳,何红,何维凌,译.杭州:浙江人民出版社,1986:5-6.

[14] 李达.李达文集(第1卷)[M].北京:人民出版社,1980:237.

[15] 李达.李达文集(第2卷)[M].北京:人民出版社,1980.

[16] 李大钊.唯物史观在现代社会学上的价值[J].新青年,1920(8).

[17] 李培林.20世纪上半叶的唯物史观社会学[J].东岳论丛,2009(1):5-11.

[18] 李迎生.发挥社会工作在疫情防控中的专业优势[N].光明日报,2020-03-06(11).

[19] 李卓,王如月,郭占锋.社会工作思想在近代中国的发端与实践——以沪江大学创办的"沪东公社"为例[J].华东理工大学学报(社会科学版),2017,32(2):30-36,46.

[20] 马克思,恩格斯.马克思恩格斯选集(第1卷)[M].北京:人民出版社,1995:56-68.

[21] 马林诺夫斯基.科学的文化理论[M].北京:中央民族大学出版社,1999.

[22] 马凌诺夫斯基.文化论[M].费孝通,译.北京:华夏出版社,2002.

[23] 米切尔.新社会学词典[M].蔡振扬,等译.上海:上海译文出版社,1987.

[24] 民政部,中央政法委,网信办,发展改革委,工业和信息化部,公安部,财政部,住房城乡建设部,农业农村部.九部门印发《关于深入推进智慧社区建设的意见》的通知[R/OL].(2022-05-21)[2022-10-30]. http://www.gov.cn/zhengce/zhengceku/2022-05/21/content_5691593.htm.

[25] 帕里罗,史汀森,史汀森.当代社会问题:第4版[M].周冰,等译.北京:华夏出版社,2002.

[26] 帕斯卡尔.思想录[M].北京:商务印书馆,1987:156-157.

[27] 人民网.中国代表强调打击恐怖主义必须要摒弃双重标准[R].(2021-08-20)[2022-11-15].http://world.people.com.cn/n1/2021/0820/c1002-32200976.html.

[28] 瑞泽尔.当代社会学理论[M].北京:北京联合出版公司,2018.

[29] 森.贫困与饥荒[M].王宇,王文玉,译.北京:商务印书馆,2001.

[30] 石中英.当代家庭教育问题的社会根源及解决之道[J].中华家教,2019(1):12-14.

[31] 世界银行集团.消除贫困不只需要经济增长[R].[2014-4-11].https://www.shihang.org/zh/news/press-release/2014/04/10/ending-poverty-requires-more-than-growth-says-wbg.

[32] 司马云杰.文化社会学[M].北京:中央文献出版社,1995:205-207.

[33] 孙本文.社会学原理[M].北京:商务印书馆,1925:306-307.

[34] 泰勒.原始文化[M].连树生,译.上海:上海文艺出版社,1992:1.

[35] 王迪.智慧社区发展的未来趋势:从设计本位到生活本位[J].福建论坛(人文社会科学版),2020(08):92-102.

[36] 王思斌.社会工作概论[M].北京:高等教育出版社,2014.

[37] 韦伯.经济与社会(第2卷)[M].阎克文,译.上海:上海人民出版社,2020.

[38] 韦伯.经济与社会(第1卷)[M].阎克文,译.上海:上海人民出版社,2019.

[39] 魏爽.近十年我国社会工作实务发展回顾与反思[J].北京工业大学学报(社会科学版).2020,20(01):47-53.

[40] 乌格朋.社会变迁[M].费孝通,王同惠,译.北京:商务印书馆,1935.

[41] 吴文藻.现代社区研究的意义和功用[N].北平晨报,1935-01-09.

[42] 希勒里.社区的定义:一致的地方[J].乡村社会学,1955(6):118.

[43] 消除贫穷国际日:联合国呼吁开展具有变革性和包容性的可持续新冠后复苏[R].(2020-10-10)[2022-10-10].https://www.un.org/zh/desa/rising-poverty-moral-indictment-our-times-guterres.

[44] 徐永祥.社区发展论(修订版)[M].上海:华东理工大学出版社,2021.

[45] 阎明.中国社会学史[M].北京:清华大学出版社,2010.

[46] 于显洋.社区概论[M].北京:中国人民大学出版社,2016.

[47] 袁志雄,柯艳娇.如何应对"离婚冷静期"[N].人民法院报,2020-06-14(3).

[48] 中国人民共和国国务院新闻办公室.抗击新冠肺炎疫情的中国行动白皮书[R/OL].(2020-06-07)[2022-10-30].http://www.gov.cn/zhengce/2020-06/07/content_5517737.htm.

[49] 周晓虹.文化反哺:变迁社会中的亲子传承[J].社会学研究,2000(2):51-66.

[50] 朱志伟.社区基金会如何动员资源——基于Y个案的考察[J].社会工作与管理,2021(6):61-69.

[51] Abrams E.，Szefler S. COVID-19 and the impact of social determinants of health[J]. The Lancet Respiratory Medicine，8(7):659-61.

[52] Giddens A. Sociology[M]. Cambridge：Polity Press,2013.

［53］Gilligan P，Furness S. The role of religion and spirituality in social work practice：views and experiences of social workers and students［J］. The British Journal of Social Work. 2006,36(4):617－637.

［54］Hansan J E. Lots of chronic paupers［J］. The Washington Post,2021(10).

［55］Harrikari T,Romakkaniemi M，Tiitinen L，et al. Pandemic and Social Work：Exploring Finnish Social Workers' Experiences through a SWOT Analysis［J］. The British Journal of Social Work，2021,51(5):1644－1662.

［56］Hillery G. Definitions of community：areas of agreement［J］. Rural sociology，1955,20: 111－123.

［57］Rachelle A，Deepy S，Andrea G，t al. The impact of the Covid－19 pandemic on social workers at the frontline：a survey of Canadian social workers［J］. The British Journal of Social Work,2021(3):1－23.

［58］Tansley A G. The use and abuse of vegetational concepts and terms［J］. Ecology,1935,16 (3):284－307.